Why Peacekeeping Fails

Why Peacekeeping Fails

Dennis C. Jett

St. Martin's Press
New York

ISBN 0-312-22698-5

Library of Congress Cataloging-in-Publication Data
Jett, Dennis C., 1945-
    Why peacekeeping fails / Dennis C. Jett.
        p.   cm.
    Includes bibliographical references and index.
    ISBN 0-312-22698-5
    1. United Nations—Peacekeeping forces.   I. Title.
JZ6374.J48   2000
327.1'7'09—dc21   99-27685
                                                                                  CIP

Design by Letra Libre, Inc.

10   9   8   7   6   5   4   3   2

For Lynda
whose inspiration and support
made this possible.

Contents

Preface and Acknowledgments

This book will attempt to identify the reasons why peacekeeping fails, principally by comparing the success in Mozambique and the failure in Angola. It will also draw on other peacekeeping experiences and consider why peacekeeping has become so difficult to do. If the chances for the success of peacekeeping can be improved, it could help shorten the suffering of those who live in countries that are attempting to bring an end to their conflicts. It might also help ensure that peace is not just a temporary respite from a war waged by those who think that if they can have power, no price is too high for others to pay.

I would like to thank those who were generous with their time and with their research. The insights they provided were invaluable in this effort. Those people include, but are not limited to, William Durch, Michael Pugh, Aldo Ajello, Richard Edis, Otto Denes, Brian Urquhart, Cameron Hume, Yvonne Lodico, Sam Barnes, Sean McCormick, Laurie Shestack, Donald McHenry, Jackie Cock, LTC Bill Price, Behoz Sadry, Erick de Mul, Tim Born, Roger Carlson, Joe Synder, Hank Cohen, Chester Crocker, Miguel de Brito, Mike McKinley, Tim Sisk, Greg Mills, Jeffrey Herbst, Laurie Boulden, Glen Oosthuysen, Adrian Guelke, Don Steinberg, Eddie Banks, Ramiro Lopes da Silva, General Sibanda, LTC John Pullinger, Richard Fritz, Herb Howe, Agostinho Zacarias, Virginia Gamba, Brazao Mazula, Don Matteo Zuppi, Tom Callahan, Norah Niland, Charles Bradley, Mary Jo McDonough, and Eric Berman.

I also drew inspiration in a sense from Paul Fauvet of the Mozambique Information Agency (AIM), the journalists of the other government-owned media such as *Domingo* and *Noticias,* and Joe Hanlon, all of whose writings so clearly demonstrate the need for more objective assessments of Mozambique, and from Bill Minter, Richard Synge, and others who also let their ideology affect their analysis. This book was prompted by a desire to provide a more objective and insightful perspective (although I'm sure some would assert still biased) on peacekeeping in Mozambique.

A long-term observer of a peacekeeping operation like the one in Mozambique cannot help being affected by it. Such first-hand experience, however, can help overcome the UN's normal lack of transparency.

This work was originally written as a dissertation for a Ph.D. in international relations form the University of Witwatersrand in Johannesburg, South Africa. I am therefore most indebted to my advisor, Dr. Chris Alden, who guided me through that process. I also owe a great deal as well to my wife, Lynda Schuster, and to my children Brian, Allison, and Noa for their support and understanding during this effort.

The Department of State has reviewed the manuscript of this book to ensure that its contents do not compromise national security. This review should not be construed as concurrence with the text. Opinions and characterizations are those of the author and do not necessarily represent official positions of the United States government.

Current Peacekeeping Operations
(as of June 1999)

Acronym	Name	Date Begun
MINURCA	UN Mission in the Central African Republic	April 1998
MINURSO	UN Mission for the Referendum in Sahara	April 1991
MIPONUH	UN Civilian Police Mission in Haiti	December 1997
UNDOF	UN Disengagement Observer Force (Golan Heights)	June 1974
UNFICYP	UN Peacekeeping Force in Cyprus	March 1964
UNIFIL	UN Interim Force in Lebanon	March 1978
UNIKOM	UN Iraq–Kuwait Observation Mission	April 1991
UNMIBH	UN Mission in Bosnia and Herzegovina	December 1995
UNMIK	UN Interim Administration Mission in Kosovo	June 1999
UNMOGIP	UN Military Observer Group in India and Pakistan	January 1949
UNMOP	UN Mission of Observers in Prevlaka	January 1996
UNMOT	UN Mission of Observers in Tajikistan	December 1994
UNOMIG	UN Observer Mission in Georgia	August 1993
UNOMSIL	UN Mission of Observers in Sierra Leone	July 1998
UNTSO	UN Truce Supervision Organization (Middle East)	June 1948

Completed Peacekeeping Operations (as of June 1999)

Acronym	Name and Location	Dates
DOMREP	Mission of the Representative of the Secretary General in the Dominican Republic	May 1965-October 1966
MINUGUA	UN Verification Mission in Guatemala	January-May 1997
MONUA	UN Observer Mission in Angola	July 1997-February 1999
ONUC	UN Operation in the Congo	July 1960-June 1964
ONUCA	UN Observer Group in Central America	November 1989-January 1992
ONUMOZ	UN Operation in Mozambique	December 1992-December 1994
ONUSAL	UN Observer Mission in El Salvador	July 1991-April 1995
UNAMIC	UN Advance Mission in Cambodia	October 1991-March 1992
UNAMIR	UN Assistance Mission for Rwanda	October 1993-September 1994
UNASOG	UN Aouzou Strip Observer Group Chad/Libya	May-June 1994
UNAVEM I	UN Angola Verification Mission	January 1989-June 1991
UNAVEM II	UN Angola Verification Mission II	June 1991-February 1995
UNAVEM III	UN Angola Verification Mission III	February 1995-June 1997

UNCRO	UN Confidence Restoration Organization in Croatia	March 1995-January 1996
UNEF I	First UN Emergency Force	November 1956-June 1967
UNEF II	Second UN Emergency Force	October 1973-July 1979
UNGOMAP	UN Good Offices Mission in Afghanistan and Pakistan	April 1988-March 1990
UNIIMOG	UN Iran-Iraq Military Observer Group	August 1988-February 1991
UNIPOM	UN India-Pakistan Observation Mission	September 1965-March 1966
UNMIH	UN Mission in Haiti	September 1993-June 1996
UNOGIL	UN Observation Group in Lebanon	June-December 1958
UNOMIL	UN Observer Mission in Liberia	September 1993-September 1997
UNOMUR	UN Observer Mission Uganda-Rwanda	June 1993-September 1994
UNOSOM I	UN Operation in Somalia I	April 1992-March 1993
UNOSOM II	UN Operation in Somalia II	March 1993-March 1995
UNPREDEP	UN Preventive Deployment Force-Macedonia	March 1995-February 1999
UNPROFOR	UN Protection Force Former Yugoslavia	March 1992-December 1995
UNPSG	UN Civilian Police Support Group—Croatia	January 1998-October 1998
UNSF	UN Security Force in West New Guinea (West Irian)	October 1962-April 1963
UNSMIH	UN Support Mission in Haiti	July 1996-July 1997
UNTAC	UN Transitional Authority in Cambodia	March 1992-September 1993
UNTAES	UN Transitional Administration for Eastern Slavonia, Baranja and Western Sirmium	January 1996-January 1998

UNTAG	UN Transition Assistance Group—Namibia	April 1989-March 1990
UNTMIH	UN Transition Mission in Haiti	August-November 1997
UNYOM	UN Yemen Observation Mission	July 1963-September 1964

Other Acronyms

AA	Assembly Areas
ACRI	African Crisis Response Initiative
AWEPA	Association of West European Parliamentarians for Southern Africa
CCF	Ceasefire Commission
CCFADM	Commission for the Joint Armed Forces for the Defense of Mozambique
CIVPOL	UN Civilian Police
CNE	National Elections Commission
COMINFO	National Information Commission
COMPOL	National Police Affairs Commission
CORE	Reintegration Commission
CSC	Supervision and Control Commission
CG	Consultative Group
DHA	UN Department of Humanitarian Affairs
ECOMOG	Economic Community of West Africa States Monitoring Group
ECOWAS	Economic Community of West African States
EU	European Union
FADM	Armed Forces for the Defense of Mozambique
FAM	Mozambique Armed Forces
FRELIMO	Mozambique Liberation Front
GURN	Government of National Unity and Reconciliation
MPLA	People's Movement for the Liberation of Angola
NATO	North Atlantic Treaty Organization
NGO	Non-governmental organization
OAU	Organization of African Unity
PIR	Rapid Intervention Police
PKO	Peacekeeping operation
PCPB	Post-conflict peace-building
RENAMO	Mozambican National Resistance
SADC	Southern African Development Community
SOFA	Status of forces agreement

UNITA	National Union for the Total Independence of Angola
UNHCR	UN High Commission for Refugees
UNOHAC	UN Office for Humanitarian Assistance Cooperation
UNRISD	UN Research Institute for Social Development
USAID	US Agency for International Development
WEU	Western European Union

Chapter One

Introduction

On February 26, 1999, Angola suffered another fatality in its civil war: the United Nations peacekeeping operation. The conflict, which has raged on and off since the country obtained its independence from Portugal in 1975, had already caused over 800,000 deaths. Ironically, the demise of the UN effort came after the longest period of relative peace in those 24 years. That peace, lasting four years, had been brokered by the UN but had begun to fall apart months earlier. Both the government and the rebels opposing it, the National Union for the Total Independence of Angola (UNITA) headed by Jonas Savimbi, had ceased any pretense of dialogue by mid-1998. The government-controlled National Assembly had branded Savimbi a war criminal and accused the international community of complacency, bias, and making it easy for UNITA to rearm and prepare for war.[1] The government also had moved aggressively to extend the area under its control, and UNITA had launched a strong counterattack. Thus, by the time the peacekeeping operation's mandate expired on February 26, the country was already at war once again.

The peacekeeping effort, like the peace, had been dying for some time before its end became official. The government of Angola had informed the UN weeks before that it would not accept a continuation of the presence of the peacekeepers after February 26. It said it wished only to deal with UN representatives on issues "related to humanitarian assistance, human rights and other matters of interest to the people of Angola."[2]

The situation had been growing steadily more difficult and dangerous for the peacekeepers, as the government's propaganda efforts against UNITA increasingly included hostility toward the UN. Perhaps as a result, two peacekeepers were stabbed to death by Angolan policemen on

February 1. This added to an already long list of UN personnel who had died trying to bring peace to Angola. Late in the previous year, two UN planes had been shot down, bringing to six the number of UN aircraft lost. Characteristically, the government and UNITA blamed each other for the incidents and even refused to help the UN investigate the crash or look for survivors.[3]

Long before these incidents, the UN had begun scaling back its presence in Angola. From an authorized strength of over 8,000 in 1995, the number of peacekeepers had dwindled to fewer than a thousand when the end came.[4] Many countries wanted the UN to continue to keep a peacekeeping presence regardless of the situation on the ground. The Secretary General, wanting to avoid the UN getting blamed for another failure, recommended withdrawal, noting that "the conditions for a meaningful United Nations peacekeeping role in Angola have ceased to exist."[5] The attitude of the parties to the conflict, especially the government, made it impossible for the Security Council to refuse to adopt his recommendation.

Thus, after the expenditure of $1.5 billion, a decade of effort, and the loss of the lives of over 60 peacekeepers, the UN Security Council officially recognized what it could no longer ignore. It approved a resolution instructing the Secretary General to close out the peacekeeping operation. Hoping to retain the capacity to have some positive effect on the situation, the council requested him to continue to work with the government to define the configuration of a follow-up UN presence.[6] And with no irony intended, the resolution also underscored the contribution of the UN to the past four years of relative peace in Angola.

But can a four-year lull in the fighting be considered an accomplishment when both sides used it simply to rearm? Fueled by the $3 billion the government earns annually on oil production and the approximately $500 million that UNITA collects from diamond exports each year, new and more sophisticated weapons are now being introduced. With the hardening of attitudes and the commonly held view that neither side has the strength to defeat the other decisively, it is expected that the fighting will continue for some time. Renewed combat, and the resulting humanitarian disaster, will translate into many more lives lost in a conflict that has already caused so many deaths. In light of this, one could ask whether fewer lives might have been lost if the UN had done nothing in Angola and whether peacekeeping, when done unsuccessfully, is worse than no peacekeeping at all.

At the same time, on the opposite coast of Africa the opposite result was achieved in another Portuguese colony. Mozambique continues to be one of the UN's biggest successes five years after its peacekeeping operation was brought to a close. The country is scheduled to hold its second democratic presidential elections in December 1999. While the candidates and the outcome may be the same and the long-term prospects for peace are not guaranteed, there is at least reason for hope and optimism.

The contrast between these two countries provides lessons that can be learned about why peacekeeping failed in one and succeeded in the other. Understanding why the two former Portuguese colonies have taken such a different path requires looking at them individually and in detail. This understanding will also be aided by looking at other peacekeeping experiences and considering why peacekeeping has become so difficult to do successfully.

Understanding Why Peacekeeping Fails

When the definitive history of peacekeeping is written, two of the most important dates in that chronicle will be December 11, 1988 and October 3, 1993. The first is the day that the UN was awarded a Nobel Peace Prize for peacekeeping. That event marked what was perhaps the apogee of expectations for peacekeeping. After a decade that saw little new activity, there suddenly seemed to be an abundance of opportunities for the UN to field multilateral armed forces in order to protect international peace and security. More over, the members of the Security Council for the first time appeared not only willing but also eager to see the UN undertake a greater number of such actions.

The second date is when 18 American soldiers were killed on a peacekeeping mission in Somalia. That day, the expectations that had been so high in late 1988 also died. Those in the international community who had foreseen many potential applications of peacekeeping were suddenly confronted with the reality of just how constrained such forces could be. This new reality had a profoundly negative effect on the enthusiasm for such ventures. Some might argue that Bosnia had a more dramatic impact on peacekeeping, but the lessons of Bosnia played out over a much longer period and were assimilated slowly. If the peace holds there, the bitter taste of so many humiliations for the peacekeepers may eventually dissipate.

The events in Mogadishu on October 3, 1993, however, were a watershed. Even though the UN continues to conduct a number of peacekeeping operations, there has been little new activity since the deaths of the Americans in Mogadishu. The UN's peacekeeping efforts have been confined mainly to long-term operations in the Middle East, Cyprus, the

Western Sahara, and Kashmir and the latest evolutions of the attempts to bring lasting peace to the former Yugoslavia and Angola.

Most of the new initiatives were small in scale and short in duration: an observer mission of 40 to Tajikistan, 15 monitors sent to verify the Libyan withdrawal from the Aouzou strip, 155 military observers dispatched to Guatemala, and 41 military observers to Sierra Leone. One medium-sized operation of 1,350 was put into the Central African Republic to help stabilize the situation. Only two major operations were launched in the next 6 years, however. These two were undertaken because the major powers that were their chief sponsors were receiving large numbers of refugees directly from the countries to which the peacekeepers were sent—Haiti in the case of the United States and Albania in the case of Italy.[7]

If the period between these dates can be described as the golden era of peacekeeping, it was a very short one. When it began in December 1988, the Cold War was all but over. Even though the Berlin Wall did not come down until 11 months later, the change in relations between the superpowers was already having an impact on the UN and its capacity for peacekeeping. A decade had passed since the start of the last peacekeeping operation (PKO), when UN troops were dispatched to Lebanon.

Suddenly there were requests for new UN missions in the Persian Gulf, Southern Africa, South Asia, and Central America, as cooperation replaced confrontation. Instead of UN action being prevented by the United States or the Soviet Union, the organization became a key mechanism for their collaboration on the world's problems. Nowhere was this more evident than in peacekeeping.

Throughout the early 1990s the demand for UN forces in their distinctive blue helmets continued to accelerate. New conflicts arose for which the international community deemed peacekeepers the appropriate response. The roles assigned this new generation of peacekeepers were quickly extended beyond the traditional task of separating the armies of two states and monitoring the cease-fire between them.

For the first time, peacekeeping seemed able to provide the answers to a whole range of international dilemmas. The application of peacekeeping forces was proposed for such varied tasks as preventive diplomacy in the earliest stages of conflicts, helping to end civil wars, confidence-building measures, disarmament, verification of arms limitation agreements, law and order assistance, combating terrorism, hostage rescue, drug interdiction, and naval peacekeeping.[8]

As many of these new missions and functions were undertaken by the UN, the number, scope, size and cost of PKOs grew. At the same time, however, the limits of such international efforts started to become apparent. The complexity of these operations inevitably led to the failure to achieve all of their mandated objectives. While the accumulation of such shortcomings affected the enthusiasm for peacekeeping, its expansion suffered its most significant setback from the single event in Somalia when the 18 servicemen were killed.

The growing number of horror stories from Bosnia was already having an effect on public perceptions, but the scenes of the bodies of American soldiers being dragged through the streets of Mogadishu greatly altered American public opinion. Never overly preoccupied with the details of foreign affairs, Americans could not understand how a mission to provide humanitarian relief had resulted in the deaths of the peacekeepers in combat. As a result, public and congressional support for any such operations in the future became far harder to muster for policymakers contemplating the involvement of American forces.

This negative image of peacekeeping was greatly compounded by the inability of the UN to bring to an end the ethnic cleansing in Bosnia and the genocide in Rwanda. Even if Bosnia and Rwanda finally find lasting peace and Somalia avoids further famine, it will be years before these legacies of failure and ineffectiveness cease to affect public perceptions.

Because of these perceptions, peacekeeping has ceased to be a viable instrument for international action in many situations where only a few years before it held such promise. If the potential for peacekeeping that was perceived in the late 1980s and early 1990s is ever to be regained to any degree, the sources of its failures must be better understood and avoided.

This book will examine why some peacekeeping operations fail. It will argue that while the factors that have led to failures in the past can be identified, increasing the chances for success is made more difficult by the way PKOs are initiated and conducted and by the way the UN operates as an organization. Many studies of the problems of peacekeeping conclude with recommendations on how PKOs could be conducted better. This will be done in this study as well, but attention will also be given to why reform is difficult and why recommendations for change may not work. What improvements are possible are limited not only by the institutional constraints of the UN and its members but by factors that are beyond the UN's control. These factors can often be influenced by the international community, however, if it has the will.

In order to consider the context in which the operations in Angola and Mozambique took place, chapter two will briefly review the history of peacekeeping and describe the evolution in the number, size, scope, and cost of such operations. It will examine how these characteristics have changed because of the end of the Cold War and a change in the nature of the world's conflicts. This evolution has contributed to the causes of failure in PKOs because it has resulted in operations of far greater complexity. As the tasks undertaken by PKOs have become increasingly ambitious, the chances of their fulfilling these expectations have diminished accordingly.

After considering how peacekeeping has changed in response to this new global reality, the next six chapters will consider the three phases through which each PKO passes—predeployment, deployment, and post-deployment. In the analysis of each of these three phases, general patterns will be supported by specific examples from a number of PKOs. In addition, the UN's experience in Angola and Mozambique will be examined in depth during each of the three phases.

Chapter three will look at how, when, and where the UN decides to intervene by using a PKO. These factors can influence the operation's chances for success even before the peacekeepers are on the scene. It will consider how elements such as Security Council politics, the PKO's mandate, and the pressure exerted by the media can affect the operation's eventual outcome.

The predeployment factors specific to the cases of Angola and Mozambique will be taken up in chapter four. These will include the histories of the conflicts, the way peace was negotiated, and the intentions and good faith of the parties. The two countries differ significantly in these conflict-specific factors even though they have many similarities. The differences in these factors contributed to making the peace agreement in Angola far more difficult for the UN to implement than the one in Mozambique.

Chapters five, six, and seven will cover the period during which the peacekeepers are deployed. At that point, a PKO enters into the second phase, and other factors come into play that can cause its success or failure. Chapter five will consider the factors that the UN can control, such as who is chosen to lead the operation, who is to participate in it, their mandate, how they interpret it, and how well they accomplish it. Chapter six will look at external factors beyond the UN's control although not beyond its influence. The willingness of the parties to cooperate and their motivation, the country's internal resources, and the external actors attempting to influence the conflict will be examined. Chapter seven will discuss the general case of humanitarian action and how that can help or hinder the effectiveness of the peacekeepers.

Chapter eight will deal with the phase that begins after the operation is over. What happens in the postdeployment period is not usually considered the fault of the peacekeepers. However, if the conditions for lasting peace have not been created, the work of the PKO can be undone rapidly following its conclusion. Enthusiasm for using PKOs in the future will certainly be affected if the international community finds it has bought only a temporary respite from a conflict after an investment that can run to a billion dollars or more.

These chapters will draw on the experience of a number of PKOs and will analyze two in particular—UNAVEM II in Angola and ONUMOZ in Mozambique—in these three phases: the period leading up to dispatching the peacekeepers, the period of their deployment, and the period following their departure.

There is good reason to compare these two countries. Both are former Portuguese colonies that had anticolonial independence movements. These movements coordinated their efforts and appealed for support in the same international fora. Both countries were battlegrounds on which the East-West conflict of the Cold War was played out by proxy. Before and after independence, various outside actors, including the Soviet Union, Cuba, the United States, South Africa, and others provided support to at least one of the combatants. This East-West struggle was an important part of the long and bloody civil wars both countries experienced after they gained their independence.

Yet despite these similar histories, the outcome of their respective PKOs could hardly have been more different. Mozambique is at peace, while Angola is at war and peacekeeping is at a minimum suspended. The detailed examination of the way these two UN operations were conducted will consider three factors that the UN can influence but not control. The three factors—the parties to the conflict, the outside actors (such as neighboring states, regional powers, and the permanent members of the Security Council), and the country's resources—can all be critically important to the success of a PKO. The degree to which the parties place more value on power more than on peace, the outside actors play a negative role, and the internal resources are used to fuel the conflict will contribute greatly to the challenge facing the UN. As this task becomes more daunting, the risk of failure grows and the UN will have to use more resources, more competence, and more force in order to succeed. The cases of Angola and Mozambique are starkly different in all three of these areas and therefore provide another reason why they can usefully be compared. The reasons why peacekeeping did not succeed in Angola can also point to factors that UN should try harder to influence in future operations if that failure is not to be repeated.

Generalization from the experience in Angola and Mozambique to other PKOs will not be automatic or easy. The variety of tasks assigned different missions and the variety of ways in which success can be defined will complicate any application of lessons learned in one PKO to another. It should not frustrate the process completely, however, and some insights can be gained.

The final chapter will attempt to draw some of those conclusions while at the same time considering whether the contrast between the two outcomes in Mozambique and Angola is as stark as conventional wisdom suggests. This last chapter will also analyze why improving the chances for success might be difficult and why the necessary changes might not be adopted. It will also consider what the future of peacekeeping might be post-Somalia and post-Bosnia. It will examine other peacekeeping options, such as whether peacekeeping forces drawn from regional organizations offer a viable alternative to forces that are more broadly recruited. In concluding, it will discuss why, despite the need, peacekeeping in the future will be underutilized because of its failure to meet all the expectations placed on it in the past.

The Need for Peacekeeping

In a 1994 article in *Foreign Affairs,* Leslie Gelb wrote about the importance of defining the new core problem in post–Cold War politics, and of developing a new strategy to address it. For Gelb, that core problem is the growing number of "teacup" wars, which he defines as "wars of debilitation, a steady run of uncivil civil wars sundering fragile, but functioning, nation-states and gnawing at the well-being of stable nations."[9]

This core problem is complicated by the fact that such wars usually involve massive levels of human suffering but rarely pose a threat to the strategic interests of the countries represented on the Security Council. These wars take place within a nation and are therefore intrastate as opposed to interstate conflicts. They most often take place in the world's less developed countries, in which political systems are as weak as the economies.

As a result, wars of this type usually pit poorly disciplined rebel forces against poorly trained armies, in which both sides are equipped extensively, and often exclusively, with light weapons. Because of their nature, these wars are difficult to end. At the same time, because of the reach of the electronic media and the human suffering involved, they are also difficult to ignore.

The initial response of the international community to these conflicts was to expand peacekeeping greatly. In the late 1980s and early 1990s, the number, size, scope, and cost of these efforts all increased dramatically. Three factors accounted for this growth. First, the end of the Cold War brought an end to the superpower confrontation that so often rendered the UN unable to act.

Largely due to this rivalry, from the mid-1970s to the mid-1980s, only one new PKO, UNIFIL in 1978, was initiated.[10] However, in the post–Cold War period, with cooperation having replaced competition, the United States, Russia, and the other Security Council members began making greater use of the UN to deal with these wars. As a result, between 1988 and 1992, 13 PKOs were begun. This was as many as had been undertaken in the previous 40 years of the UN's existence.[11]

A second factor was the change in the type and frequency of armed conflicts. The decolonization and independence of so many countries since the end of World War II resulted in a surge in civil wars as political elites within these new nations struggled for dominance. The collapse of the Soviet Union and the end of the Cold War only added to the number of trouble spots.

Van Creveld notes that these political changes produced a fundamental shift in the nature of the world's conflicts.[12] Instead of wars in which two nations with organized armies face each other across defined geographic lines, today's conflict is usually an internal struggle, with irregular forces, light weapons and guerrilla tactics. Because these wars take place within a failed state rather than between two states, they become much more difficult to resolve. Political power and legitimacy within a country are harder to determine than a geographical settlement between two countries.

Another characteristic of this increasingly common type of war is that the victims of the conflict are far more likely to be civilians than in the past. About 50 percent of war-related deaths from the eighteenth century up to 1970 were civilian. In the 1970s, this figure rose to 73 percent and had climbed to nearly 90 percent by 1990.[13] As the number of conflicts and the proportion of casualties that are civilian have grown, so has the cost of dealing with the humanitarian disasters they have created.

According to one U.S. government study, between 1985 and 1995 the number of regional conflicts increased from 4 to more than 20. The study concluded that these wars caused 42 million people to become refugees or displaced within their countries.[14] The annual expenditure required for humanitarian relief to deal with this situation amounted to $4 billion, or double what the international community spent for such aid in 1980.[15]

The third factor in the growing popularity of peacekeeping arose out of humanitarian concerns. As the international community struggled to deal with human suffering caused by the growing number of intrastate conflicts, policy makers saw peacekeeping as an alternative to the Hobson's choice between doing nothing or engaging in military intervention.[16]

The spread of the global electronic village and the "CNN effect" also brought this suffering to the attention of people throughout the world as it happened.[17] The public response to such scenes made it harder for policymakers to ignore these problems, even if their root causes and solutions were little understood.

The international response to these humanitarian disasters was encouraged by the growth in the number of non-governmental organizations (NGOs) that could assist the traditional UN and other governmental entities in dealing with such situations. The UN-affiliated Union of International Associations currently recognizes over 14,500 different international NGOs.[18]

Not only the number of NGOs but their influence and resources have steadily risen for the last decade. For instance, the share of official U.S. assistance channeled by the Agency for International Development (AID) through NGOs had been averaging about 28 percent in the early 1990s, but was scheduled to rise to 40 percent in the latter half of the decade. In 1992, some 13 percent of aid to developing countries, totaling $8.3 billion, was funneled through NGOs.[19] They became not only a more important source of administrative and logistical capabilities in cases of great humanitarian need but an increasingly effective lobby for a response when such a need arose. Since the humanitarian needs usually sprang up much more quickly than a stable cease-fire between the warring parties, peacekeepers were often given the task of creating and maintaining the conditions in which the NGOs could do their work.

Thus, in the immediate post–Cold War period, peacekeeping became more possible, more necessary, and more desired. The statistics demonstrate the effect of these three factors on the growth of peacekeeping. In 1987, the UN had five PKOs under way with a combined manpower of some 10,000 soldiers and an annual budget of $233 million. By the beginning of 1995, the UN was conducting 17 peacekeeping missions with over 75,000 troops, at an annual cost of $3.6 billion.[20]

The decidedly mixed track record of these endeavors has brought this growth trend to a halt. There were successes to point to, such as Namibia, Cambodia, El Salvador, and Mozambique. These successes, however, were overshadowed by some spectacular failures, and it was the latter that drew most of the media attention and international concern.

Because the failures did far more to tarnish the reputation of the UN than the successes did to enhance it, proponents of peacekeeping have to contend with the legacy of Somalia and Bosnia when they argue for future operations. Few could understand why, in the former country, the most powerful army in the world could not tame a gaggle of war lords. In the latter, scenes of peacekeepers unable to protect themselves, let alone stop the gross abuse of civilians, were equally incomprehensible to the public.

In part due to the experiences in Somalia and Bosnia, Rwanda provided a clear demonstration of international reluctance to become involved in peacekeeping missions, even in the face of widespread suffering. In November 1996, President Clinton decided to send U.S. troops to Zaire as part of a Canadian-led, multinational effort to help deliver aid to Rwandan refugees there. This mission was explicitly described as being restricted in scope to providing aid and in time to a duration of four months.

Having been under political pressure to clearly define when the U.S. would support and participate in peacekeeping operations, President Clinton had issued Presidential Decision Directive 25 on February 22, 1996. It listed a number of factors that were to be taken into consideration before the U.S. would vote for a PKO and even more stringent requirements for the U.S. to send troops to participate in one. While not all the factors were considered essential for U.S. involvement, the launching of even the limited effort in Rwanda required the prospect of nearly a million people in imminent risk of starvation and intense pressure on President Clinton from Canada, France, and the UN Secretary General. He consented, but only after long hours of heated discussions within his administration. When the operation finally did begin, because of changes in the situation on the ground, it was cut back to 300 Canadian troops and a handful of military liaison officers from other countries. Even this limited effort lasted only a few weeks.[21]

Therefore, while in the early 1990s peacekeeping became more possible, more necessary, and more desired, because of the change in the nature of the conflicts and the operations initiated to deal with them, peacekeeping also became much harder to do successfully. By the mid-1990s, the failures brought about by the increasing complexity of PKOs made the international community much less willing to use this instrument. In addition, complexity was not the only deterrent. The rapid growth in the cost of PKOs dampened even further the enthusiasm of those countries that had to pick up the tab.

The Cost of Peacekeeping

The diminished enthusiasm for peacekeeping brought about by its failures was compounded by growth in the cost of PKOs and the problem of how that cost was to be shared. The growth in the number and cost of PKOs in the early 1990s outstripped the willingness of the international community to pay for them to the point that the UN was confronted with a major financial shortfall.

This was not the first time the problem of paying for peacekeeping threatened the effectiveness of the UN. In 1960, the UN mounted its largest PKO to date in the Congo. The UN faced a genuine cash crisis when member states failed to respond to appeals for voluntary contributions to fund the operation. It was not until 1973, after more than 15 years of inconclusive debate, that a formula was worked out whereby the majority of the financial burden for peacekeeping was to be borne by the five permanent members of the Security Council.[22]

As the number and size of PKOs has grown, however, the budget for them increased fourteen-fold. Put another way, the cost to the UN of peacekeeping in 1993 equaled what it had spent on PKOs in the entire preceding 48 years of the organization's existence.[23] While this was a large increase in relative terms, many argued that in absolute terms the amounts spent on peacekeeping were small, especially in comparison to military expenditures worldwide. The cost of UN peacekeeping reached a high of nearly $4 billion in 1993 and dropped significantly since then. It was $1.4 billion in 1996, $1.3 billion the following year, and estimated at under $900 million for 1998.[24] Total military spending in the world during 1995 and in 1996 was estimated at around $750 billion each year.[25]

UN member states were nevertheless slow to pay the growing assessments for peacekeeping, and the amounts owed to troop-contributing countries grew as fast as the arrears. When those countries providing the manpower were not given reasonably prompt reimbursement, they also began to lose their enthusiasm for peacekeeping.

As the expense of peacekeeping has risen, so has the political profile of the budget issue. Nowhere is this more true than in the United States. After years of bearing 31.4 percent of peacekeeping costs under the formula worked out in 1973, the U.S. Congress approved a measure limiting the American share to 25 percent.

In addition, Congress wanted the U.S. portion of the regular UN budget reduced from 25 percent to 20 percent, and insisted on significant managerial reforms before it would agree to payment of over $1 billion in arrears. When Secretary General Annan introduced a package of reform measures in July 1997, initial congressional reaction was not enthusiastic. It remains to be seen how quickly the U.S. will move to pay its UN debt.[26] The U.S. is not the only country in debt to the UN. When the Secretary General introduced his reform proposals in mid-July, only 75 of the UN's 185 members had paid their dues for the year in full. This constant state of near bankruptcy prompted him to include with those proposals the establishment of a $1 billion revolving credit fund to help the UN pay its bills.[27] No country seemed eager to fill this financing gap, however, calling into question how the international community would pay for future PKOs if it were once again to make greater use of them.

The cost factor has given a major impetus to the increasing interest in having peacekeeping conducted by other organizations. While few PKOs are currently carried out by organizations other than the UN, alternative arrangements are gaining greater attention. Regional groupings such as the Organization of African Unity (OAU), the Economic Community of West African States (ECOWAS), and the Southern African Development Community (SADC) have been mentioned as more sources of peacekeeping forces, in part because they may be cheaper.

The ECOWAS-organized PKO (ECOMOG) in Liberia offers one recent experience on which to judge the viability of a regionally based peacekeeping effort. Chapter nine will discuss whether this alternative might prove as effective as and less expensive than a PKO conducted by the UN, or whether in peacekeeping the international community is likely to get only what it pays for. Who pays is not the only issue under debate, however. An even more basic question is what the international community hopes to buy.

Defining Peacekeeping

Any discussion of peacekeeping is complicated by the fact that there is no common definition of the term; indeed, this may be one of the causes of failure in PKOs. Nowhere in the 111 articles of the Charter of the United Nations is the word used. It has been applied by journalists, diplomats, academics, and others to a wide variety of situations.

Clearly, monitoring the separation of military forces in Cyprus is a very different task from nation-building in Namibia or trying to prevent ethnic cleansing in Bosnia. Arriving at a definition of the term has also been made more difficult by the evolution in the size, scope, and mandate of PKOs.

As the mandates of peacekeeping operations have grown, so have the number of ways to define them.

The International Peace Academy defined a PKO's role as "the prevention, containment, moderation and termination of hostilities between or within states, through the medium of a peaceful third-party intervention organized and directed internationally, using a multinational force of soldiers, police, and civilians to restore and maintain peace."[28] Such a definition is sufficiently broad to apply to virtually any conflict in which international intervention is contemplated. It is therefore of limited utility in defining the limits of the debate about just what it is the peacekeepers are supposed to accomplish.

Perhaps because of this difficulty with definitions, UN Secretary General Boutros-Ghali in July 1992 described four different types of operations:

> Preventive diplomacy: action to prevent disputes from arising between parties, to prevent existing disputes from escalating into conflicts, and to limit the spread of the latter when they occur.
>
> Peacemaking: action to bring hostile parties to agreement, essentially through such peaceful means as those foreseen in Chapter VI of the UN Charter.
>
> Peacekeeping: the deployment of a UN presence in the field, hitherto with the consent of all parties concerned, normally involving UN military and/or police personnel and frequently civilians as well.
>
> Peacebuilding: action to identify and support structures which will tend to strengthen and solidify peace in order to avoid a relapse into conflict.[29]

The Secretary General's attempt to categorize the different missions into four groups has not been the last word on the subject, however. In a collection of essays written by American military experts in the wake of the Somalia experience, Quinn asserted that among the various parts of the U.S. government involved in peacekeeping, a general consensus had emerged about the following terms:

> Peacekeeping: non-combat military operations (exclusive of self-defense) conducted by UN authorized forces with the consent of all major belligerent parties, designed to monitor and facilitate an existing truce agreement.
>
> Aggravated peacekeeping: military combat operations conducted by UN authorized forces and designed to monitor and facilitate an existing truce agreement; initially begun as non-combat operations (exclusive of self-defense) and with the consent of all major belligerents, but which subsequently, due to

any number of reasons, become combat operations where UN forces are authorized to use force not only for self-defense but also for defense of their assigned missions.

Peace enforcement: military combat operations conducted by UN authorized forces in which combat power or the threat of combat power is used to compel compliance with UN sanctions or resolutions.[30]

Lewis, writing in the same collection of essays as Quinn, puts forth a slightly different set of definitions and asserts that they have gained general acceptance. They are the most descriptive, as they break down peacekeeping, in the broadest sense, into five distinct types of operations:

Peacemaking: using mediation, conciliation, arbitration or diplomatic initiatives to peacefully resolve a conflict such as with the Vance-Owen initiatives in Bosnia-Hercegovina.

Peacekeeping: traditionally involving military personnel as monitors/observers under restricted Rules of Engagement once a cease-fire has been negotiated. Examples of this type include Cyprus and the Golan Heights.

Peace enforcing: using military force to complete a cessation of hostilities or to terminate acts of aggression by a member state. Enforcement of "No Fly Zones" in Iraq and Bosnia, and actions in Somalia are cases in point.

Peacebuilding: rebuilding institutions and infrastructure within a country to create conditions conducive to peace, such as in Cambodia and Somalia.

Protective engagement: employing military means to provide safe havens or a security environment for humanitarian operations.[31]

These five types of operations also cover the chronological spectrum embodied in the three phases discussed earlier, although not all of them fall neatly into one phase. Peacemaking can take place before or while the peacekeepers are deployed. Obviously, peacekeeping, peace enforcing, and protective engagement are possible only with peacekeepers in the field. Peacebuilding could begin even before deployment, but must happen during and after it. Such international nation-building efforts are essential to prevent the conflict from simply resuming after the peacekeepers depart.

Diehl, Druckman, and Wall, in a broader and more theoretical discussion of ways to define peacekeeping, came up with 12 different categories of missions and measured them by ten different characteristics.[32] For purposes of this book, Lewis's five types of operations are sufficient. The fact that the experts in the field can come up with such a variety of ways to define the objectives of a PKO is indicative of the complexity of peace-keeping today and the difficulty of generalization. As will be seen with the different ways to measure success, measuring a mission's performance can be equally challenging.

Differences in defining the roles peacekeepers are to play are important, as they have led to misunderstandings and false expectations. These expectations can compound the perception of failure when they are not met. As U.S. Senator John McCain put it: "Neither the UN Secretary General, the Security Council, the General Assembly, nor for that matter, the Clinton administration could define the concept in the same way from one day to another or from one country to another. To Americans, peacemaking in Somalia meant feeding a starving people. To the UN Secretary General, it meant warlord hunting."[33]

Clearly, the lack of a common definition can contribute to a PKO's failure. At a minimum, it will complicate communications between civilian officials and military officers, as the latter try to prevent the former from yielding to "mission creep"—the process whereby the goals of the PKO are constantly redefined and expanded, leaving the military faced with trying to accomplish an ever-changing mission.

Some lack of specificity will be impossible to avoid, as the situation in the next country requiring a PKO will never be exactly the same as the last. Any attempt to draw a definition so broadly as to be all-inclusive will be general and vague to the point of being meaningless, which is the reason the five different categories described by Lewis are necessary. These five types of PKOs vary widely in their size, cost, complexity, purpose, length, and rules of engagement. As described in the next chapter, they also vary widely in the extent to which they will be applied by the international community in future conflicts.

Peacemaking is usually the easiest and the cheapest form of peacekeeping, because it has the smallest number of people engaged. It can involve as few as a handful of people and can consist mainly of preventive diplomacy by a special representative of the Secretary General. This type of operation can be initiated quickly once the potential for conflict is foreseen and the decision made to try to avert it. Peacemaking implies a mediator's role, although, as will be discussed, there is some question as to whether the UN can perform such a function effectively.

Peacekeeping under Lewis's definitions is what is often referred to as "classical" or "traditional" peacekeeping. The thesis will not concern itself to any great extent with "classical" peacekeeping other than to describe its important role in the history of PKOs and its effect on the thinking of those considering new missions. Classical peacekeeping requires the insertion of UN troops between the armies of two countries along well-defined geographical lines, after a cease-fire has been agreed to by the parties to the conflict. It is not these interstate but the intrastate conflicts that pose the most serious peacekeeping challenge in the post–Cold War era.

In civil wars, the army of the government in power is typically pitted against one or more rebel groups in a guerrilla struggle without geographical limits. These conflicts present the problem not simply of monitoring a cease-fire but also of nation-building. Because they are fought with light weapons, disarmament and demining often become essential elements of the PKO, even though they greatly complicate the job of the peacekeepers. Since it entails so many different tasks, a PKO of this type is referred to as a multifunctional or multidimensional operation. This multifunctional effort (what Lewis refers to as peacebuilding) was what was attempted in Angola and Mozambique. Such operations present the peacekeepers with far more complex challenges than "classical" peacekeeping. To start with, UNAVEM and ONUMOZ had to deal with the legacy of many years of civil war. In both countries, thousands of combatants had to be assembled and demobilized, weapons collected, a single, unified army formed, and the first democratic elections held.

A multidimensional PKO is largely concerned with what Lewis refers to as peacebuilding, but is not likely to be limited to that one definition. It could at different times incorporate elements of all five different types of peacekeeping. In both Angola and Mozambique, while there were peace treaties signed by the parties, the UN had to spend a great deal of its time and effort at peacemaking trying to get the various sides to live up to their commitments. Both PKOs included tasks that would fall under classical peacekeeping as well as many others that were peacebuilding. The efforts at peacebuilding came with an implementation schedule that added considerable time pressure on the peacekeepers as well as the parties.

Rules of engagement vary from one multidimensional PKO to another and even more among the five different types of operations as defined by Lewis. The peacekeepers in Angola and Mozambique did not have mandates to use the force required in peace enforcement or protective engagement, but that is not always the case in a multidimensional operation. As Durch notes, while PKOs of this type "usually operate with the full consent of the local parties, their military component may be authorized to use limited force against local elements that may actively hinder implementation of the peace accord."[34]

The use of force will vary from one multidimensional PKO to another because each requires its own rules of engagement depending on how it combines elements of the five different types of operations defined by Lewis. Peacemaking, peacebuilding, and peacekeeping all assume the consent of the parties to the conflict, the strict impartiality of the peacekeepers and the nonuse of force. A peace enforcement or protective engagement operation does not, and obviously could not be launched under such assumptions. Authorization under Chapter VII of the UN Charter, which stipulates that all necessary means including military action may be used, would be necessary for peace enforcement and could be required for protective engagement.

Because of this need to use force, and in light of recent experience, the international community is not enthusiastic about initiating an operation where there is a high risk that the peacekeepers will become involved in the conflict. As the Secretary General put it: "In war situations, the international community should authorize the combat forces needed to deal with it. Where a cease-fire is in place, and where the consent and cooperation of the parties is reliable, peacekeepers should be deployed."[35] Because of the experience in Somalia, another UN official put it more succinctly: "The UN is out of peace enforcement for good."[36]

Considering past peacekeeping experiences and contemplating future ones, it is clear that the difficult issue of how much force the peacekeepers should be authorized to use will not be resolved simply by avoiding peace enforcement situations. Even if the UN is out of the peace enforcement business, the use of force must be contemplated in the future for protective engagement actions. If not, the lack of the cooperation of one or more of the parties may preclude the provision of humanitarian assistance by the international community. As shown by the agony of Rwanda and its potential repetition in Burundi, resolving this dilemma will be neither clear-cut nor easy.

While the UN may be out of peace enforcement and its future with regard to protective engagement unclear, other questions will arise about the future of its other peacekeeping roles. Peacemaking and classical peacekeeping, when it is confined to observer missions, will continue since the costs, personnel requirements, and risks involved are all low.

A large-scale PKO, whether or not its chances for success are complicated by a complex nation-building mandate, will travel a much rougher road to approval than in the recent past. Even in classical peacekeeping, once the mission is expanded beyond observation to the close monitoring of a cease-fire, the size, cost, and risk of a PKO can go up quickly. As these factors increase, so will the resistance to new initiatives, particularly those in which the duration of the operation is unclear and the exit strategy of the peacekeepers undefined.

Perhaps the most interesting question is whether there is a future for large, complex, and costly peacebuilding missions like the one that succeeded in Mozambique and the efforts that failed in Angola. If not, the international community will have lost an important instrument that, under the right circumstances, can help restore order in a failed state. If Kaplan is right, anarchy is a growth industry, and there will be no shortage of future opportunities for such efforts.[37] Even if his pessimism proves excessive, peacebuilding is an option that the UN will need to consider in its attempts to ensure international peace and security. But before peacebuilding can be seriously considered, an understanding of the reasons for failure in the recent past should be reached. Only then can attempts be made to ensure that peacebuilding succeeds in the future.

Defining Failure

Just as there have been attempts to arrive at a consistent set of definitions of what constitutes the different types of peacekeeping, there have also been efforts to define when a PKO is a success. And as in defining peacekeeping, the experts cannot agree on how best to do it. One of the most significant discussions of success criteria was only able to conclude that "different actors and constituencies have different objectives and criteria for evaluating success."[38] The most comprehensive definition of success has been by Bratt, who lists four distinct criteria for measuring success: completion of the mandate, facilitation of conflict resolution, containment of the conflict, and limitation of casualties.[39]

Even such a complete set of criteria should be used with some caution. Mozambique qualifies as a success in terms of all four indicators. In Angola, however, there were four separate, although sequential, PKOs. Looking at completion of the mandate results in the conclusion that in Angola there was a success (UNAVEM I), a failure (UNAVEM II), and two partial successes (UNAVEM III and MONUA) that fulfilled parts of their mandate, but failed to prevent a return to war.

Containment of the conflict may not be a real accomplishment of the PKO if expansion of the conflict is not a real danger. There was some potential for it in Mozambique, but this was eliminated when the peacekeepers arrived and troops guarding transportation corridors from

Zimbabwe and Malawi went home. Angola had a spillover effect on all its neighbors and especially on Zaire, which the peacekeepers could do little to prevent.

Limiting the number of casualties can be a debatable achievement, especially if the PKO is not brought to an end or is terminated without an end to the conflict. There was almost no fighting in Mozambique after the peacekeepers arrived, but they were able to do little to prevent renewed hostilities in Angola.

Facilitation of conflict resolution is perhaps the most important thing a PKO can achieve, since it was conflict that brought the operation into being in the first place. Even this is not the ultimate measure. As will be discussed, in classical peacekeeping in intrastate conflicts, limiting casualties and containing the conflict are often sufficient reason to justify the continued existence of the PKO and to consider it a success by three of the four measures.

ONUMOZ did help ensure that the conflict was resolved in Mozambique and the peace agreement implemented, but it is unclear whether the international community will do enough following the departure of the peacekeepers to ensure the peace lasts. In Angola, conflict resolution has been a series of temporary fixes that have ultimately broken down repeatedly over the issue of how political power is to be shared. As will be seen, this issue has yet to be resolved, and Angola may not know lasting peace until it is.

Chapter Two

A Brief History of Peacekeeping

In the fifty years since the creation of the United Nations, peacekeeping has gone through several distinct phases. After an initial start-up era in the years immediately following World War II, these phases have alternated between periods of rapid growth and periods of inactivity. The first two expansion periods saw a significant increase in the number of new PKOs launched, mainly in response to conflict in the Middle East. Tension between the two superpowers brought these two expansion periods to a close. Both of them were followed by eras in which peacekeeping was confined almost solely to the continuation of ongoing missions. A third cycle of the ebb and flow began with the end of the Cold War. The expansion phase of the most recent cycle was the most ambitious in the UN's history. When failed operations demonstrated how overly ambitious this expansion of peacekeeping had been, the current period of relative inactivity began.

In his case-by-case assessment of the history of peacekeeping, Wiseman divided peacekeeping operations into five different eras: (1) the Nascent Period, 1946–1956, (2) the Assertive Period, 1956–1967, (3) the Dormant Period, 1967–1973, (4) the Resurgent Period, 1973–1978, and (5) the Maintenance Period, 1978–1985.[1] To these five, Fetherston's more recent analysis of peacekeeping history contributed one more: the Expansion Period, 1988–1993.[2] To bring us to the present and to complete the third cycle of expansion followed by a sharp reduction in the number of PKOs initiated, one more period must be added.

This final phase could be labeled appropriately the Contraction Period, because in the post-Somalia world of peacekeeping, there has been little new activity and a steady decline in the number, size, and scope of existing missions. Since 1993, the most significant PKOs begun were the latest iterations of previously unsuccessful efforts in the former Yugoslavia and Angola. Peacekeeping in the former Yugoslavia evolved into several separate operations—UNPROFOR and UNMIBH in Bosnia, UNCRO and UNMOP in Croatia, UNPREDEP in Macedonia, and UNTAES in Eastern Slavonia. Following the failure of UNAVEM II, the Angola operation moved into its third generation as UNAVEM III and then became MONUA.

The few completely new initiatives begun after October 1993 were generally small and often brief. An observer mission (UNMOT) of 40 was sent to Tajikistan, 15 monitors (UNASOG) went to the Aouzou Strip in Chad for two months to verify the Libyan withdrawal, 155 military observers (MINUGUA) were dispatched to Guatemala for less than 5 months, and 41 military observers are in Sierra Leone (UNOSMIL). One medium-sized operation with an authorized strength of 1,350 was put into the Central African Republic (MINURCA) to help stabilize the situation. Only two new major PKOs have been launched since October 1993 and can be considered to have been undertaken because of special circumstances. Both operations were begun mainly because the countries that were their chief sponsors had been receiving numerous refugees from the countries where the peacekeepers were sent—Haiti (UNMIH followed by UNTMIH) in the case of the United States, and Albania in the case of Italy.[3] Indeed, it appears that only when a situation generates a significant number of refugees directly onto the shores of a major power is it deemed serious enough to necessitate the initiation of a PKO with personnel numbered in the thousands. This seems to be the unwritten policy at present during the Contraction Period.

A number of missions have been either closed or downsized during the Contraction Period, reflecting a desire to reduce the size and number of PKOs. UNMIH became UNTMIH with the "T" added to indicate it was a transition mission. UNAVEM III became MONUA—an observer mission. In addition to UNASOG, UNPROFOR, and UNCRO, the missions terminated since 1993 include those in El Salvador (ONUSAL), Somalia (UNOSOM II), Mozambique (ONUMOZ), Liberia (UNOMIL), and Rwanda (UNOMUR and UNAMIR). This last mission was launched just before the deaths in Mogadishu, and its failure to prevent the genocide in the Rwandan conflict added further significant damage to the image of peacekeeping.[4]

The Contraction Period seems to be more than the scaling back that followed the UN's disastrous experience in the Congo. Somalia, Bosnia, and Rwanda have created so many doubts about peacekeeping that the international community finds itself in an era of both self-doubt and self-constraint, and it is an open question how long this era will last. Until the next period begins, new missions will be rarer, their size small, and their mandates narrowly focused.

To understand how peacekeeping got to where it is today and where it might go in the future, it is necessary to consider its past in greater detail.

The Nascent Period, 1946–1956

In its initial ten years of existence the UN launched only a few observer missions and commissions, to which the term "peacekeeping" was not even applied. The first two operations undertaken—UNTSO in Israel and UNMOGIP in Kashmir—are still in existence. In both, the number of personnel involved is less than a couple of hundred and their annual costs are correspondingly low: about $30 million and $8 million respectively. Both of these operations involve classical peacekeeping duties in intrastate conflicts. In addition to its mandated tasks, one important role played by UNTSO over its long history has been to provide a ready source of experienced personnel for the start-up of other PKOs. Since each new PKO has generally been started on an ad hoc basis on short notice, this contribution has been significant.

The Assertive Period, 1956–1967

This next decade in peacekeeping history was one of innovation and activity second only to the Expansion Period that ended in 1993. Renewed conflict in the Middle East and one of the early struggles toward decolonization provided new opportunities for peacekeeping. Eight new PKOs were launched that included not only observer missions (UNOGIL in Lebanon, UNYOM in Yemen, DOMREP in the Dominican Republic, and UNIPOM in India-Pakistan) but three major operations with more complex duties (UNEF I in Egypt, ONUC in the Congo, UNSF in West New Guinea, and UNFICYP in Cyprus).

Because it was being applied under different circumstances than in the past, peacekeeping during this period broke new ground in several respects. For the first time, the UN assumed temporary authority over a territory in transition to independence, added civilian police to a PKO, became involved in a civil war, established a large-scale operation, and allowed the peacekeepers to carry arms.

UNEF I was the first of the large, armed PKOs and was established in response to the 1956 Suez Crisis. The first operation explicitly labeled "peacekeeping," it placed at risk not only nearly 6,000 neutral troops but the credibility of the UN as well. UNEF I proved the UN could do more than serve as a forum for debate, and it helped keep the peace in the Sinai for longer than a decade. That credibility suffered, however, when the operation was withdrawn in the rising tensions that preceded the June 1967 war. At least one writer has concluded that because of this experience, the UN has been reluctant to withdraw once engaged, even when it would have been better to do so.[5]

UNEF I also brought about another important innovation. It gave rise to the drafting of a set of key principles that were to guide most subsequent PKOs for years to come.[6] These principles provided that peacekeeping missions would be: (1) established with the consent of the parties to the dispute; (2) allowed to use force only in self-defense; (3) composed of troops voluntarily furnished by neutral countries; (4) impartial; and (5) under the day-to-day control of the Secretary General.

When UNEF I succeeded in fulfilling its mandate to secure the ceasefire and monitor the withdrawal of foreign forces, optimism about the potential for peacekeeping rose. This optimism suffered a severe setback in 1960 when ONUC, the operation in the Congo, set some other firsts. It was the first time the UN had intervened in a civil war, although this was done primarily to prevent the superpowers from coming to a confrontation over the Congo. While it eventually succeeded in keeping the Congo together and putting down the secession attempt by Katanga Province, ONUC was in several respects the UN's first major peacekeeping failure.

During ONUC, the UN violated most of the five principles that had been established during UNEF I. The nonuse of force, impartiality, and the consent of the parties were all ignored, as the UN forces were directed to "take all necessary steps in consultation with the Congolese government to provide it with such military assistance as may be necessary."[7]

Armed with this vague mandate, the peacekeepers tried to restore order to the Congo, sometimes by force. In the process, 126 of them were killed, along with Secretary General Hammarskjold and an unknown number of Congolese. As the operation became more costly, both in lives and dollars, discussions in the Security Council as to whether ONUC should proceed reached a deadlock. General Assembly resolutions were then invoked to enable ONUC to continue. This maneuver provoked bitter disputes about how ONUC was authorized, run, and funded. For their own reasons, the Soviet Union, France, and others refused to help pay the operation's $411 million cost, and the UN was brought to the verge of bankruptcy before ONUC was ended in 1964.

Thus ended the UN's first attempt at multidimensional peacekeeping. Rikhye (1974) believed that had the extent of the cost been foreseen, the operation would not have been undertaken. He also speculated that a PKO of this type would probably never be repeated, not so much because of its size but because of the complexity and dimensions of the tasks involved.[8] Rikhye's prediction remained true for some time. Three decades would elapse between the start of ONUC and the initiation of another PKO of similar size and complexity.

Durch (1993) lists three basic conditions determining when peace-keeping should be attempted and what would give it a chance for success: first, consent of the parties; second, a change in the objectives of the parties from winning everything to salvaging something; and third, the support of the Great Powers. At one time or another ONUC violated all three and has been described as the UN's Vietnam.[9] Whatever the correct analogy, in its wake the UN Secretariat and the member states appeared mainly interested in forgetting the experience. Instead of learning from it and seeking to execute such operations better, the institution seemed intent on simply avoiding similar commitments in the future.[10] This inability to identify and assimilate lessons learned and the retreat to simpler mandates was to be seen again in the future.

The Dormant Period, 1967–1973

In part because of the reaction to the Congo experience, the first era of peacekeeping inactivity ensued. Seven years passed with no new PKOs launched. The period did not lack conflicts, but none reached a crisis stage sufficient to prompt the UN to act or to overcome the legacy of ONUC. Wiseman also suggests that efforts by the newly founded Organization of African Unity to use its own regional security measures and superpower rivalry contributed to this hiatus in initiating new missions.[11]

Rikhye, writing at the end of this period, subscribed to the latter as the primary reason for the pause. He lamented the fact that "the deadlock between the Super Powers over matters of procedure and principle and the inflexibility of their positions in the Security Council have prevented any real progress in developing new concepts for peacekeeping."[12] Rikhye nonetheless argued that the UN was still the international institution best organized and equipped to conduct such missions.

The Resurgent Period, 1973–1978

Renewed conflict in the Middle East prompted a resurgence of peacekeeping activity, as three large-scale PKOs were launched during this period. All were in the Middle East (UNEF II in the Sinai, UNDOF on the Golan Heights, and UNIFIL in Lebanon); in fact, from 1965 through to the end of this period, no PKOs were begun outside that region. This supports Durch's argument that successful peacekeeping requires, among other things, the backing of the Great Powers.

Over the years the Middle East was an area where peacekeeping not only had the support of the United States and the Soviet Union but was consistently desired and applied by them irrespective of the state of their bilateral relations. The United States saw peacekeeping as a way to help assure the security of Israel, and the Soviet Union saw it as a way to lessen the cost of defeat to its Arab allies. This resurgence was limited in function, however, if not in size. All three of these new operations were limited to classical peacekeeping. Not yet having recovered from the Congo experience, the UN once again confined itself solely to the simpler task of assisting the resolution of interstate conflicts. While classical PKOs have less complicated mandates, their duration can be very long. UNDOF and UNIFIL are still active, with force levels of over a thousand in the former and over five thousand in the latter.

The Maintenance Period, 1978–1988

The next decade marked the second period of dormancy when no new PKOs were begun. The increased tensions between the superpowers during the Reagan administration once again resulted in a corresponding decline in what the UN was able to attempt. There were also no new conflicts in the Middle East that the Great Powers considered ripe for peacekeeping. When Israel's incursion into Lebanon took place, UNIFIL was already on the scene but able to do little to prevent the fighting. Peacekeeping activity in this period was restricted to the maintenance of ongoing operations in the Middle East (UNTSO, UNDOF, UNIFIL) and those in Cyprus and Kashmir. All of these PKOs were classical peacekeeping efforts and all of them continue performing this function today.

The Expansion Period, 1988–1993

A new era of activity began as the Cold War ended with more PKOs begun by the UN during the next five years than in all of the previous forty. This explosive growth in peacekeeping took place due to the convergence of three factors. First, the termination of the Cold War meant that the Soviet Union and the United States no longer needed to use the UN simply as a forum for acrimonious debate and blocking each other's initiatives. Instead, it was possible for them to cooperate on the world's problems and to use the UN as an effective instrument to deal with them.[13]

Hume describes how this new level of cooperation started with the efforts to bring about the end of the Iran-Iraq war and the launching of UNIIMOG, the observer group to monitor the cease-fire. He notes that "by the summer of 1990, Iraq's invasion of Kuwait triggered a reaction that revealed a new pattern in place."[14] In just four months, the Security Council—for the first time—moved through the progressive steps specified in Chapter VII of the UN Charter and authorized the use of force. Operation Desert Storm was the culmination of this process, and it showed that the international community could now agree on aggressive peace enforcement efforts as well as classical peacekeeping missions.

The second factor was the change in the nature and number of conflicts. In his 1991 book on the transformation of war, cited earlier, which describes the changes in the nature of the world's conflicts, Van Creveld asserts that the world is entering a new era. This is a time not of peaceful economic competition between trading blocks but of warfare between ethnic and religious groups.[15] It is an era in which conventional armies, states, and frontiers diminish in importance and wars are waged by groups that in the past were called terrorists, guerrillas, or bandits. The distinction between soldiers and civilians fades, and a population base is more important than a territorial one. Within Van Creveld's scenario, war becomes a much more direct experience for most civilians. Or, as another writer puts it, "Civilians, rather than soldiers, are the tactical targets, and fear, brutality, and murder are the foundation on which control is constructed."[16]

When the Charter of the UN was written, however, the drafters made two assumptions about the post–World War II era. It was believed that most conflicts would be between states and that the permanent members of the Security Council would work jointly to lead international efforts to contain such conflicts. For much of the Cold War, the first assumption proved correct, while the second did not. In the post–Cold War period, ironically, the situation has reversed. The level of Security Council cooperation has never been higher, but there are few interstate wars to resolve.

As Van Creveld noted, none of the perhaps two dozen armed conflicts being fought all over the world involved a state on both sides. Evans, writing a couple of years later, maintained that 29 of the 30 conflicts under way were within state borders and that the incidence of civil war was not abating. He explained the decline in interstate conflict as a result of a new global norm to resist territorial aggression, the increasing effectiveness of economic power in advancing a nation's interests, and the decreasing ability of military power to do so.[17]

The growing number of civil wars rarely took place within countries in which the Great Powers felt their vital interests were at stake, however. Unilateral military intervention was therefore not usually an option given serious consideration, except occasionally by the French in their former colonies. This left it to the international community to take action on a multilateral basis, and the UN was almost always the organization best able to act. The increase in intrastate conflicts gave it ample opportunities to do so.

The growth of peacekeeping and the decline of war as a conflict between states can both be seen in the statistics: only one of the five PKOs in existence in early 1988 was involved an intrastate conflict. In the 21 missions established between 1988 and 1995, 13 related to intrastate conflict, including nine of the last 11 initiated. Of the 10 established during 1996, 1997 and 1998, all dealt with internal conflicts if one assumes Croatia's problems with the other remnants of the former Yugoslavia are internal.

Not only the number but the responsibilities of PKOs grew as intrastate conflicts increased. Whereas PKOs dispatched to deal with interstate wars engaged in classical peacekeeping, those that dealt with civil wars often had to involve themselves in the multidimensional aspects of nation building.[18]

Aside from the complexity and expense of nation building, these intrastate conflicts presented other challenges to the peacekeepers. Because they were often fought by rebel groups using guerrilla tactics against poorly funded, third-world armies, light arms and land mines became the weapons of choice. These factors made the conflicts harder to control and more likely to place the peacekeepers at risk.

In addition to peacekeeping becoming more possible and more necessary, the third factor that came into play was that it became more desired.

Public opinion would not allow policy makers to ignore the humanitarian disasters this new type of war created. Many writers attribute this to the "CNN effect"—the creation of the global electronic village in which the same images were transmitted simultaneously to millions of households. Thus news of the latest conflict came to the attention of the world as it was happening, and in living color.

Some government officials found this influence constructive. President Clinton's National Security Advisor commented in a speech: "We know that when the all-seeing eye of CNN finds real suffering abroad, Americans want their government to act—as they should and we should."[19] A former Secretary of State made a more cautious assessment: "We have yet to understand how profoundly the impact of CNN has changed things. The public hears of an event now in real time, before the State Department has had time to think about it. Consequently, we find ourselves reacting before we've had time to think. This is now the way we determine foreign policy—it's driven more by the daily events reported on TV than it used to be."[20]

Clearly the CNN effect brings pressure to bear on government officials to do something in these situations and to do it quickly. To meet this growing imperative for action, peacekeeping more frequently became the "something," as it provided the middle option between doing nothing and unilateral military intervention. This type of response by the international community can be problematic, however. While the international community will want to do something to deal with the humanitarian effects of an intrastate conflict, rarely will it be willing to do what is necessary militarily or politically to bring these internal wars to a definitive end. Occasionally a neighboring country or a former colonial power will be willing to step in, but that will be the exception. There will remain a wide range of situations that prompt pressure for action but that do not contain the conditions necessary for peacekeeping to succeed.

Furthermore, while the eye of CNN is all-seeing in the sense that it can reach anywhere, it can focus on only one image at a time. Those problems that are within its view get increased attention, sometimes to the exclusion of more pressing, but less visible, crises. For example, considerable attention was paid to Liberia in the early months of its civil war, but this interest evaporated when Iraq invaded Kuwait. Thus, the decision to intervene with peacekeepers is increasingly driven by what is on television rather than where that intervention is most needed or most likely to prove fruitful. Under such conditions, the pressure of events does assume more importance than thoughtful analysis.

It should also be kept in mind that the eye of CNN changes its focus from day to day, if not hourly. As a result, as Pearce described it: "The reporting of a crisis, especially one that is serious enough for the commitment of US troops to be a potential issue, presents a particular problem because it tends to generate a public opinion bell curve—with a sharp upside as horrors and atrocities are revealed, stirring public concern, discussion, and calls for action. The downside comes in an equally sharp drop-off of support for sustaining a troop commitment, once made—especially if casualties occur with no clear interest at stake and no clear exit in sight."[21] The resulting short attention span dictated by this bell curve is not limited to American audiences. With 130 million viewers in 140 countries, CNN has globalized the problem.

The growing number of civil wars during this period, in many cases involving ethnic differences, began taking a greater toll on innocent civilians. CNN's airing of these humanitarian disasters has had at least one constructive effect. National sovereignty, one of the principles underlying the UN charter, became a much less effective argument for those who claimed the international community had no right to intervene, even to end such suffering. Mandelbaum asserts that the declining inhibition against intervention results from the end of the Cold War (which eliminated much of the potential for superpower confrontation in these interventions) and the increasing acceptance of the protection of individual rights as an international norm.[22] This increasing acceptance is clearly encouraged when CNN demonstrates to the world the extent to which individual rights are violated in civil conflicts.

Whether it was due to the greater cooperation within the Security Council, the growth in the number of conflicts, or the increased attention paid to them because of CNN, the distinctive light blue helmets of the UN peacekeepers began to appear in many more places around the world. From a level of 9,000 in 1988, they increased to over 80,000 by 1993. During the Expansion Period, PKOs were sent to Afghanistan and Pakistan (UNGOMAP), Iran and Iraq (UNIIMOG), Iraq and Kuwait (UNIKOM), Uganda and Rwanda (UNOMUR), the Western Sahara (MINURSO), the former Yugoslavia (UNPROFOR), Georgia (UNOMIG), Liberia (UNOMIL), Haiti (UNMIH), Rwanda (UNAMIR), Angola (UNAVEM), Central America (ONUCA), Cambodia (UNAMIC and UNTAC), Somalia (UNISOM), and Mozambique (ONUMOZ). The inability of all of these missions to realize their objectives led to the current phase, in which the enthusiasm of the international community for new initiatives has greatly diminished.

The Contraction Period, 1993–?

The host of new operations undertaken during the Expansion Period, with more complex mandates operating under more difficult circumstances than in the past, resulted in significant successes but in major failures as well. The failures captured far more attention, however, as the scenes of a nation continuing to tear itself apart make more dramatic footage than those of a country trying to rebuild itself. While CNN contributed to peacekeeping's expansion, it also helped to usher in the present era of contraction. Not only did the peacekeepers not bring peace to Somalia, Bosnia, and Rwanda, but they were made to look totally ineffective or worse. Neither the public nor many analysts and commentators could understand why the peacekeepers often could not even defend themselves, let alone bring war lords to heel, end genocide, or prevent ethnic cleansing. As the international community struggles to deal with the growing potential for another episode of genocide in Burundi and faces other crises in the future, it will be constrained by this legacy of failure.

The Contraction Period has not prevented the continuation of the decades–old missions in the Middle East or the evolution of the efforts in the former Yugoslavia and Angola into different operations. The only new tasks given peacekeepers in the post–Somalia period have generally been small, brief observer missions with an authorized strength numbered in the dozens. Tajikistan, Chad, and Guatemala benefited from these PKOs. There were only two large PKOs launched in which the peacekeepers numbered in the thousands. These were in Albania and Haiti, however, and were initiated largely because they generated a major exodus of refugees directly into Italy and the United States respectively.

The peacekeepers completed their tasks, or at least gave up trying to complete them, and left Afghanistan, Mozambique, Central America, Cambodia, Somalia, Iran/Iraq, Rwanda, and some parts of the former Yugoslavia. A few statistics tell the tale of peacekeeping's shrinkage in recent years. Where there had been 82,000 blue helmets around the world in 1993, there were 70,000 in 1994. By 1995, there were 60,000 military and civilian personnel serving in 17 PKOs, at a total annual cost of $3.5 billion. By the end of 1996, although there were still 16 PKOs underway, only 26,000 peacekeepers were involved and the annual cost was down to $1.6 billion.[23]

The contraction in this period affected not only the number of individuals and the cost involved in peacekeeping but the functions the peacekeepers were asked to perform as well. During the Expansion Period, all five of the various peacekeeping roles defined earlier were undertaken. As long as the Contraction Period lasts, new PKOs will be limited in scope with some functions unlikely, if not impossible. Preventive diplomacy in the form of peacemaking and classical peacekeeping at low force levels will continue because the costs and risks are low. These were the kind of tasks given the three small observer missions in Tajikistan, Chad, and Guatemala.

A peace enforcement mission by the UN will probably not be tried again unless a situation arises similar to the instance in which it worked before—the American-led coalition in Operation Desert Storm. There the threat to American and other interests in not reversing Iraq's invasion of Kuwait was too great to ignore. Approval of either a protective engagement mission or another peace building-operation is also unlikely, except in a few special cases such as Haiti and Albania. In the former, little of perma- nence would have been accomplished without a serious attempt at nation building. In the latter, the mission was billed as protective engagement to permit humanitarian assistance and to help democratic elections take place. The lack of interest in a long term commitment to nation building efforts may make the success of this operation only temporary.

Albania is a good example of the type of PKO with limited goals and limited duration that may be typical of the Contraction Period. When "pyramid" savings schemes in that country collapsed and left thousands penniless, anarchy broke out, resulting in widespread violence and thou- sands of refugees.[24] After requests from Italy and the Albanian president, the Security Council authorized the establishment of a "temporary and limited multinational protection force to facilitate the safe and prompt de- livery of humanitarian assistance, and to help create a secure environment for the missions of international organizations in Albania, including those providing humanitarian assistance."[25]

Not only was the mandate limited, but the operation was given only three months from the adoption of the enabling resolution to the time when its existence was to be reevaluated. Two other aspects of the opera- tion demonstrated the differences in approach in the Contraction Period. Faced with a situation of anarchy but no real organized conflict, the peace- keepers were nonetheless given Chapter VII rules of engagement. As such, they could use the force necessary to ensure the security and freedom of movement of the operation's personnel and the mission's rapid completion of its mandate. The second notable aspect was the fact that the cost of the operation was to be borne solely by the participating member states.[26]

Italy wanted the peacekeeping force because it would help stabilize a neighbor and stem the flood of Albanians seeking refuge there from the economic and political chaos in Albania. Albanian President Sali Berisha wanted the peacekeeping force because he thought it might help him hang onto power. Even though he had completely lost control of the country, he sought to keep his job by delaying elections scheduled for June 29, 1997. While elections were the only hope for reconciliation, he knew he was sure to lose them. The Albanian people blamed his government for the fraudulent investment schemes that had robbed so many of their savings.[27]

The peacekeepers' mandate was so narrowly defined that they were not charged with disarming ordinary civilians, despite the fact that the government armories had all been looted and tens of thousands of weapons and millions of bullets had been stolen.[28] French, Italian, and Spanish peacekeeping troops began landing in Albania on April 15, 1997, even though there remained doubts about how they were going to carry out their vague but limited mandate.[29]

The elections were held on schedule, and, after some initial resistance, Berisha accepted his defeat. The elections were an implausible success given Albania's complete lack of democratic tradition. Many observers felt that it would be impossible to ensure free and fair elections, especially as there were parts of the country considered too dangerous and remote for the peacekeepers to enter to protect foreign election monitors.[30] The peacekeepers, who had numbered 7,000 at the time of the elections, began to depart as soon as the elections were over. The new prime minister, Fatos Nano, who would not be installed for another month, promised to end the chaos and restore stability without the help of the foreign troops.[31]

The mission's mandate had been extended by the Security Council until August 12. That date marked not only the end of the mandate, but, as one diplomat observed, "It is also the day the last one of the peacekeepers is out of here." Nano's willingness to do without foreign troops was therefore "simple realism, recognizing the reluctance of European governments to keep their soldiers in Albania any longer."[32]

The UN mission in Albania lasted from March 28 to August 12, 1997, and came and went so fast it did not even acquire its own acronym. It took a direct threat to the well-being of a major country like Italy to provide the impetus for the dispatch of the peacekeepers. The fact that the political solution was built on the shakiest of foundations was not enough to get them to stay. Although Italy did plan to send some 600 personnel to help train the police and the military, the country had very few units of either force intact when the peacekeepers departed.[33]

Such limited mandates and limited time frames as seen in Albania may have become the norm for PKOs in this era of scaled-down expectations and operations. How long the Contraction Period will last and what will come next are at this point unclear.

The Next Era

Over the history of peacekeeping, the first two periods of relative inactivity were brought to an end by a new round of conflict in the Middle East. The most recent dormant era was ended by the three post–Cold War factors that combined to produce the dramatic growth of the Expansion Period. New fighting or new peace agreements in the Middle East could prompt additional peacekeeping efforts. But it is hard to conceive of a scenario of conflict or compromise in that region requiring larger numbers of peacekeepers than the ones that have been there for years.

Peacekeeping could have a major resurgence if it were to be applied to the multidimensional tasks of peace building once again. There will be plenty of candidates for such multilateral rescue missions. A study of why states disintegrate found that the most likely candidates for failure were poor countries with the accompanying characteristics of a closed economy, high infant mortality, and a surplus of young men. A democratic rather than autocratic system of government only added to the potential for instability when the country lacked development.[34] Since underdevelopment is not something that can be cured in the short term, there is likely to be no shortage of failed states in which to try new efforts at peacekeeping. In such situations, however, the doubts created by recent experience will have to be overcome or forgotten before peacekeeping can be seen as a possible remedy.

The first six periods of peacekeeping lasted between five and eleven years with an average of just over seven years. A better understanding of why peacekeeping has succeeded or failed could bring the Contraction Period to an end sooner and allow the next era to begin.

Chapter Three

Failing Before Beginning

The success or failure of a peacekeeping operation can be preordained even before the arrival of the blue helmets on the scene of the conflict. These predeployment factors can be either particular to the UN and the way it operates or specific to the conflict in question. Among the former, the organizational factors, are the UN's process of deciding where to intervene, the mandate given the peacekeepers, who is chosen to lead and participate in the PKO, and how the mission is planned. The latter factors, the conflict-specific ones, will be examined in chapter four. How the UN operates, how it decides to become involved and what mandate it gives the peacekeepers are all elements that can affect the chances for achieving the mission's objectives prior to the actual start of the operation.

Organizational Factors

No one at the UN sits down and evaluates whether a conflict is a threat to international stability and whether the UN can intervene effectively. Instead, the UN responds to requests for peacekeeping, and those can come from several directions. In looking at PKOs initiated prior to 1991, Durch describes three sources of requests for UN peacekeeping missions: Security Council initiatives to quell a conventional conflict, independent requests from the local parties, and agreements brokered by third parties who then sought UN assistance in implementing those agreements.[1] The Security Council initiatives before 1991 were all begun in response to wars in the Middle East and represented about a quarter of PKOs undertaken. Requests from local parties made up another quarter and arose mostly from interstate conflicts that occurred during the early part of the Cold War. The remaining half of the PKOs begun before 1991 resulted from requests to help implement brokered agreements between the parties in a civil war.

Since 1991, the sources of requests for peacekeeping missions have changed dramatically as a result of the changing nature of war described earlier. Interstate conflicts have virtually disappeared, with Iraq's invasion of Kuwait being one of the rare exceptions. Of the PKO's launched since 1991, only three had classical peacekeeping responsibilities involving problems between two states—Iraq/Kuwait, Chad/Libya, and Rwanda/Uganda. The remaining PKOs were all within the borders of an individual state and usually had a multidimensional mandate. In most of these cases, the PKO resulted from a brokered request for UN assistance, usually because of a civil war.

Other peacekeeping initiatives came about because of a new level of Security Council activism stemming from the post–Cold War cooperation between the superpowers. Unlike the Security Council initiatives described by Durch, these new initiatives were peace enforcement or protective engagement efforts in the absence of a brokered agreement between the warring parties within a country. These attempts at peacekeeping in the absence of peace, or a clear desire from all the parties for UN intervention, are where the UN has had its most spectacular failures.

This type of peace enforcement operation, similar to the ones in Bosnia or Somalia, is not likely to be tried again soon by the UN, unless the interests of a major power are directly threatened. As the Secretary General has noted, neither he nor the Security Council "has the capacity to deploy, direct, command and control operations for this purpose, except perhaps on a very limited scale." He added that "it would be folly to attempt to do so at the present time when the Organization is resource starved and hard pressed."[2] Therefore brokered requests are likely to be the inspiration for an even greater percentage of peacekeeping efforts in the future. In such cases, the UN will be asked to implement an agreement without having had an opportunity to influence greatly the terms of that agreement. Thus the UN will be faced with turning down or accepting a request for a peacekeeping mission largely defined by others.

Deciding to Act

While in the words of one U.S. official, "the UN has a hard time turning its back on any country,"[3] making a choice as to whether to deploy peacekeepers is now both more necessary and more difficult than in the past.

The current budgetary environment and lack of enthusiasm for major new commitments make it clear that UN peacekeeping is no longer an option freely available in response to every international or humanitarian crisis. In the past, when the financial burden and limitations of peacekeeping were less well known, the UN's choice of where to get involved responded to a greater variety of factors. Security Council politics, especially the interests of the permanent members, the pressure generated by media attention, and the distractions at that point in time of other, more pressing international issues were more important than operational or economic limitations.

In the wake of the unsuccessful efforts in Somalia and Bosnia, the Security Council has attempted to recognize these new limitations and deal with them. One way was to spell out what it considered some of the conditions necessary for successful peacekeeping. At the same time, the council did not want to describe the minimum conditions required for initiation of a PKO, since this could limit itself too much. An internal UN assessment of the start-up phase of peacekeeping operations described these conditions as follows:[4]

> On May 3, 1994 the President of the Security Council stated on behalf of the Council that, in responding to situations on a case-by-case basis, and without prejudice to its ability to respond rapidly and flexibly as circumstances require, the Council considered that the following factors, among others, should be taken into account when the establishment of new peacekeeping operations was under consideration:
>
> (a) Whether a situation exists the continuation of which is likely to endanger or constitute a threat to international peace and security;
>
> (b) Whether regional or subregional organizations and arrangements exist and are ready and able to assist in resolving the situation;
>
> (c) Whether a cease-fire exists and whether the parties have committed themselves to a peace process intended to reach a political settlement;
>
> (d) Whether a clear political goal exists and whether it can be reflected in the mandate;
>
> (e) Whether a precise mandate for a UN operation can be formulated; and
>
> (f) Whether the safety and security of UN personnel can be reasonably ensured, including in particular whether reasonable guarantees can be obtained from the principal parties or factions regarding the safety and security of UN personnel.

These guidelines were felt necessary because both the Security Council and the Secretary General had recognized that there were three particularly important principles of peacekeeping—the consent of the parties, impartiality, and the nonuse of force except in self-defense.[5] Such factors and principles remain only guidelines and can be ignored if the pressure of other forces is sufficient. In the view of one U.S. official, "If a Security Council member really cares about initiating a PKO in a particular instance, it can get its way."[6] Or as Hume observed, "There is a collegial spirit among the SC's 15 ambassadors."[7] This spirit is reflected by the fact that much of the work of the council is done in informal sessions. Each council member gives due consideration to the interests of other members, and this is likely to be even more important in deciding on future operations, particularly if the PKO is a large one, as was the case in Haiti and Albania. Launching a PKO therefore requires the support of at least one major council member and the opposition of none.

In deciding when and where to deploy peacekeeping forces, the Security Council used to operate with several underlying assumptions—that a negotiated settlement is always preferable to a military victory, that ending the violence is always an immediate priority since it will save lives, and that the presence of peacekeepers will help achieve both of those aims. As one writer described it, the essential element in all peacekeeping operations is to sustain a controlled impasse until the political differences that gave rise to the conflict can be resolved.[8]

The present aversion to large PKOs may call for the reconsideration of some of these assumptions. The tendency now is to deploy small groups of observers with the hope that the parties will need only loose monitoring to maintain a cease-fire. There is also a tendency to use humanitarian aid as a substitute for taking the more difficult steps needed to achieve a political or military solution.

Reconsideration of the underlying assumptions is warranted, not only because peacekeeping is more difficult in practice than is assumed, but because they simply may no longer be valid. While they may have been true in the classical peacekeeping efforts in interstate conflicts, there is reason to doubt these assumptions in today's intrastate wars. Licklider has pointed out that not only have civil wars become more common and more violent since the end of the Cold War, but they are also less likely to be resolved by negotiation. In addition, when a negotiated settlement is arrived at, it is more likely to break down than a military one. He draws the tentative conclusion that the long-term casualties of negotiated settlements are likely to be greater than those of military victories.[9]

Licklider distinguishes between civil wars involving identity groups, which are becoming increasingly common, and those fought for political or economic reasons. He concludes that where the motivation for the fighting is ethnic or religious, a military victory is more likely to result in genocide. On the other hand, he finds that if a negotiated settlement in an identity civil war lasts for five years, it is likely to hold over the longer term.[10] While Licklider's findings are somewhat ambiguous, they should be taken to imply that peacekeeping guarantees neither better chances for a negotiated settlement nor lower casualties over the long term. At a minimum, a better understanding of the causes of the conflict might improve the chances for successful peacekeeping.

Pressure to initiate a peacekeeping operation can come from many directions. Triggers include what is appearing on CNN, concerns raised by member states, particularly those on the Security Council, or the suggestions of the Secretary General. Any serious assessment of whether the peacekeepers will contribute to a long-term solution to a conflict, and more importantly whether they might not, seems to be only one factor among the many considered in deciding whether to insert them.

The Mandate

Since there are no provisions within the UN Charter for peacekeeping operations, the legal basis for each operation is the mandate given to it.[11] The Security Council sets the parameters of the operation when it determines its mandate. The mandate can doom the PKO to failure if it sets objectives that cannot be achieved, especially if it is unaccompanied by sufficient resources to achieve those objectives. Mandates can also suffer from too much ambiguity or from leaving the parties themselves with too much to accomplish on their own.

In other words, a mandate can suffer from being unrealistic, unsupported, too vague, or too weak. Sometimes it is intentionally so. As Durch noted, "mandates tend to reflect the political play in the Security Council."[12] The Security Council members, because they were acting either in accordance with their own interests or on the basis of faulty assessments of the situation, have been responsible for all four mandate-related failures in recent operations.

Peacekeeping efforts in the former Yugoslavia have been criticized by a number of writers for a failure by the UN to construct a mandate that addressed the problem and for allocating inadequate resources to support that mandate. Ignatieff, in reviewing two new books on Bosnia, asserted that "Having failed diplomatically, the West then fell back on a peacekeeping strategy whose mandate was woefully inadequate to the realities on the ground."[13]

Finnegan makes an even harsher assessment. He believes Bosnia should not be construed as just another UN-peacekeeping failure, and that the UN accomplished its job, if that job "is understood to be providing political and diplomatic cover to Britain, France, Germany, Russia and the United States for their inaction in the face of ongoing aggression." He notes that "the UN went into Bosnia with a mandate limited to providing humanitarian relief and with a doctrine of neutrality that made little distinction between the aggressors and victims."[14] Meisler agrees with Finnegan, saying that in Bosnia, America and its allies used the UN peacekeeping efforts as a fig leaf to disguise their unwillingness to take strong action.[15]

Others have criticized the mandate in Bosnia not for a lack of political will but for a lack of material and human resources. Eliasson has pointed out that the Security Council agreed to only 7,000 troops when UN military experts had projected that the protection of the safe areas in Bosnia would require 34,000 soldiers.[16] One UN commander in Bosnia bemoaned both a lack of will and resources. He stated shortly before resigning that "There is a fantastic gap between the resolutions of the Security Council, the will to execute those resolutions and the means available to commanders in the field."[17]

Even a mandate that does not lack the will or resources to be implemented can still fail because it is either too vague or too weak. A UN assessment of peacekeeping in Somalia identified the former as the problem with the mandate there. It observed that "evaluation of UNOSOM at all levels has concluded that the operation's mandate was vague, changed frequently during the process and was open to myriad interpretations."[18]

MINURSO, the peacekeeping operation in the Western Sahara, is an example of the mandate's being too weak, but this was by design, not by accident. Beginning in the mid-1980s, UN mediation was intended to arrive at a plan whereby Western Saharans could choose between independence and a merger with Morocco. By 1988, the government of Morocco and the Polisario independence movement had agreed in principle to a UN-supervised referendum, but they remained far apart on the details of its implementation. In such a situation, only the full cooperation of both sides with the objectives and procedures specified in MINURSO's mandate would have permitted the referendum to be carried out properly.

The success of the mission also depended on the loser's willingness to accept defeat, but neither side expected, or could afford, to lose.[19] Morocco was prepared to see a referendum held only if it would destroy the Polisario's claim to political legitimacy and for all practical purposes withdrew its consent and cooperation when the outcome of the referendum could not be assured. Even MINURSO's impartiality became a problem, since Morocco viewed this as a threat to achieving its goal.[20] The Polisario, on the other hand, needed to ensure that the referendum was conducted in such a way as to maximize the chances that those voters who were likely to support independence would be in the majority. They were therefore disposed to cooperate with the UN only to the extent that such cooperation helped assure that outcome.

The two great powers most concerned with the situation, France and the United States, had other interests in play besides the successful outcome of a peacekeeping operation. In diplomatic circles in Rabat the assumption was that losing the referendum would cost King Hassan his throne.[21] Since the possible loss of a moderate Arab leader and important ally could not be taken lightly, the mandate contained no enforcement mechanisms such as economic sanctions, due to French and American objections to such provisions.[22]

It is not surprising, therefore, that MINURSO was stymied at each step by a Moroccan government that saw the PKO only as a mechanism for achieving through negotiation what they could not accomplish militarily.[23] Morocco went so far as to place severe limits on the resupply of the peacekeepers, and Moroccan troops have placed the peacekeepers' safety at risk on more than one occasion. Thus 330 peacekeepers costing over $5 million a month preside over a stalemate that has continued since the operation began in 1991. Some would consider this an acceptable outcome, since the mission has kept the peace and fighting has not resumed. In this context, the PKO is, according to one American official, simply "part of an overall approach to keep the lid on."[24]

The former Secretary General pointed out that this situation could not continue indefinitely and suggested guidelines under which the referendum could be held. The Polisario rejected the formula proposed by the Secretary General to determine who would be eligible to vote. They were no doubt influenced by what one writer called "widespread reports of a pro-Moroccan bias by Boutros-Ghali, a personal friend of King Hassan."[25]

In addition to suspicion of the Secretary General's motives, the Polisario suffered from being unable to have greater influence over the drafting of MINURSO's mandate. Its situation is not unique. Nearly all of the governments of the nation states in the world have representatives at the UN, while few rebel movements do. Because of this and the fact that the UN

Charter is based on the principle of national sovereignty, a government is therefore better represented and probably more able to influence events than a guerrilla group or independence movement. This is often reflected in mandates, UN resolutions, and reports that favor the government's position or make generous allowances for its sense of sovereignty by playing down its failure to meet its commitments.

Tilly, in describing revolutionary situations, writes about de facto multiple sovereignties that arise due to the presence of a weak state, challengers to that state, and some measure of support for those challengers among the citizenry.[26] This is an apt description for most civil war situations in which the UN is considering launching a PKO. Nonetheless, the government will have greater influence on the mandate given to the PKO than the challengers to that government. And at the same time as they are inviting several thousand blue-helmeted troops into their country to help resolve a situation they have not been able to contain, the government, in the name of national sovereignty, will often try to limit the scope of the mission and the ability of the peacekeepers to carry it out. Such arguments often succeed in producing a flawed mandate and reduce its chances of successful implementation.

Not having a flawed mandate would help an operation's chances for success, but the perfect mandate from the peacekeepers' point of view may be difficult, if not impossible, to achieve. Berdal points out that:

> Security Council mandates, by their very nature, will continue to embody political compromises reflecting the competing interests of member states. As such they are unlikely ever to satisfy a ground commander's wish for an "unambiguous mission statement," a wish that in any UN-mounted peacekeeping operation is likely to be unfulfilled.[27]

The Role of the Secretary General

On June 19, 1996, reporters were summoned to a press conference at UN headquarters in New York. There the Secretary General's deputy spokesman, Ahmad Fawzi, put to an end the months of speculation regarding whether the Secretary General would run for a second term. Fawzi announced that Dr. Boutros-Ghali had taken the decision to run for reelection "in view of the strong encouragement that he has received from member states."[28]

While some member states may have wanted Boutros-Ghali to run again, one important member did not. The next day, the White House press secretary, Mike McCurry, told reporters that the U.S. would oppose a second term for the Secretary General and would use its veto, if necessary, to ensure he did not have one. In justifying this tough stance, one unnamed senior U.S. official maintained that Boutros-Ghali had "fought tooth and nail" against efforts to reform the UN bureaucracy and improve the efficiency of UN operations.[29]

Boutros-Ghali's declaration of his desire for a second term came as a surprise to few, despite the fact that he was originally elected with the understanding that he would serve only one. A mid-February 1996 *Washington Post* article described the near-unanimous belief among UN diplomats and officials that he intended to run for office again.[30] Initially the Clinton administration sought to avoid a public confrontation over the issue and refused to take a position in the absence of an announcement by the Secretary General. Republicans in Congress, however, attempted to force the debate into the open and use it as an issue in the presidential political campaign.[31] When administration officials reacted to this maneuver by hinting that they would oppose a second term, Boutros-Ghali brought the issue to a head rather than wait until nearer the end of his term.[32]

The Secretary General's reelection became a domestic political issue in the United States, not only because it got caught up in President Clinton's own bid for reelection. Criticism of the Secretary General in the American Congress was bipartisan and almost universal. He was widely regarded in Congress as a leader who had proved incapable of making radical changes in an unwieldy and inefficient organization.[33] A large measure of that congressional criticism also stemmed from the feeling that Boutros-Ghali bore much of the blame for the failure of UN peacekeeping in Bosnia.[34]

Clearly the Secretary General, as the top UN official, has a responsibility for peacekeeping, but how that responsibility is defined and carried out is open to debate. The UN Charter identifies the Secretary General as "the chief administrative officer" of the UN, permits him to "bring to the attention of the Security Council any matter which in his opinion may threaten the maintenance of international peace and security," and instructs him to perform those functions entrusted to him by UN organs.[35]

In an article in *Foreign Affairs*, Boutros-Ghali described that definition as far from precise and leaving much about the responsibilities of the position a mystery.[36] He asserted that it was the duty of the Secretary General to take a public stand on "orphan conflicts," which he defined as those wars that lack international attention, concern, and effort. He justified this stand by saying such conflicts demand and deserve that the international community commit the needed political, financial, humanitarian, civil, and, in some cases, military resources.[37]

In July 1995, the "safe haven" of Srebrenica had fallen, captured Muslim males had been led off to an uncertain fate, and Dutch peacekeeping troops had been taken hostage. As the UN was undergoing this humiliation in the former Yugoslavia, the Secretary General was on a plane to Africa. Asked why he did not cancel his trip in the midst of this latest Bosnian crisis, Boutros-Ghali replied that if he did, all the African countries would tell the world that while there is genocide in Africa, he was paying attention only to a village in Europe.[38]

In a subsequent newspaper article, the Secretary General justified taking the trip at that time by maintaining he had to draw the world's attention to the "underdog conflicts" that do not get the focus of the media and the attention of international public opinion. He also stated that "For the United Nations, the suffering of all peoples is equal. I also wanted to reassure African governments and people—especially those in crisis situations—that the United Nations attaches equal importance to their immense sufferings."[39]

The Secretary General had been successful in calling attention to at least one "forgotten" conflict in the past. One writer noted that "it was only after Boutros-Ghali made his controversial statement contrasting international responses to Bosnia and Somalia (the so-called 'rich white man's war' statement) that the United Nations was stirred into action."[40] One American official admitted that when the charge of racism was made in the key debate on Somalia, the American representative had no effective counterargument, and that debate marked a turning point in the UN's involvement in that country.[41] Apparently the lessons of Somalia did not dampen the Secretary General's enthusiasm for calling attention to such conflicts.

Boutros-Ghali was able to implement this higher level of UN activism because his five-year term as Secretary General coincided with the bulk of the Expansion Period, when the number, cost, and size of peacekeeping operations grew exponentially. It was also during those years that the UN's reach exceeded its grasp in Somalia, Bosnia, and Rwanda, resulting in the onset of the Contraction Period.

The Secretary General was running for reelection, however, and was not interested in losing votes by rejecting requests for peacekeeping. Whatever his motivation, the Secretary General can use his position as a bully pulpit to call attention to the world's forgotten conflicts—be they underdogs or orphans. While a Secretary General's compassion may be limitless, however, the abilities of his organization are not. Those limitations require decisions on when to engage the prestige and resources of the UN and when not to do so.

Certainly the Secretary General should bring to the attention of the Security Council situations that threaten international peace as provided for under the UN Charter. However, not every conflict threatens the international order. Furthermore, the UN does not have the financial, administrative, or military capacity to get involved in every conflict, even if one assumes a role for the UN to play in all of them. Durch has postulated that a PKO needs the support of the Great Powers, particularly the United States, to succeed.[42] That support will be governed by the interests of the Great Powers, which will not be materially affected by every conflict. In fact, the very definition of the increasingly common "teacup" wars that Gelb described is that they do not involve the interests of the Great Powers.

The question of a second term for the Secretary General was resolved only after the United States cast its veto against Boutros-Ghali on November 19, 1996.[43] Despite all the controversy about the reelection of Boutros-Ghali, a consensus candidate was found. On December 13, 1996 the Security Council unanimously agreed on the appointment of the Under Secretary General for Peacekeeping, Kofi Annan, for a five-year term as Secretary General beginning January 1, 1997.[44]

Annan, the first black African to hold the post, came with a career of UN experience and proven managerial ability.[45] Within six weeks of his assuming his office, however, at least one newspaper article questioned whether he would move quickly enough to change the organization sufficiently to satisfy its critics in the American Congress.[46] The fear expressed was whether someone known for having a cautious, consensus-building approach could bring about real reform within the UN. Thus while the new Secretary General could not have better qualifications in terms of peacekeeping experience, it will remain to be seen whether his proposals for reforming the UN will persuade American legislators to pay the over $1 billion the United States owes in back dues.

Annan did begin immediately to make some changes. Under Annan, the UN has taken a decidedly different approach to peacekeeping than that of Boutros-Ghali. In its assessment of its peacekeeping activities in 1996, the UN concluded that the defining feature of UN peacekeeping was "a determination to apply the difficult experiences of the decade's first half to the future."[47] The same report notes:

> Faced with a humanitarian and security crisis in the Great Lakes region of Africa, in November 1996, the Security Council endorsed an independent

multinational force—not a peacekeeping operation—led by Canada to facilitate humanitarian assistance and the voluntary repatriation of refugees in eastern Zaire as well as assistance to displace persons. The Secretary General, proposing such a multinational force in options he submitted to the Security Council, acknowledged that the UN lacked the capacity to deploy a sufficiently strong force quickly enough to cope with the situation. By year's end, amid considerable uncertainty, the Secretariat was making plans, as requested by the Security Council, for a UN operation to take over when the planned multinational force left the Great Lakes Region.[48]

The admission that the UN was incapable of dealing with the situation was at least refreshingly realistic. However, the alternative of letting a non-PKO composed of an ad hoc force try, in essence, to provide peacekeeping functions proved not to be a workable solution. As will be seen in the discussion on humanitarian assistance, the Canadian force never amounted to much and stayed a very short time. Nor was it subsequently replaced by a UN effort.

While the UN has become more selective about where it engages, it still faces problems about how to do that effectively. When the UN does decide to get involved in peacekeeping, for instance, it will always have difficulty coming up with the best people for the job.

Picking the Right People

At least one writer believes that "Selection of individuals or units to participate in multinational operations is, arguably, the most critical step in the operation."[49] Whether it is critical or merely important, picking the right people or the wrong ones can greatly affect the prospects for the success of a PKO. The most important of these personnel decisions is choosing the person to lead the operation.

The head of a PKO carries the title Special Representative of the Secretary General (SRSG). While the degree of administrative and political support from New York and competent staff at lower levels are important to a PKO's success, the key actor is obviously the person in charge on the scene. With the proliferation of conflicts to which peacekeeping has been applied and the more active use of preventive diplomacy, there has been a corresponding increase in the number of Special Representatives. In mid-1995, there were 22 SRSGs. Of that number, 7 were operating as traditional envoys for contacts with the parties to a particular dispute, and 9 were resident in zones of conflict. The duties of the latter usually included leading a peacekeeping mission.[50] By August 1997, there were 25 Special/Personal Representatives or Envoys of the Secretary General, perhaps reflecting the fact that individual emissaries are easier and cheaper to dispatch than peacekeeping operations.[51]

Hume describes four main challenges for an SRSG who is in charge of a multidimensional PKO: ensuring the parties remain committed to peaceful dialogue and renew their consent to the UN operation on a regular basis; revising the process of implementation as necessary, to meet changing circumstances or altered perspectives of the parties; maintaining international support for the plan, and making that support evident on the ground; and keeping the political, military, and economic elements of the implementation plan moving forward in a coordinated and coherent manner.[52]

Such tasks require considerable diplomatic, political, and administrative skills. SRSGs tend to be either senior statesmen or drawn from the ranks of career UN officials. The former are more likely to be used as special emissaries for specific contacts or negotiations of limited length. It is the latter who are often asked to reside in an area of conflict and spend months, and often years, leading a complicated PKO.

If the SRSG is one of the keys to a PKO's success, the manner of and motivation for his or her selection is an important factor. Even more than in most bureaucracies, the decision-making process in the UN on personnel issues is less than transparent from outside the organization. To outward appearance, those selected to head large PKOs seem to be senior UN officials with whom the Secretary General has a special relationship, or for whom there is a particular "political" argument that would justify the appointment.

For instance, one of Boutros-Ghali's first acts as Secretary General was to name Yasushi Akashi to lead UNTAC, the PKO in Cambodia. Akashi had worked for the UN since 1957 but had no direct peacekeeping experience during his lengthy career. He was chosen, nonetheless, in deference to Cambodian leader Prince Sihanouk's preferences and because it was hoped his selection would increase Japan's involvement in UN peacekeeping.[53]

While a long career operating within the UN bureaucracy appears to be considered useful experience when it comes to the complex task of heading a peacekeeping operation, there is reason to question whether it is a sufficient qualification to ensure a good chance of success. Some would argue that the role of SRSG calls for more than just a successful career at the UN, and that it requires certain political skills not necessarily possessed by all senior UN bureaucrats. As will be seen in the cases of Angola and Mozambique, senior management at the UN often seems to assume that a long UN career is both a necessary and sufficient condition for being an SRSG. The actual experiences of those two PKOs tend to support the argument that length of service is not enough.

Although the choice of the man or woman at the top is critical, the rest of the staff of a PKO also contribute to, or detract from, a PKO's chances for success. In a multidimensional effort, there will be large numbers of civilians as well as military contingents. There are many dedicated and competent international civil servants, but not all UN employees are capable and committed. To understand why this is so requires some explanation of the bureaucratic culture of the UN. In the words of one senior UN career official:

> There is a culture of secrecy in the UN and especially in the Secretariat in New York. Officials establish themselves and virtually cannot be removed. You would have to kill someone to get fired. The secrecy stems from self-interest and the Cold War fear that one's career could become a victim of a Super Power confrontation. The Secretariat is like the politburo used to be in a Communist government. Everything is inward looking and New York oriented. There is some contact with the field, but the outside world is far away. The majority of the staff are not there because of a commitment to the ideals of the UN. They got their job because they represent a geographic interest group and they keep their job because they are protected by their group or some other patron.[54]

Another very senior former UN official put it somewhat more succinctly: "During the Cold War, countries would send people to work in the Secretariat who were often either spies or the dead wood they wanted to get rid of from their own bureaucracies. Now it's just the dead wood."[55]

Mohammed Sahnoun, who was the first of five SRSGs to tackle Somalia, also described this generalized problem:

> The legacy of the Cold War is being felt both in the ineptitude of the UN's structures and in the waste of its human resources. Much of the recruitment of UN staff is done through governments and embassies, and the recruitment process does not necessarily respect the criteria of competence and experience. Even less regard is given the criterion of commitment.[56]

Sahnoun also noted that the problem is enshrined not just in tradition, but in Article 101(3) of the UN Charter, which states: "Due regard shall be paid to the importance of recruiting the staff on as wide a geographical basis as possible."[57]

The problems of the organization are not limited to recruitment but extend to advancement as well. The UN's formal personnel management system has been described as dysfunctional.[58] Evaluation of efficiency is made meaningless by the fact that 90 percent of the staff gets excellent ratings.[59] Instead of a merit system for promotion, there exists an informal network of patron-client relationships.

Since virtually everyone gets excellent efficiency reports, under such a system getting promoted becomes more a question of whom you know rather than what you do and how well you do it. Given this and the inward-looking, headquarters-oriented mentality within the UN, it is not surprising that PKOs are not considered to be on the fast track to bureaucratic success. As Durch noted, "the system does not reward Headquarters personnel who agree to serve in UN field missions."[60]

The problem of the quality of the personnel is amplified in a PKO. The career UN official cited earlier was even more explicit about the personnel quality problem for PKOs. According to that official: "No one volunteers for a field mission, unless they are interested in the financial incentive. Those assigned to a field mission are often sent because their supervisor saw it as an opportunity to get rid of dead wood." Or as another senior UN official with considerable peacekeeping experience put it: "PKOs are the dumping grounds for placement problems."[61] That is certainly not to say that all in a PKO are incapable, but even a few who lack commitment or ability can compound the problem of achieving the mission's aims. The trust between the parties to the conflict is always weak and is not enhanced by peacekeepers who are incompetent or corrupt.

Lack of competence and commitment affects not only the civilian personnel serving in PKOs. The military contingents have also had significant quality problems. On a national level, a study of the first 18 PKOs initiated up to 1990 concluded that a state's participation in peacekeeping resulted more from national interest than an idealistic commitment to the global community and international peace.[62] The range of these national interests grew as the number of PKOs increased during the Expansion Period, along with the number of troops required and the number of countries contributing them. As the number of contributing countries grew, the potential for divergence between national interests and international ideals did as well.

Prior to 1990, 33 countries had participated in 3 or more of the 18 PKOs initiated.[63] Of those, just over half were first-world countries. By 1994, the number of countries had doubled and in 1996 there were 70 contributing countries. Of these, only 22 had developed economies.[64] In the past, a troop-contributing country was likely to be from the first world. During the Expansion Period, this was true less than one third of the time. This distinction speaks to both the motivation and the capability of such forces. With armies, one gets what one pays for. Soldiers from first-world countries are better fed, led, and equipped because their governments can afford to make them so. That is not to say that such contingents are always problem-free, as is demonstrated by any number of incidents in various PKOs.

Economic factors, as well as expansion, may account for the growing percentage of second- and third-world soldiers among the military contingents of PKOs. Countries contributing troops to a PKO typically receive about a thousand dollars a month per soldier from the UN. In a first world army, this covers only a fraction of the country's costs of maintaining an individual soldier, and engaging in peacekeeping is therefore a considerable additional expense. In some second- and third-world armies, the amount received from the UN more than covers the support costs of the individual soldier, and the government in question can actually come out well ahead. For military observers, the cost to the UN is even higher, as they receive a per diem rate that will be a hundred dollars a day or more.

How much a government makes from contributing troops to peace-keeping is up to the government. Soldiers from Zimbabwe on peacekeeping missions receive one third of what the UN pays, while their government keeps the rest. India and Pakistan retain the entire amount and give nothing extra to their troops, with a predictable impact on motivation and morale.[65]

The cost to the UN of armies from first-world countries participating in peacekeeping is different from the cost of third-world armies in another respect. The former usually have a great deal of equipment to bring with them. The latter, on the other hand, are usually equipment-deficient, especially in transportation assets. The UN must either accept this lower capability or pay to remedy it.

The problem of the quality of peacekeeping troops is another element that the UN finds difficult to manage. While it can ask for an individual soldier to be repatriated, the UN lacks the authority to discipline those who serve in its name. The UN compounds this problem by ignoring such situations or at least never publicly identifying those responsible. To do so would risk embarrassing a member state, and such confrontations are avoided by the UN even when it means tolerating unacceptable actions or substandard performance.

The UN's unwillingness to deal more assertively with bad behavior can undermine the credibility of peacekeeping forces that depend on their image as much as anything for their own protection. Nevertheless, the *International Herald Tribune* reported:

> Corruption among soldiers in the UN peacekeeping mission in the former Yugoslavia always has been a problem, and troops from the former Soviet Bloc nations are said by military and UN officials to be the most active in black marketeering, running prostitution rings and facilitating military maneuvers and resupply operations by the Serbs. UN efforts to stamp out the malfeasance have generally been ineffectual, partly because Russia, a permanent member of the UN Security Council, has hampered investigations and partly because the culture of the $1 billion-a-year UN operation in the Balkans has often turned a blind eye to the problem.[66]

The problem and the UN's inability to deal with it are not unique to the former Yugoslavia. Of the 81 military personnel sent home from the PKO in Cambodia for disciplinary reasons, 56 were Bulgarians. Yet a UN spokesman said that although the Bulgarians "behave in a manner that makes all of us blush," they could not be sent home en masse because "it would be a terrible insult."[67] In addition to the quality of the peacekeepers, another problem that often faces the UN is the quality of the peace.

What Kind of Peace to keep

The kind of peace and how it is arrived at will have a profound effect on the chances for successful peacekeeping. A UN expert on war-torn societies postulated four possible routes to arriving at peace: first, when one side defeats the other militarily; second, when a peace agreement has been negotiated but one or more sides continue to seek victory through other means; third, when peace has been imposed by an outside party; and fourth, when a negotiated settlement has been arrived at and accepted by the parties and is endorsed by the external actors who instigated and supported the conflict.[68]

Licklider concludes that while most civil wars end in military victory, the first type of peace, about one quarter of the 57 civil wars he studied, ended through negotiated settlements.[69] He also notes, however, that negotiated settlements of civil wars are more likely to break down into large-scale violence than are military victories. Ending a civil war through

negotiation is difficult because the stakes are so high and because no institution can be trusted to enforce agreements.

If civil war has been ended through military victory, peacekeeping is
probably unnecessary or unwanted, since it would infringe on the sovereignty of the victors. Peacekeeping is often desired when a civil war ends
through a negotiated settlement, since the parties will want a neutral party
to assist in its implementation. But if the settlement was imposed from the
outside or the parties are insincere, the peacekeepers can become pawns in
a game in which the parties pursue victory through other means. Thus the
second and third types of peace can often result in a return to fighting despite the efforts of the peacekeepers. It is only in the fourth type of
peace—in which the parties and external actors have arrived at a negotiated settlement and have settled for attaining some but not all of their
goals—that there will be reasonable prospects for peacekeeping to succeed.

Even when the parties are sincere, they may base their participation
in an agreement on assumptions that prove incorrect and may cause
them to rethink or renege on their commitments. When implementation
gets to the point of actually surrendering some measure of power, be it
military, economic, or political, the parties may balk. Every election has
a loser, and accepting that outcome is not easy for a party new to democracy. In fact, some parties seem to define a free and fair election as one
they did not lose.

How the peace was brokered can also affect its chances of lasting and
the prospects for peacekeeping efforts designed to ensure it does. Third-
party mediation and third-party facilitation have become more commonly
used in the post–Cold War era as mechanisms for conflict resolution.[70]
Third-party mediation is a process in which parties to a dispute attempt to
reach a mutually agreeable solution under the auspices of a third party.
Often mediators are not indifferent to the possible outcomes of negotiations and can have power and influence over one or both of the parties.
The mediator need not be impartial but simply acceptable to both parties.

Third-party facilitation, on the other hand, ideally works in a cooperative, nonhierarchical and noncoercive fashion. A facilitated resolution pro-
motes compliance by the parties because the solution is one they arrived
at themselves.[71] In the case of Mozambique, Hume observed, "Perhaps the
commitment of the parties to these arrangements will be more genuine
because the mediators had no leverage to impose solutions."[72]

Touval writes that despite some successful attempts at mediation between 1987 and 1991, the UN is not an effective mediator of international
disputes. He points to Afghanistan, Angola, Haiti, Somalia, and the former

Yugoslavia as conflicts that UN negotiators have tried and failed to resolve. He attributes this to the UN's inability to perform many of the basic functions of an effective mediator. Touval described the problem as follows:

> The UN does not serve well as an authoritative channel of communication. It has little real political leverage. Its promises and threats lack credibility. And it is incapable of pursuing coherent, flexible, and dynamic negotiations guided by an effective strategy. These limitations are ingrained and embedded and no amount of upgrading, expansion, or revamping of UN powers can correct those flaws.[73]

Instead he concludes that it is time to recognize the UN's shortcomings and stop giving the organization tasks it cannot perform.

What does the kind of peace and how it is arrived at imply for the success of peacekeeping? The less the degree of commitment and sincerity on the part of both sides to the conflict, the less likely it is a PKO will succeed. An agreement that has been facilitated, rather than mediated, inherently has a better chance for success because the parties have greater responsibility for the agreement's shape. Even so, the parties may attempt to assume too much control over, and responsibility for, the peace process. As a result, they may prove unable or unwilling to live up to their commitments when the time comes to implement them. The UN may be saddled with helping to implement the agreement whether or not it helped facilitate or mediate the outcome. In light of this, it becomes important to gauge the sincerity of the parties prior to a peacekeeping effort and to ensure that the UN has the authority it needs to succeed. Once the process is under way, the UN must be willing to use whatever leverage is available to keep things on track and to keep the parties in compliance with their own peace accords.

Planning, Logistics, and Rapid Reaction

Two often cited faults of UN peacekeeping efforts are: 1) inadequate planning once the mandate for a new mission is written, and 2) an inability to get troops to the scene rapidly. But do these easy and obvious criticisms have that much to do with the ultimate achievement of the mission's goals? Will rapidly plunging the blue helmets into the midst of a conflict and making sure they have sufficient paper clips and more essential supplies needed by a large military and civilian bureaucracy significantly affect their chances of success? Or is rapid reaction simply a formula for finding failure faster?

The planning problem arises, in part, from the natural tension between the planners, who want to take into account various contingencies, and the administrators, whose task it is to keep the budget down. The problem can also result from the occasional clash between civilian and military mindsets. Some believe planning problems to be critically important. One article in Daniel concluded:

> Our central contention is that the lack of functional political-military machinery within the UN, to assist in framing of resolutions under Chapters VI or VII and to manage any military aspects of their implementation and control, is a fundamental institutional gap that must be filled if the use of collectively sanctioned military measures is to be effective.[74]

The UN's own internal reports note the need for better planning. One 1995 UN report stated: "There is, as yet, no doctrine on the planning of UN peacekeeping operations."[75] One conclusion drawn by the UN's assessment of the lessons learned from the operation in Somalia: "It is essential to have an integrated mission plan covering political, humanitarian and military aspects, each dovetailed into and complementing the other."[76]

In a strictly military operation, such as a mission under Chapter VII like Desert Storm, which liberated Kuwait, logistics and planning can determine whether the opposing force is overcome. In a more limited but mainly military mission, such as an observer mission engaged in preventive diplomacy or a classical peacekeeping operation, planning will again be important to ensure the peacekeepers arrive at the right place at the right time in order to be able to keep the peace.

In a multidimensional effort designed to bring a permanent end to a civil war, however, there are other important factors besides planning. If the wrong people are given the wrong mandate, or if the parties have simply switched their tactics instead of their goals, good planning may make the bureaucratic machinery run more smoothly, but it will not save the operation.

If planning is important but not critical, what about the argument that a rapid reaction capability is vital to the success of peacekeeping? In his 1995 address to the General Assembly, the former US Secretary of State identified the need to "improve the UN's ability to respond rapidly when new missions are approved."[77] Many have suggested that this quicker response capability should take the form of a standing force. The Secretary

General has called on the United Nations "to give serious thought to the idea of a rapid reaction force."[78] A Canadian government proposal called for the creation of a force of 5,000 soldiers and civilians.[79] One think tank came up with a far more grandiose scheme, which called for the creation of "a 43,000–person standing UN Legion."[80]

Brian Urquhart, a career UN official with many years of peacekeeping experience, once suggested that the UN should have its own force of volunteers. In his view, such a force would not engage in preventive diplomacy, traditional peacekeeping, or large-scale peace enforcement but could usefully engage in immediate, small-scale peace enforcement actions.[81] He attributed the origin of this proposal to the UN's first Secretary General, Trygve Lie, who wrote that "even a small UN force would command respect, for it would have all the authority of the United Nations behind it."[82]

Urquhart made his proposal in 1993, just as the Expansion Period was about to be brought to a close. He had previously argued the other side of this issue. In his autobiography, published six years earlier on the eve of the Expansion Period, he pointed out that after the initial success of the UN's first major PKO, UNEF I, Secretary of State John Foster Dulles and a unanimous resolution of the American Congress both called for a standing UN peacekeeping force. Urquhart noted that Dag Hammarskjold resisted this "ephemeral tide of success and optimism." In his 1960 Secretary General's annual report, Hammarskjold wrote that "the organization of a standing UN force would represent an unnecessary and impractical measure, especially in view of the fact that every new situation and crisis is likely to represent new problems."[83]

The upbeat mood of the Expansion Period may have encouraged Urquhart to shift from Hammarskjold's caution to Lie's optimism with regard to the viability of a standing UN force. Reality has a way of clashing with the best of intentions, however, and Somalia, Bosnia, and Rwanda have negatively affected the arguments in favor of a standing force. The central problem is what kind of mandate the international community is willing to give the peacekeepers if they have to fight to keep the peace. It is unclear whether even with a UN version of the Foreign Legion the international community would be willing to see peacekeepers kill and be killed in large numbers in order to save others.

Lie's contention that even a small force would be sufficient since it had the might of the UN behind it may have been true in his time. In an interstate war with disciplined armies, the sight of light blue headgear might provoke respect. In today's "teacup wars" this is not the case. A Liberian teenage rebel, high on drugs or alcohol and wearing a dress and a wig to frighten his enemies, does not react in the same way that a disciplined soldier would. In the uncivil civil wars of today, the sight of UN peacekeepers is as likely to provoke resentment, contempt, distrust, and aggression as it is to generate respect.

Even if the mandate is a manageable one, there is reason to doubt whether a more rapid arrival increases the chances for success of a PKO. In two nation-building exercises that are considered successes, it was not. Heininger notes that in Cambodia "ironically, the lack of a strong presence in those early months may ultimately have worked in the UN's favor."[84] In Mozambique, the former SRSG, Aldo Ajello, believes the seven months it took the UN to field substantial numbers of troops was useful because it gave the former guerrillas time to organize as a political party and to create a base for implementing the peace accords.[85]

If the safety of the peacekeepers is an important consideration, and the intentions of the parties to a civil war are untested, does the earlier insertion of the UN forces bring any advantage? In an interstate war, in which two large armies with sophisticated weapons could make a miscalculation, a quick reaction on the part of the international community could help lower the risk of renewed fighting. In a civil war, in which guerrilla tactics are used, the fighting mainly directed at civilians, and the sincerity of the parties often in question, a stable cease-fire should be a precondition unless the UN is ready to fight to establish one.

Policymakers usually want to see action once a decision is made, especially when the motivation for that decision arises from public pressure and what is being seen on CNN. While some argue about the importance of the "CNN effect," others see a clear effect on policy and policymakers. In reviewing CNN reporter Peter Arnett's book, *Live from the Battlefield*, Shalev notes that "what emerges from this book is the power the media has in influencing policy—not because of a conscious motive, but by doing what Arnett has tried to do: describing what can be seen directly to the people who need to see it."[86] The problem is that a reporter standing in the midst of a battlefield provides a worm's-eye view of events that is usually devoid of context, analysis, or opposing points of view. It is these images, however, that often determine how and when decisions are made. When that happens, there is the danger, as Berdal noted, that "peacekeeping activities become merely a substitute for addressing the root cause of ethnic and communal violence and are not closely linked to an ongoing political process aimed at conflict resolution," in which case those activities "may prolong the war itself."[87]

The pressure to act, even when doing nothing would be the better course, will remain strong and will not always be resisted. As James noted:

> Sometimes the United Nations should be willing to stand back from involvement; or leave a situation which seems temporarily beyond recall. It is, perhaps a modicum of modesty and humility which is called for. Regrettably, a sojourn in New York—especially as a member of the Security Council—seems to sit uneasily with such characteristics and to inculcate an insistence on action, come what may.[88]

Conflict-Specific Factors

The most important ingredients in a recipe for civil war would include antagonistic local actors willing to fight each other, internal resources worth fighting over that can fuel the conflict, and outside forces that are willing to aid one side or the other. While the last two are not essential, the first one is. As noted earlier, the war can end because of military victory by one of the parties or because of a peace agreement. A peace agreement can be negotiated between the parties or be imposed from outside. If it is negotiated by the parties, their sincerity will be put to the test eventually and will be critical to the success of a PKO. As one UN study observed:

> Many parties in civil wars sign peace agreements for tactical reasons without intending to live up to their obligations. Movements and leaders may define the stakes in all or nothing terms. They may be willing to sign and implement an agreement if it suits their immediate interest, but will defect if the agreement will not bring them complete power.[89]

That a peace agreement can suddenly become more attractive for purely tactical reasons is illustrated by an article about the crisis in eastern Zaire in March 1997. As rebels advanced toward the country's third-largest city, Kisangani, President Mobutu quickly accepted a UN peace plan he had previously criticized. A Zairian government statement demanded "the deployment, without delay, of an international force to implement the peace plan of UN Special Envoy Mohammed Sahnoun to verify on the spot the withdrawal of all foreign forces."[90] The rebels, who were demanding Mobutu's departure from power, had achieved an uninterrupted string of military victories and were not interested. Ultimately, Mobutu was ousted without any peacekeepers having been thrown into the breach and perhaps manipulated to try to keep him in power.

The UN study cited earlier also points out that two other factors may come into play. Leaders can feel pressured to sign an agreement, but may suffer from "various decision-making pathologies that prevent them from implementing it."[91] Another potential problem arises from the fact that organizationally, the parties in civil wars are usually weaker than the opposing forces in interstate wars. Even if the leaders are sincere and capable of living up to their word, their movement may splinter, with some factions pursuing their own objectives that might make peace impossible.

Thus the intentions, capabilities, and unity of the parties can affect the chances for successful peacekeeping. The Secretary General has observed that in all of the UN's recent peacekeeping successes the consent of the parties, impartiality and the nonuse of force were present, and in most of the less successful missions at least one of those three principles was not.[92] For peacekeeping to succeed, however, the parties must do more than merely consent to the presence of the peacekeepers. As Durch hypothesized, "peacekeeping requires a prior alteration of the local parties' basic objectives, from winning everything to salvaging something."[93] Such basic changes in the goals of the combatants are more easily announced than genuinely made. Agreeing to a PKO can be an element in an alternative strategy, in which the goal is still to gain power, or simply an effort to gain time before the parties resume the armed struggle.

The UN is not particularly adept at assessing or dealing with the true motivations of the parties or at imposing a cost on the parties for their duplicity or failure to live up to their commitments. Diplomacy and impartiality seem to preclude identifying one side as dishonest or disingenuous. In a study of 81 conflicts between 1945 and 1985, Miall concluded that the UN is more successful in dealing with interstate rather than intrastate disputes, and that it is ill-equipped to cope with internal conflicts in which intangibles such as value differences are the primary cause of the problem. He believes diplomats are better at negotiating territory and resource conflicts than ones in which basic values are at stake.

Clearly territory and resources can be divided up and distributed more easily than political power or basic values and identities. The history of the conflict and the character and goals of the principal players are therefore relevant to determining these basic values. After that, an assessment should be made as to whether or not the determining values can be changed sufficiently to create space for successful peacekeeping.

Two elements that can hasten or impede any such change in values are internal resources and external influences. If the country in question is rich in natural resources, these can provide both an incentive for the parties to continue fighting and the revenue to make the arms purchases to do so. In the words of a former Liberian finance minister, talking about his country's civil war: "It is easy to get the impression that some people don't want this situation to end. This country was founded as a plantation state, and it remains a private farm in the eyes of many of those in charge."[94]

In a similar way, the external actors can make resolution of the conflict, and therefore the job of the peacekeepers, possible or impossible. In Cambodia, independent decisions by China and Vietnam to withdraw support from the factions they were backing "made the framework for a peace agreement possible and allowed each foreign patron to end its military supply relationship with its surrogate."[95]

The actions or perhaps just the acquiescence of neighboring states can have negative impact as well. The Liberian civil war was launched from neighboring Cote d'Ivoire, and that country and Burkina Faso were the conduits for most of the weapons used by at least one of the rebel factions. Aside from standard warnings in any number of UN resolutions for "all states to comply strictly with the embargo on all deliveries of weapons and military equipment to Liberia imposed by Resolution 788 of 1992,"[96] neither country has come under any criticism for its inaction. Whether it is external actors, internal resources or the parties themselves, as will be seen in the cases of Angola and Mozambique, such factors are critical to the success or failure of peacekeeping.

Chapter Four

Similar Histories, Different Outcomes

There are a number of factors particular to each conflict that can greatly affect the chances that peacekeepers will be able to help find permanent peace. They include the conflict's history, what kind of peace there is to keep, how that peace was negotiated, and the intentions and good faith of the parties. Mozambique and Angola differed significantly in all of these conflict-specific factors, even though both countries obtained their independence from Portugal at the same time and in much the same way. The differences in local actors, internal resources, and external forces all contributed to making the peace agreements to end their civil wars very different and, in the case of Angola, far more difficult to implement than in Mozambique.

Local Actors and Their Leadership Styles

The war in Angola started as two separate and largely spontaneous revolts in 1961, first in Luanda and then in the north.[1] The groups leading these revolts differed in every respect—ideology, regional base, foreign affiliations, racial attitudes, language, and experience in exile.[2] When the war reached a stalemate five years after it began, a third group was created based on a third socioeconomic network of subnational interests. The differences among these three liberation groups—the Popular Movement for the Liberation of Angola (MPLA) in Luanda, the National Front for the Liberation of Angola (FNLA) in the north, and the National Union for the Total Liberation of Angola (UNITA) in the south—were far from absolute but were reinforced by the leadership styles of their leaders and the foreign backers that supported each of them.[3]

Following the military coup in Lisbon in 1974, the new military government in Portugal abruptly decided to give its five African colonies their independence. In June 1975, the Portuguese signed the Alvor Accord with the MPLA, FNLA, and UNITA, which called for a coalition government composed of all three parties. This transitional government was to be short-lived, as the accord called for general elections in October 1975 and full independence the following month. Despite this short timetable, the Portuguese provided no institutional support for the transitional government, no system for the disarmament of insurgent forces, and no policy framework for keeping the parties together. Since Luanda was its regional stronghold, the MPLA filled most of the executive government posts. The other two parties were, not surprisingly, dissatisfied and distrustful of that result, even if it was to be temporary. Soon after the transitional government took office, heavy fighting broke out among all three rival groups.[4]

While there were three different political forces among Mozambique exiles, unlike Angola, where each leader formed his own movement, the Mozambicans were "initially united under the fatherly umbrella of Eduardo Mondlane."[5] This measure of initial hegemony within what was called the Mozambican Liberation Front (FRELIMO) was in dramatic contrast to the situation in Angola, with its competing liberation movements.[6] Mozambican nationalists were able to conduct their ideological debates within a single framework and to talk about unity in exile, before the conflict turned to violence.

Minter describes the contrast between the different leaders in Angola and Mozambique:

> Mondlane's unifying style of work (as head of FRELIMO), supported by (Tanzanian President) Nyerere's similar orientation, had a continuing impact after his death (in 1969.) Roberto's non-cooperative leadership style was notorious, raising the question whether other FNLA leaders might have been more receptive to reconciliation with the MPLA. Savimbi's monomaniacal quest for the top position and undying resentment of Luanda society, as well as his skill at ingratiating himself with different constituencies and sponsors, arguably played decisive roles in leading UNITA into alliances with the Portuguese military, South Africa and other external sponsors. Neto's poetic sensibility and personal dedication were coupled with an introverted leadership style which hampered communication with internal and external opponents.[7]

Minter draws a different conclusion about the two countries even after taking into account the question of leadership. He notes "the unity that emerged in the Mozambican independence movement could easily have failed, given different leadership and a different exile environment. It seems unlikely, however, that even drastically different leadership configurations could have overcome the many factors promoting disunity within Angolan nationalism."[8]

The peaceful debate and the unity among Mozambicans seeking independence did not last for long. As would frequently happen in the future, Angola served as an example that would inspire action within Mozambique. Fearing that a spontaneous insurrection might break out at any time, as had happened in Luanda, FRELIMO's leaders decided to launch their own armed action.[9] Disagreement with this decision and its subsequent failure to bring about a military victory increased the ideological and ethnic tensions within FRELIMO. A rival group based in Zambia called COREMO was established, and though it was militarily active only briefly in 1971, it remained "a potential alternative focus for nationalist sentiment."[10]

Hoile maintains that FRELIMO was unilaterally installed in government, despite the existence of several democratic opposition groupings enjoying similar political support, due to the sympathies of the leftist Portuguese administration in Lisbon at the time.[11] Hoile, a member of Britain's Conservative Party, is unsympathetic towards FRELIMO. Most Mozambican experts have different ideological leanings and arrive at a different interpretation of Mozambique's history.[12] They tend to see FRELIMO as the logical and legitimate inheritor of the reins of government.

Whether it was forethought or simply haste, Portugal gave FRELIMO power almost unconditionally through an agreement signed in Lusaka on September 7, 1974. It required a handover to a FRELIMO-dominated transitional government without elections, or even a referendum, and only nine months of interim administration before independence.[13] Even though the rapid chain of events within Portugal that led to the transition caught FRELIMO by surprise,[14] what opposition there was to the Lusaka agreement was contained. FRELIMO simply jailed, and in some cases executed, the members of rival parties. Despite violent efforts by some colonialists to turn back the clock, the initial resistance to FRELIMO's rule was easily overcome, and in contrast to Angola, one party was firmly in control from the beginning. This control did not remain unchallenged for long, however. Mozambique's white-ruled neighbors helped organize the Mozambican National Resistance (RENAMO) to punish FRELIMO for supporting liberation movements and thereby encouraged a civil war.

Internal Resources and External Forces

While there were differences in the number of groups and leadership styles of those fighting for independence, in both countries there was an initial period of relative calm after its attainment. In neither case did this calm last for very long. Bender describes the first nine months following the Lisbon coup as "the most peaceful phase of decolonization in Angola. The transitional government was barely in place, however, before the internecine conflicts which had dominated relations among Angolan nationalists during the past two decades were resumed."[15]

From the outset the fighting was fueled by Angola's vast diamond and oil resources and outside actors, including both superpowers. The MPLA drew on support from the Soviet Union and Cuba. The United States backed the FNLA and UNITA, and South Africa supported the latter. Their assistance involved more than arms and ammunition. Foreign troops took part on a massive scale, with the Cuban forces reaching a level of 50,000 supporting the MPLA, and thousands of South Africans fighting alongside UNITA.[16] Neither superpower nor the regional powers were willing to see their side lose.

The country's internal resources provided the funds to buy whatever outside aid might not have provided. Angola's oil wealth allowed its government to become the largest arms purchaser in sub-Saharan Africa. Mortgaging its future revenue from oil production, the Angolan government spent an estimated $3.5 billion on weapons imports in 1993 and 1994 alone. For its part, UNITA used the revenue from diamond mining in the areas under its control to buy weapons from private arms dealers and foreign governments.[17] Both sides, thanks to their internal resources and external benefactors, were able to make extensive use of heavy weapons and millions of land mines.

Mozambique was, in a perverse sense, blessed by the fact that it had far fewer internal resources with which to fuel its civil war or to encourage outsiders to do so. In comparison with Angola's oil and diamonds, which had enormous value and strategic importance, Mozambique's biggest exports were cashew nuts, cotton, and shrimp. All of these economic activities were valuable sources of foreign exchange for the government but were greatly curtailed both by postindependence economic policies and the war. A devastating drought, which affected all of southern Africa, may have been the final blow to any desire to continue the war. As the one diplomat intimately involved with the peace process observed: "It was perhaps nature itself which was the final catalyst in bringing the parties to agreement. Agricultural production virtually collapsed, inflicting a fatal blow to the Government's financial position and bringing widespread famine to the country side which hit RENAMO-controlled areas worst."[18] The international community did not rush to alleviate the effects of the drought in those areas under RENAMO's control. Food assistance might have prolonged the conflict by sustaining the rebels but there was little such aid. RENAMO's reputation for human rights abuses was so bad that relief agencies began to consider aid to the areas under its control only toward the end of the negotiation process.[19]

Besides fewer internal resources, Mozambique also benefited from far less external intervention, although it was to suffer greatly from the intervention of its neighbors. Birmingham notes that "the superpower involvement in Mozambique was predominantly covert." Although he does not explain what covert action actually occurred, he contrasts this with Angola, where "a war-by-proxy between the United States and the Soviet Union replaced Vietnam as one of the foci of Cold War confrontation between East and West."[20] Like Angola, Mozambique had an initial, postindependence period without major conflict. This was also short-lived, however, because despite the relative inactivity of the superpowers, Mozambique was by no means free from the influence of outside actors.

FRELIMO's opposition to minority rule in Rhodesia and South Africa caused those countries to begin providing organization, arms, and training to opposition forces inside Mozambique. Rhodesia continued to channel assistance to RENAMO from 1976 until 1980, when Zimbabwe became independent. At that time RENAMO "was transferred lock, stock and barrel"[21] to South Africa, who not only continued, but expanded the level of assistance.[22] Despite the signing of the Nkomati Accord in 1984, under which South Africa pledged to end support to RENAMO, the assistance continued, and diminished only once President de Klerk took office in 1989.[23]

While both sides in Mozambique benefited from external assistance and arms, the role of foreign troops in the conflict was far less significant than in Angola. While RENAMO had some help from foreign advisors, it did not have the assistance of foreign troops. Zimbabwean, Malawian, and Tanzanian forces and Soviet advisors did provide limited help to FRELIMO, but the vast majority of the effort by Mozambique's neighbors was aimed at keeping the transportation corridors through Mozambique open.

Minter concludes that if there had not been external support arising from the Cold War and the regional struggles to end white rule, Mozambique would probably have had no war and the one in Angola would have been shorter and more decisive.[24] Such a conclusion is at least debatable as he assumes the political differences within those countries could have been resolved with no, or at least much less, violence. However, it is clear the outside actors greatly exacerbated the situation.

The question of whether the absence of outside support would have precluded the creation of RENAMO is one that is often addressed in writings on Mozambique and is almost a litmus test of the ideological leanings of the writer. Those sympathetic to FRELIMO's ideology saw RENAMO not as a political movement but as a military unit developed by and under the control of the Rhodesians and subsequently the South Africans.[25] While the importance of outside support and organization is denied only by the most ardent RENAMO supporters, it is another thing to say that there would have been no war without it. One French anthropologist concluded that FRELIMO's style of governing made armed opposition inevitable.[26]

The suspicion that RENAMO was solely a creation of white minority governments in the region carried over into insisting that RENAMO had no popular appeal within Mozambique. For some it became such an article of faith that when one foreign correspondent reported that RENAMO's 38 percent of the vote in the parliamentary elections of 1994 demonstrated its support, one of his colleagues called his editor and tried to get him fired.[27] One academic researcher, who had been a high-ranking officer in the Mozambican air force, admitted however:

> It is fair to say that FRELIMO's policies, the war itself and FRELIMO's increasingly militaristic and authoritarian responses to it, paved the way for the transformation of RENAMO from an instrument of external aggression into the strongest expression of internal opposition, as suggested by the results of the October 1994 elections.[28]

Some measure of outside influence will always be a factor in civil wars. Only a country that is an island would have much of a chance of escaping that. Neighboring countries and regional powers will be tempted to intervene to encourage the outcome they favor. Nevertheless, whether it was external support, internal resources, or the leadership styles of the local elites, all three factors contributed significantly to making the civil war in Angola far more intractable and difficult to resolve permanently than in Mozambique.

Mediation and the Mandate

The way the conflict was mediated, the peace agreements that were concluded and the mandate that was given the peacekeepers were all profoundly different in Angola than in Mozambique. Together with the history of the conflict, these factors went a long way toward ensuring that the peacekeeping in the former would be a formidable, if not impossible, undertaking.

In the Mozambican conflict, the peace talks conducted in Rome were not the first attempt at reaching an agreement. In 1984, the South African government tried to mediate the first negotiations between RENAMO and FRELIMO. While the South African government had signed the Nkomati Accord with Mozambique, which required South Africa to cease providing support for RENAMO, the South African military continued to equip RENAMO via direct airlifts and via Malawi. As a result, the South African-brokered talks between the two sides collapsed almost immediately.[29]

Additional years of conflict proved to both sides that they could not win a military victory. Contacts between the Catholic Church and RENAMO in May 1988 began to explore the possibility of direct negotiations leading to peace. Governments, including those of Malawi, Kenya, Portugal, and Zimbabwe, offered to mediate, but their attempts made little progress. Over two years after the initial contacts with the Catholic Church were made, the two sides had their first meeting in Rome under its auspices. The talks benefited greatly from the financial support of the Italian government and the facilitation of the Community of Sant'Egidio, a Catholic lay society.

Sant'Egidio had no power over the parties or any vested interest in the outcome. It could only facilitate the process and could not mediate it in the strictest sense of the word. This arrangement allowed Sant'Egidio to help the parties arrive at their own agreement. The UN was not brought into the process until the final stages of the negotiations, in part because of the Mozambican government's concern about the implications such a UN role would have for national sovereignty.[30] As Berman notes: "the real reason for the delay in requesting UN assistance lay in the strong desire of the Government to marginalize the role of the UN in the negotiations."[31]

Although the UN was eventually asked to help implement the General Peace Agreement signed by both parties, it did not have significant influence on its design. Despite this fact, the agreement gave the UN a comprehensive range of tasks, including overall supervision of the peace process.[32] This result occurred more by luck than design. According to one observer, after two years of extensive negotiations in Rome, "the parties simply did not know the detailed implications of what they were signing."[33] The government of Mozambique was shocked to learn of the Secretary General's plans to deploy 7,300 blue helmets, since it had assumed that the UN would field somewhere between 100 and 300 unarmed military observers. It had not expected and did not want such a large force. The Security Council, however, was determined to avoid another costly embarrassment like UNAVEM II in Angola.[34]

The Mozambican government had to acquiesce in a UN role that carried with it significant authority. As the UN subsequently described it in its official history of the operation:

> Although not all aspects of the General Peace Agreement specifically required United Nations monitoring, the supervisory role allocated to the Organization carried the implication of responsibility for the entire peace process in Mozambique. The implementation of each part of the process was likely to come under the purview of the Supervisory and Monitoring Commission and therefore of the United Nations.[35]

In Mozambique, the UN had the distinct advantage of drawing on and learning from the experience in Angola. There the mediator, the peace agreement, the resulting mandate given to the UN, and the outcome were all vastly different. Angola had, like Mozambique, a long history of failed negotiations and mediators. In 1989, for example, President Mobutu brought President Dos Santos and Savimbi together for the first time at Gbadolite. The two Angolan leaders talked, shook hands, and gave their consent to an agreement calling for a cease-fire. Mobutu intended to visit Washington soon after the summit and was determined to get an agreement quickly. The MPLA maintained that Savimbi had, in an unofficial side document, agreed to integrate UNITA into the MPLA, to stop receiving foreign aid, and to go into exile for two years. Savimbi vigorously denied he had consented to his own political demise and the "Gbadolite Declaration" was stillborn.[36]

The following year, Portugal undertook the role of mediator. Portugal was chosen because it was acceptable to both parties and to the superpowers. In addition, Portugal wanted the opportunity to offset history's judgment about its responsibility for creating the conditions that had brought about Angola's civil war, and to demonstrate that Portugal still had influence in southern Africa.[37]

The protracted negotiations with Portuguese mediation made little initial progress. Lacking the diplomatic, economic, and military leverage to play the part of a mediator and advance the process, Portugal was also denied the time to act as a disinterested facilitator.[38] Neither Washington nor Moscow wanted to see its protégé defeated, but in the interests of a wider détente and a desire to resolve the related problem of Namibia, both wanted a quicker solution. The Angolan parties were therefore brought to the table by outside pressure and not by a desire to reconcile among themselves.[39]

To get the talks moving, the United States and the Soviet Union decided to introduce a new sense of urgency and eventually Secretary of State Baker and Foreign Minister Shevardnadze became personally involved in helping the parties work out the remaining details. Several additional rounds of negotiation ensued before a peace accord was finally signed on May 31, 1991, in Bicesse, Portugal. The Bicesse Accords, as they became known, were exceedingly detailed and comprehensive. They called for a multiparty political system, a new national army, termination of outside military assistance, a cease-fire, and internationally monitored elections. The MPLA, which had accepted the principle of a multiparty democracy only the month before, had wanted a three-year delay before elections, while UNITA pushed to have them within a year. A compromise was reached that required the elections to be held between 15 and 18 months following the cease-fire.[40]

Stemming perhaps from their continuing deep distrust of each other, the parties assigned themselves the key roles and responsibilities in the implementation of the peace agreement and gave only a very limited role to the UN. This was clearly spelled out in the Bicesse Accords, which state:

> The overall political control of the cease-fire process will be the responsibility of the Angolan parties acting through the Joint Political Military Commission (CCPM). The verification of the cease-fire will be the responsibility of the international monitoring group. The UN will be invited to send monitors to support the Angolan parties at the request of the Government of Angola. The governments that send monitors will be selected by the Angolan parties acting through the CCPM.[41]

The mandate of UNAVEM II was therefore to verify that the former combatants were faithfully monitoring the cease-fire and monitoring the neutrality of the Angolan police. The UN was also requested to provide technical assistance to the Angolan government and to observe and verify the electoral process, which was to be organized and directed by the National Electoral Council.[42] The UN neither chaired nor was even a member of the CCPM, which had overall responsibility for overseeing the peace process. It was permitted only to be an observer at CCPM meetings if invited.

UNAVEM I had comprised only 70 military observers, whose task was monitoring the withdrawal of Cuban troops. It was considered an important breakthrough because it was the first international presence in Angola and succeeded in its task. The Secretary General attributed this success to the mission having enjoyed the full cooperation of all the parties involved.[43] Given the expanded but still very limited mandate of UNAVEM II, the UN authorized the deployment of only 350 military observers. The mission's function (verification of the implementation of the peace accord by the parties) required only a limited number of blue helmets.

In addition to limited numbers, UNAVEM II also suffered, however, from competition from the UN's other peacekeeping activities. The Expansion Period had reached its most expanded point, and high-level attention and resources were in short supply. As Lodico explains:

> UNAVEM II's budget was too low and reflected the lack of political attention and concern that it received in comparison to other missions. During the time period in which UNAVEM II was launched, it competed for resources and attention with the missions already established in El Salvador, Western Sahara and Kuwait in the spring of 1991 and the very large missions established in Cambodia and Croatia in early 1992.[44]

The short supply of resources (and attention at the political level) might explain why the UN accepted such a limited mandate. Getting the cooperation of the parties made UNAVEM I a success, but that required only monitoring the departure of foreign troops. With the decline of Soviet support and Cuban enthusiasm for the war in Angola, the UN was required only to be a witness to the inevitable. For UNAVEM II to succeed, on the other hand, the two sides would have to complete a process that left one of them with the lion's share of political and economic power. At any point either of the parties could get cold feet and begin to renege on its commitments. At least a large UN presence would have made this backsliding more apparent if it happened.

UN peacekeeping had not really had a major failure since the Congo operation decades before. Even though the parties themselves had assumed all the major responsibilities for implementing the peace agreement and asked the UN only to verify their compliance, the UN felt compelled to agree. Given the time required to reach a peace agreement, and the efforts of Portugal and the superpowers to conclude it, the UN was reluctant to ask for modifications in the agreement that would make its conditions easier for the UN to enforce.

The combination of a weak mandate and few resources to implement it was further complicated and compounded by the UN's selection of the people assigned to carry out this mission impossible.

Picking the Right People

While all have been speaking with the benefit of hindsight, no one the author has talked to has described Margaret Anstee, who was named to head UNAVEM II, as the right person for the job.[45] More than one career UN official characterized her as a "development type" lacking the political skills necessary to implement a difficult mandate. Yet another asserted that she compounded this lack when she chose her staff badly and wound up having to rely on election experts rather than "political types." Other sources criticized her for not being aggressive enough and for accepting a situation in which the parties were obviously not fulfilling their commitments.

It is fair to ask whether anyone could have fulfilled the mandate assigned Anstee with the resources given her. It is also fair to question any alleged failure to choose the right people, since SRSGs seem to have only very limited influence over who works under them. Force commanders are named by the Secretary General, and New York can dictate to an SRSG who key members of a PKO are to be. One SRSG, despite his objections, was forced to take a procurement chief whose nickname, for obvious reasons, was "Mr. Ten Percent."[46]

Whatever Anstee's real or imagined faults, she did bring an impressive résumé to the job. She had nearly 40 years of distinguished UN service behind her, working mainly for the United Nations Development Program (UNDP), when she was offered the position in Angola. She suggests a reason for her being chosen when she notes that "the 'woman thing' also came into the picture" in her decision to accept the post.[47] Anstee, a self-described pioneer in many areas not previously open to women, had just written a chapter for a book, pointing out that peacekeeping was one area that women had not yet penetrated. One motivation of the UN management in selecting her may therefore have been to address just that criticism.

Whatever the motivation, it was a move that was made with haste in early 1992, even though the decision to appoint an SRSG for Angola had been made in principle the previous autumn. Anstee received the call offering her the job late on February 5, 1992, at her residence in Vienna, without any prior indication that she was under consideration for the post. The offer was made and she was given 24 hours to decide. She said yes on February 6, the appointment was announced the next day, and she was on a plane for Luanda nine days later.[48]

The selection of Aldo Ajello as the SRSG for Mozambique half a year later provides equally little assurance that it was a carefully considered decision. Called into the office of Under Secretary James Jonah in New York, Ajello was offered the job after a brief conversation. The discussion did not indicate why Ajello was chosen but instead consisted of Jonah asking for a few of the most basic facts concerning Ajello's background. Ajello's tongue-in-cheek explanation for his getting the position links it to the fact that Rome was the site of the peace talks that ended the conflict. Ajello speculated the UN management decided the SRSG should be an Italian because the talks were being heavily subsidized by the Italian Government. He added, not entirely in jest, that he believes he got the nod because his name came up first on the alphabetical list of senior UN officials with that qualification.[49]

Ajello's background—only ten years with UNDP but a number of years spent as a journalist and as an elected politician in Italy—appears to have had little bearing on the UN's decision. However, whether honed in Sicilian politics or not, Ajello's political skills were to prove instrumental in the success of ONUMOZ. In fairness to Anstee, it must be said that Ajello had a far stronger mandate and a mission strength of over 7,000 instead of several hundred. As will be discussed in the next chapter, this deficiency in manpower was exacerbated by the parties, who proved to be difficult in Mozambique but hopeless in Angola. Lastly, Ajello had one other advantage over Anstee. He arrived in Maputo just as the peace process collapsed in Angola and fighting broke out again. Anstee's experience showed just how difficult the role of SRSG could be, and those lessons were very helpful to Ajello in conducting his PKO.

The selection of the SRSG and her key staff members were not the only personnel issues for UNAVEM II. It suffered from a more generalized difficulty. In an operation that was kept to a minimum number of staff, any weak performers could have a major impact on the ability of the PKO to accomplish its mission. ONUMOZ had its share of incompetent staff, but it had a strength of over 7,000. Ajello could therefore work around those who could not do their jobs and assign their responsibilities elsewhere regardless of what the organizational charts said.

Anstee no such flexibility with so few people. In addition, as she described it, her efforts to recruit good people suffered from "the competition among several different peacekeeping missions being mounted at that time, some in more desirable sounding locations," and the fact that "Angola usually ranked last on lists of preferences of the volunteers."[50] Thus UNAVEM II lost out to other PKOs not only in the contest for attention and resources from New York but in the competition for the best people as well.

Anstee's efforts to find a good staff were also stymied by the UN quota system according to which a person's nationality is a more important qualification for a position than ability. Anstee notes that "the overriding consideration made very clear to me early on was that the Secretary General wished me to give preference to staff from developing countries and particularly Africans."[51] Outside recruitment was virtually excluded for budgetary reasons, and this "inevitably led to compromises, some of which were later to make an already difficult mission even harder to handle." Her efforts to find people who could speak Portuguese or even Spanish also met with little success. She points out that as a result "very nearly all senior officials of UNAVEM II could operate only through interpretation, which, however proficient, can never satisfactorily substitute for direct face-to-face exchanges, especially in delicate political negotiations."[52]

Whatever the shortcomings of the staff, the stage was set for the deployment of the peacekeepers. In Angola, UNAVEM II was launched with a small staff with serious shortcomings, few resources, and a weak mandate. It had to deal with a conflict that had a long history of massive external intervention, ample internal resources to fuel additional fighting, and local leaders who had only grudgingly been brought to agreement. Under such circumstances only the total cooperation, good faith, and scrupulous implementation of the Bicesse Accords by the Angolan parties could assure success. If not, all the UN could do was witness the peace coming apart.

In Mozambique, a country dependent on donor aid for survival in the midst of the worst drought of this century, ONUMOZ had a large staff, ample resources, and a mandate that gave it overall responsibility for the peace process. It had a much greater ability to influence the outcome and to certify convincingly that the parties had adhered to rules of the game. These predeployment differences alone go a long way toward explaining why the outcomes of the two PKOs were so different.

Chapter Five

Failing While Doing

As discussed in the last two chapters, a peacekeeping effort can be preordained to fail by predeployment factors such as the way its mandate is written. Once the peacekeepers are deployed, however, the operation enters its most critical phase. When the mission is under way, the causes of and chances for failure are most numerous. The PKO can fail at this stage either because the efforts of the peacekeepers are inadequate or because other factors prevent those efforts from succeeding. Failure can arise either within the UN as an organization or outside it. This chapter will look at the internal factors or how well the peacekeepers do their job. The subsequent two chapters will consider the effect of the external factors that the UN cannot entirely control and the role of humanitarian action and its potential for affecting the outcome of a PKO.

The internal factors have much to do with the way the UN and its bureaucratic culture operate. Once the peacekeepers are on the ground, how they do their job and the support they get from the Secretariat and the Security Council in New York can become causes of mission failure. In a multidimensional PKO, the blue helmets are handed a variety of tasks, and it would be difficult, if not impossible, to do them all well. If the key tasks are not completed, then fighting can break out anew and the PKO will have failed. Even a failure to accomplish some of the minor objectives may taint the operation enough to dampen the enthusiasm of the international community for launching future operations.

The tasks of a PKO can be broad or narrow, depending on the mission's mandate. This chapter will look at the major components and tasks of the peacekeeping operations in Angola and Mozambique to see where they succeeded and where they failed. In Angola, UNAVEM II was charged with verifying that three things were being accomplished: military demo-bilization, police neutrality, and the holding of fair elections.[1] The parties utterly failed to achieve the first two, despite UN attempts to persuade them to do so. The elections went ahead nonetheless, and while they were declared generally free and fair, UN monitoring efforts were inadequate to convince everyone that they were. When the loser called foul, there was sufficient confusion for his assertion to be believed by some. The war resumed shortly thereafter.

In Mozambique, the tasks assigned ONUMOZ were much broader and numerous, but the mandate and resources were much stronger. In addition to the three objectives in Angola, ONUMOZ had to supervise the cease-fire between the two parties, coordinate and monitor humanitarian assistance throughout the country, provide security for key transportation corridors, assist the reintegration of the demobilized soldiers, and oversee the formation of a single, unified army.[2] ONUMOZ accomplished the key elements of its mission. It was not an unqualified success, however, as will be seen by a closer look at how it operated and how well it went about fulfilling its many and varied responsibilities.

The Internal Factors

A multidimensional PKO designed to bring a permanent resolution to today's intrastate conflicts can include thousands of peacekeepers who have been given an array of responsibilities. A more limited mission can attempt to bring about the same result, but it will be given only a few functions and a couple of hundred people to accomplish them. Mozambique was an example of the former. Initially, Angola was an example of the latter, but after the failure of UNAVEM II, the effort there evolved into UNAVEM III—a mission as large and nearly as complex as ONUMOZ. An evaluation of each task assigned to these PKOs is useful in understanding where they succeeded and where they did not. This also requires considering how a PKO functions as an organization and how it relates to the rest of the UN.

The most important person in a PKO, whether small or large, is the one in charge. As the last chapter indicated, when a Special Representative of the Secretary General (SRSG) is selected to head a PKO, competence seems a secondary consideration. Mozambique was extremely fortunate, however, to have had Ajello as the head of ONUMOZ, although many of the key Mozambican players would be loath to admit it.[3] As one post-ONUMOZ assessment described it: "Unlike some other SRSG's who are selected more because of intra-UN bureaucratic politics than competence, Ajello was able and willing to use the political muscle at his disposal to push the process forward, to challenge the UN bureaucracy, and to deal squarely with foot-dragging by both Mozambican parties."[4]

Ajello not only had a strong mandate and ample resources, he was also willing to use both of them in a very flexible and, when necessary, aggressive manner. Such qualities are the antithesis of those possessed by the usual career diplomat or international bureaucrat, who will prize caution and discretion over initiative and boldness. Operating far from the New York bureaucracy, with local parties who were only recently opposing each other on the battlefield is a difficult, dynamic, and often dangerous environment. Ideally, it requires a person who has done more than make a career out of pushing paper and avoiding risks.

Ajello, fortunately, was cut from different cloth. For instance, when Afonso Dhlakama, the leader of RENAMO, was reluctant to come into Maputo for the first time during the peace process, Ajello proposed providing a heavy presence of UN soldiers along the roads Dhlakama would travel to give him some sense of security. The Brazilian general, who was in command of ONUMOZ's military component, argued strongly against taking on this task. He asserted that such a move was clearly outside the ONUMOZ mandate.

Ajello insisted, however, since there were no UN police or other forces available to do the job. Not to have done it would have left Dhlakama's welfare entirely in the hands of the government's police force. Ajello saw the deployment of the ONUMOZ blue helmets for this purpose as essential to getting over an important obstacle at a critical juncture in the peace process.[5] A more cautious UN civil servant would not have taken the gamble of overruling his military commander.

This was not the only example of Ajello's willingness to bend the rules when it was critical to the success of the mission. He was also able to make good use of the trust fund set up to provide resources to help RENAMO convert from a guerrilla group to a political party. While UN rules normally dictated that receipts should have been provided for all expenditures, a portion was provided to Dhlakama each month without such a requirement. While such creativity might give an accountant heartburn, it was another key factor in keeping the process going and keeping RENAMO a part of it.[6]

Nor was Ajello afraid to confront the parties when they failed to live up to their obligations. Early in the peace process, RENAMO was the more recalcitrant of the two former combatants. By the beginning of

1994, once the troops began to gather in large numbers in their assembly areas, RENAMO seemed to have definitely given up its military option. At that stage, it appeared committed to going ahead with the peace process or, at a minimum, it was unable to stop it. The government, on the other hand, became more difficult as the process unfolded. As a result, relations between the government and Ajello became progressively worse during the first half of 1994. As the government tried to slow down the assembly of its troops for demobilization, the army chief of staff accused ONU-MOZ of partiality toward RENAMO and even asserted that ONUMOZ was to blame for the refusal of his soldiers to join the new army.[7] In the end, after considerable international pressure orchestrated by Ajello, the government gave all of its remaining troops the option to join the new army or demobilize immediately. In overwhelming numbers, the men opted to become civilians.

Relations between ONUMOZ and the government were still strained, however, and the peace process appeared on the point of coming apart just as the registration of voters was getting under way. A delegation of Security Council representatives was dispatched from New York to review the situation. Upon their arrival on August 7, 1994, Ajello handed them each a blue binder entitled "Chronology of the Evolution of the Confrontational Attitude of the Government of Mozambique Towards ONUMOZ, April–August 1994," complete with 17 supporting documents. In its report on the trip, the mission noted, with the diplomatic understatement that characterizes such documents, that there was "a certain amount of friction between the Government and ONUMOZ, essentially because of the complexity of the situation." The report added that:

> With events moving rapidly, the Government has occasionally felt overlooked, unconsulted, and even blamed for delays. Overall, ONUMOZ maintains a good level of cooperation with all the parties, including the Government, but must remain sensitive to those perceptions. The situation appears to be under control.[8]

The Security Council mission seemed more concerned about the bruised feelings of the government than with supporting its man on the scene. The government had clearly been responsible for the delays and had offered only hollow excuses. It took international pressure and the rioting of its own troops to get the government to move ahead with this critical element of the peace process. Ajello's tough approach was not only not inappropriate, it was essential. As one assessment of ONUMOZ noted:

The local actors have too much historic and political baggage to overcome their mutual mistrust and implement faithfully agreements they have signed. They need to be constantly prodded and not be allowed to claim national sovereignty as a reason for delay or failure to implement.[9]

It was just such prodding by Ajello that eventually ensured that both sides lived up to their obligations. Such confrontational tactics are not the UN's usual style. The organization often seems unable to call anyone to task and incapable of simply pulling out when the parties disregard their commitments. This is even more true when the government of a member state is the guilty party than when the rebels are, since the former is almost always represented in the UN and the latter are not. If an insurgent group is well financed it can send an observer to the deliberations in New York, but such an observer can rarely be as effective as the government's ambassador, who is on the scene full time.

In Angola, both the style of the head of the PKO and the results achieved were quite different from Mozambique. To be sure, the SRSG in Angola, Margaret Anstee, had nowhere near the mandate or the resources that Ajello enjoyed (not to mention the hindsight that Anstee's experience provided Ajello.) While they both bore the same title, their marching orders and manpower were as different as the outcome of their PKOs.

The series of events that led to UNAVEM II's failure has at least been well documented. Anstee has rendered a major service to students of peacekeeping in writing a memoir of her experiences in Angola.[10] Rich in detail, it describes the conditions under which she labored and the difficulty of her task. As the title of the book—*Orphan of the Cold War*—implies, she believes that "the real nail in the Angolan coffin was that the solution of the conflict never enjoyed high priority on the agenda of the countries that mattered."[11] This explanation for UNAVEM's failure is a recurrent theme in the book. Elsewhere she comments: "Had there been an international resolve to do so, then peace could have been brought to Angola and its people."[12]

Both her book and subsequent events make clear, however, that it was a lack of internal, not international, resolve that led to the failure to find peace. To begin with, the Angolan government and UNITA intentionally limited the UN role when they negotiated the peace accord and then failed almost totally to fulfill their obligations to implement what they had signed. Anstee's book, like most memoirs, seeks not just to chronicle but to explain and justify the author's actions. It raises the question, which Anstee has asked herself, whether the outcome could have been different if her actions had been different.[13] She concludes that she could not have done her work differently unless she had refused to take on the assignment in the first place.

She may well be right, given the mandate, the resources, and the parties with whom she had to work. The contrast between her style and Ajello's nonetheless makes the question relevant. Ajello was able to manipulate the parties, the UN, the donors, and the media to attain the desired outcome. Anstee gives the impression through her own words of having been more of a spectator who was buffeted by all four of these groups. She notes that she also exceeded her mandate at times, but the instances she cites seem somewhat less than daring. In one case, she describes the response to the government's charges that UNITA had a hidden army. Joint teams comprised of government and UNITA representatives were dispatched to check out these serious allegations, but were able to do so only because "UNAVEM, once more exceeding its mandate, provided transport."[14] Since verification of demobilization was a key part of UNAVEM's mandate and given the participation of and a request from both parties for assistance, this hardly seems like a radical departure from her marching orders. Ajello often remarked that he rewrote his mandate almost on a daily basis and would probably not have considered such an occasion worthy of mention.

While it was in part dictated by her limited mandate and resources, Anstee's interaction with the Angolan parties was different than Ajello's with the Mozambicans. Ajello chaired the key committee implementing the peace process, whereas Anstee was simply an invited observer. However, she may have overplayed this passive role. According to one UN official, in meetings while Anstee was waiting for the parties to express their opinions, the parties were waiting for her to resolve their differences.[15]

She was certainly well aware of the problem. She writes that she reported to New York early on that the Joint Political Military Commission (CCPM in Portuguese), the key body in the process, met only sporadically and made little or no progress when it did. Aside from saying that this was "par for the course" and that the CCPM was "a very strange animal," she gives little indication she was able to do much to correct the situation other than by politely cajoling both sides.[16] Whereas Ajello confronted the parties when they failed to fulfill their obligations, Anstee simply documents their failures. Her view was that "the United Nations could only work through, with and by the consent of the two parties."[17] While this may have been correct given the weak mandate she had to work with, it was also a style that guaranteed failure under the circumstances.

The messages Anstee was receiving from New York only reinforced her self-limiting role. She was told not to ask for a larger budget for the operation, because funding was determined not by the mission's needs but by what the traffic (the main donors) would bear.[18] When she discussed the lack of resources with a Portuguese official, she received "a thinly veiled rebuke" from the Secretary General, presumably for going outside the UN with her concerns. When she tried to come up with an innovative way to obtain much needed additional contributions on a voluntary basis directly from the donors, the Secretary General blocked her course of action.[19]

Anstee's efforts to influence the main donors or to use them to influence the parties also met with little success. On a whirlwind trip to Washington in July 1992, she had to rely on a young academic to open "practically all of the most important doors in Washington."[20] She mentions little in the way of other efforts to rally international support or exert pressure on the parties. Ajello met at least weekly with the key donors and briefed the other diplomatic representatives in Maputo on a regular basis. This helped form a political consensus among the diplomatic representatives on the scene and was used to present a united front to the parties when it was necessary to force a change in their behavior. This unity also had the effect of influencing the debate at the UN in New York.

If the parties, the UN, and the main actors in the international community were not going to respond, one might think that Anstee, out of frustration if nothing else, would have used the media to call attention to the growing prospect of failure in Angola. Although Anstee cites a "negative CNN effect," in which the lack of media attention resulted in a lack of international interest, she does not describe any effort to use the international media to call attention to the impending disaster she foresaw.[21] While Angola was not featured on CNN, presumably some in the media would have been interested in the fact that the $118 million annual budget for UNAVEM II was supporting a failing mission.

Anstee was an advocate of quiet diplomacy. While asserting that this did not imply that one should never resort to public criticism, she argued it must be used sparingly and in carefully selected cases.[22] One has to wonder how selective she had to be. Even in the face of vicious personal attacks by the official government press (and on other occasions by UNITA's propaganda machine), she concluded that "it was best to ride out the storm as coolly and calmly as possible and that the necessary defense of UNAVEM must avoid putting it on a collision course with the President and the Government."[23] Not only did Anstee not use the media to respond to the attacks on her, she failed to use it to point out that the peace process was largely a sham and hanging by a thread—a thread that broke quickly after the results of the elections were rejected by the loser.

Anstee was ever the optimist and willing to take the Angolans at their word, even when experience would indicate otherwise. As Matloff describes it:

> She erred in that she treated Savimbi as a reasonable man who acted in good faith. The fact that he had lied to her and that his people had threatened to kill her did not inhibit Anstee's determination to negotiate. She kept pushing for a meeting between the UNITA leader and Dos Santos, naively believing Savimbi might acquiesce. She miscalculated, not understanding that Savimbi was a man who operated by force and responded only to force.[24]

Anstee's approach, resources and mandate contrast sharply with those of her successor, Alioune Blondin Beye. The original authorized strength of UNAVEM II was 350 military observers, 126 police observers, 87 international and 155 local civilian staff, and 400 electoral observers.[25] In UNAVEM III, Blondin Beye commanded resources equivalent to what Ajello had at the peak of ONUMOZ—about 7,000 peacekeepers costing a million dollars a day. With the termination of other peacekeeping efforts, by 1996 Beye was in charge of the UN's largest PKO.[26]

The new SRSG had a much stronger mandate to work with as he managed UNAVEM III. Under the Lusaka Protocol, responsibility for the supervision, control and general verification of the cease-fire was given to the UN. Blondin Beye's way of dealing with the parties was different as well. While one person described him as a cheerleader for the process, another observer noted that Blondin Beye would never go into a meeting with the parties without knowing its outcome in advance, and would postpone a session if he were not sure what would result.[27] As will be discussed, the differences between the mandate, resources, and style of Anstee and Blondin Beye did not result in complete success for UNAVEM III.

Anstee's mandate, resources, approach. and signals from New York all contributed to a situation in which she saw herself as having taken on an impossible challenge with "little room for manoeuvre."[28] Instead of individually or organizationally confronting the parties, Anstee and the UN deferred to the Angolans. As Lewis notes in an article about the peace process in Angola: "International organizations like the UN tended to buckle under the weight of appearing not to infringe the sovereignty of their hosts."[29] As a result, UNAVEM II went forward toward the elections with the peacekeepers fearing failure but feeling powerless to avert it. The best the UN could do was hope for success. It was, as Anstee described it, a situation in which "Everyone was very apprehensive, everyone had their fingers firmly crossed."[30]

But peacekeepers must do more than cross their fingers. How well they accomplish the various functions they are assigned will have much to contribute to a successful outcome. UNAVEM II had three principal tasks and failed consistently at all three. ONUMOZ, heralded by the Secretary General as "a major success story in UN peacemaking, peacekeeping and humanitarian and electoral assistance,"[31] was given a mandate to perform many more functions but with far more resources. It also had a much more uneven record than the Secretary General's comment would imply. Providing a measure of internal security, monitoring the police to prevent human rights violations, demobilizing and reintegrating most of the former combatants, reshaping those that remained in uniform into a unified army, providing humanitarian aid, demining, facilitating disarmament, and monitoring elections were all undertaken, but with widely varying degrees of success. Looking at each of the tasks individually will provide a description of how well each PKO carried out its mission.

Too Many Soldiers with Too Little to Do

Since the majority of the personnel in a PKO are soldiers carrying out military tasks, what those tasks are and how well they are done are critical determinants of the mission's effectiveness. As of January 1993, the military forces in ONUMOZ consisted of 6,552 soldiers from 22 countries. They were divided into three groups: 6,011 in the armed contingent, 327 unarmed military observers, and 214 on the military staff, mainly at ONUMOZ headquarters in Maputo.

The principal mission of the armed contingents was to provide security along the main transportation corridors. The Bangladeshi soldiers were deployed in the north along the Nacala Corridor, the Botswanans in the northwest along the Tete Corridor, the Italians in the central region along the Beira Corridor, the Uruguayans in the south along National Highway 1, and the Zambians in the far south along the Limpopo Corridor and the highways from Maputo to Swaziland and South Africa.[32]

Providing security for the transportation corridors was essential at the start of ONUMOZ, to ensure that they remained open and to allow the Zimbabwean and Malawian troops that had been guarding them to leave. Once the troops in the armed contingents of ONUMOZ were deployed, however, there was little flexibility used in determining their location or their use. Both seemed set in concrete, having been determined by military planners in New York months, if not years, before. Developments on the ground that affected where the troops were needed and where they were not, as well as the capabilities of individual units, never became part of the equation or provoked any revisions of the original strategy. The mission's military commander had his orders and was not interested in looking for ways to rewrite them. With few exceptions, the SRSG had little incentive to do so either, knowing he would face resistance not only from his military commander but from New York as well.

The armed contingents were supposed to "assume immediate responsibility for verifying and ensuring the security of strategic and trading routes, adopting the measures necessary for the purpose."[33] Some measures for ensuring the security of these routes were deemed less necessary than others. When a group of Italian troops patrolling the Beira Corridor came across an armed robbery in progress, they detained the thieves and turned them over to the police. The general in charge of ONUMOZ's military contingent reprimanded them and told them they should have simply continued on their way and reported the incident when they next encountered the police.[34]

This was not the only example of an excessively narrow definition of what the soldiers were supposed to do. An officer from one of the African contingents noted that the rules of engagement reduced his troops to noting the license plate number and numbers of passengers in vehicles full of weapons that passed through their checkpoints.[35]

Once the foreign troops had left and the assembly and demobilization of the Mozambican troops began, it became increasingly questionable whether so many troops were needed to defend corridors that were not threatened by more than the occasional highway robber. This was doubly true if all the UN soldiers were permitted to do was observe and report to the police any robberies or weapons they came across. Very few modifications were made, however; the authority, responsibility and initiative were lacking on the local level, and New York was too far removed geographically and psychologically to care. The only significant change in troop levels during ONUMOZ was reduction of the Italian contingent. This came about only in response to donor pressure to achieve some savings in the face of the additional cost of the police monitors that were being added at that time.

So while the conditions and needs changed over time, the location and function of the military contingents of ONUMOZ did not. In addition, the sites selected for the five battalions corresponded more with the logistical necessities of the units than the military requirements of the mission. With 22 countries represented, the capabilities among these units varied greatly. Engineering and logistical units were often deployed without the equipment or training to accomplish their tasks. Infantry units differed in ability, from NATO standard to a bare ability to function. Yet these considerations could rarely be compensated for and adjustments made. Altering the original deployment plan by moving the weakest units to the least critical areas would have caused the contributing country considerable embarrassment. Since recruiting peacekeeping troops in the midst of the Expansion Period was becoming increasingly difficult and because offending a member state was always avoided, the UN basically treated all units as if their capabilities were equal.[36]

UNAVEM II did not suffer from such difficulties. It had no armed contingents, since it consisted of only a few hundred unarmed military observers. After UNAVEM II failed and Angola returned to war following the elections in 1992, a new peace treaty was eventually negotiated in Lusaka and signed in November 1994. This time the Angolan parties asked for a more active and robust UN presence. The agreement called for "the supervision, control and general verification of the reestablished cease-fire to be the responsibility of the United Nations acting in the framework of its new mandate with the participation of the Government and UNITA."[37] On February 8, 1995, the Security Council authorized the establishment of UNAVEM III, with a maximum deployment of 7,000 military personnel in addition to 350 military observers and 260 police observers.[38]

The deployment of the armed continents under UNAVEM III was not without familiar problems, reflecting how little is learned from one PKO and applied to the next. One observer in Luanda described the deployment of the various battalions as being mainly for cosmetic purposes, largely in provincial capitals and without relation to the quartering areas for the demobilizing troops or to routes of retreat in case fighting broke out again. The deputy force commander had drawn up and authorized the deployment plan and would accept no changes. When his nominal superior subsequently wanted to work out a more rational structure and reduce the number of deployment areas, he had to do it by going around his deputy.[39]

Thus, the largely self-imposed limitations made the military contingents less effective than they could have been in Mozambique and hindered their efforts in Angola during UNAVEM III. They were not the only peacekeepers in uniform who made less of a contribution to the peace process than they should have, however; their police colleagues in both operations fell even further short of the mark.

Calling the Wrong Cop

In both Angola and in Mozambique, assuring the neutrality of the local police was an important responsibility of the peacekeepers and was critical to maintaining the integrity of the peace processes. This was another area in which both PKOs failed to accomplish what was necessary because the UN was not up to the job. As with the military contingents, it was too often the case that the wrong people were in the wrong place doing the wrong things.

Keeping tabs on the police had not originally been part of ONU-MOZ's responsibilities, because the need for police monitors had been rejected by the Mozambican government when the PKO was initiated. As the peace process unfolded, RENAMO feared its supporters would be harassed by the police during the electoral campaign and also saw that FRELIMO was creating a considerable military capability within the Rapid Intervention Police (PIR). When RENAMO demanded that the UN ensure the police remain neutral, the government eventually dropped its objection. The government was still reluctant to permit UN oversight of its police, but it calculated that with UN monitoring, the police would find it easier to expand the government's control into areas still controlled by RENAMO.

As a result, beginning in early 1994, a total of 1,086 United Nations civilian police (CIVPOL) from 29 countries were deployed to the mission area.[40] The Security Council resolution authorizing the creation of the police component had called for up to 1,144, but ONUMOZ never reached this level because the UN could not find enough qualified police officers willing to serve.[41]

While CIVPOL may have provided needed reassurance to RENAMO at an important point in the peace process, it accomplished very little else. Most of the UN police monitors lacked the language skills, the qualifications, or the inclination to curb police abuse. Even when they did find wrongdoing, they were powerless to do anything about it because of the bureaucratic arrangements that had been established. CIVPOL investigated 511 complaints, of which 61 were related to human rights violations, but did so very slowly. When it did complete its work, CIVPOL did not make public what it found, and was empowered only to turn over its findings to the National Commission on Police Affairs (COMPOL).

COMPOL was created to oversee CIVPOL's work and was composed exclusively of Mozambican members from both sides.[42] Unlike most of the other commissions in the ONUMOZ structure, this commission was not chaired by the UN. As a result, after CIVPOL had investigated, documented, and forwarded the cases of human rights violations, COMPOL did nothing. By the conclusion of ONUMOZ, COMPOL had failed to take a single disciplinary or preventive action.[43]

COMPOL's failure to take any action on CIVPOL's findings was not the only problem with the police contingent. The post-ONUMOZ assessment by the U.S. Embassy describes the integration between CIVPOL and the UN civilian staff as poor. It also notes that:

> One senior UN diplomat described the 1000–strong CIVPOL as worse than useless (to be fair they received no cooperation from the Mozambican Government.) Far too many of the police knew a lot about guarding tourist sites (in their home countries), but very little about protecting human rights. While it did provide some psychological assurance to RENAMO, CIVPOL's idea of monitoring the police was to drop by the station for coffee at the same time each week. The vast majority did not speak Portuguese (or any common language) and some could not even drive, with predictable consequences for ONUMOZ's vehicle fleet. As with the military contingents, the emphasis was on finding the numbers planned with little attention to whether they could actually do the job required or whether the planned number was appropriate.[44]

CIVPOL members were drawn from 29 countries and even though they underwent "an extensive human rights training programme, the first of its kind provided to a UN police force,"[45] they were simply not up to the job. The lack of cooperation from the government was a major factor, but the qualifications of the monitors was another. Their failings could have been compensated for to some degree by a stronger mandate or the insistence of the international community that they receive the full assistance of the government. However, this would have provoked a confrontation with the government that the UN preferred to avoid.

Perhaps equally important is the requirement that the UN should approach the task of recruitment as an exercise in filling the quota with whomever is available. Large numbers of policemen cannot be mobilized like military units. To find enough bodies, the UN took whatever it could get and the policemen, like the military units in ONUMOZ, were drawn more from third-world countries than from the first world. Even if they were from countries where human rights were respected, policemen may not be the best human-rights monitors. Also, it should be more important to have a trained monitor who speaks the language and knows the culture than a person in a uniform. Thus far the UN has not adopted this approach to the problem, in part, perhaps, because the host government might like civilian police monitors even less than uniformed ones.

As CIVPOL demonstrated its ineffectiveness, RENAMO's and the general public's confidence in both CIVPOL and the UN's ability to ensure the neutrality of the police quickly dissipated. Not only did CIVPOL not provide adequate protection against human rights violations or ensure such acts did not go unpunished, it may have made things worse. One human rights organization interviewed several Mozambican policemen about intimidation of RENAMO supporters by the Rapid Intervention Police. The policemen admitted that malpractice was common, but they "justified it by saying they felt it was internationally acceptable police practice: they said many CIVPOL monitors engaged in corrupt practices and did not comment on their policing style, although they frequently visited their stations."[46]

The failure of CIVPOL did not undo the peace process, but it did very little to help it succeed and added considerably to the cost of the mission. The thousand plus monitors were each making over $100 per day in per diem payments alone. These policemen were originally seen as a confidence-building measure to protect RENAMO supporters and others from abuse by the government's security forces. CIVPOL's inability to investigate cases of abuse rapidly or to ensure that the guilty party was punished did not go unnoticed by the Mozambican police alone. The civilian population was equally aware of these failings. This did nothing to help build confidence that the elections could be held in a free and fair manner, without police harassment. About half of the CIVPOL members did serve effectively as election observers, but overall CIVPOL's other faults ensured that it made far less of a contribution to the successful outcome in Mozambique than it should have.

In Angola, the record of the police component was even more dismal than in Mozambique. This failure was due more to the actions of the Angolan parties, however, than to the UN police observers themselves. The peace agreements signed by the Angolan parties called for the creation of a neutral police force under the supervision of joint government and UNITA police monitoring teams. Each of these teams was to include a UN police affairs expert to verify the neutrality of the Angolan police.

The Angolans never established the neutral police monitoring teams, however, thus denying the UNAVEM police any opportunity to carry out their primary function. As in so many other aspects of the Angolan peace accords, the parties reserved for themselves the responsibility for implementation and allowed the UN only a verification role. In this instance, as in so many others, the parties proved unable or unwilling to fulfill the obligations to which they had committed themselves. Worse still, they often refused to let the UN take over, or even to play its limited part effectively. In the case of the police, some think this failure was more by design than accident. Anstee states frankly that "it was hard to believe that either side was genuinely committed to building a joint police force."[47]

As in Mozambique, many Angolans thought policemen, even those from the UN, should act as enforcers of law and order and were disappointed and disillusioned when they did not. The local populace were not the only ones unhappy with the function of the police component in Angola. Many of the UN police themselves resented it when their role evolved into being human rights observers without their having had any training for the task. As the elections neared, many of them spent more of their time working either with the military elements of UNAVEM or for the electoral elements.[48] While these efforts were positive contributions, they were minimal ones, and the original mission of the police component was never accomplished.

Although many Security Council statements and resolutions spoke about the importance of making the police monitoring operation work properly, these exhortations were ignored by the Angolan parties.[49] Thus, what should have been a confidence building measure not only failed to build confidence but became a major source of mistrust. The Angolan government decided to set up an "antiriot" police group and to import weapons from Spain to equip them. UNITA began to criticize the move as an attempt to create a hidden military force and asserted that some army officers had simply changed uniforms and joined the police group. Despite the seriousness of these charges, the Secretary General noted in his report to the Security Council only that monitoring of the police was fragmentary and that few UNITA members had been integrated into the force. He also sent letters to UNITA leader Jonas Savimbi and President Dos Santos, politely calling attention to the importance of establishing a neutral police force.[50] His letters failed to induce the Angolan leaders to correct the situation, and the police remained a serious bone of contention between the parties.

The close relations between the Mozambican and Angolan governments gave the former various opportunities to learn the wrong lessons from the latter regarding implementation of a peace agreement. In the case of the police, there was an attempt by the Mozambicans to copy their Angolan counterparts by creating in the PIR a significant military force that excluded RENAMO members. While this represented a less flagrant attempt to subvert the peace process than the antiriot police group in Angola, the UN reaction was even more tepid.

When the visiting Security Council delegation in August 1994 flew by helicopter to tour a voter registration site north of Maputo, it missed its destination. The pilot, who had only very vague instructions on where he was to land, set down in the middle of a group of buildings that he thought was in the correct location. Once on the ground, the delegation saw several large groups of men in khaki uniforms carrying automatic weapons quickly march away from the landing area. The site was a police training facility that ONUMOZ was completely unaware of, yet it was never mentioned in the visiting delegation's report on its trip.[51]

Even the pro-government newsletter about the peace process published by AWEPA, the European Parliamentarians for Southern Africa, noted that "RENAMO's real fear is of the PIR. The visiting Security Council team discovered that it has heavy weapons and is receiving what is effectively military training."[52] While fighting never broke out again and the government did not have to call on its "hidden" military capability, the UN again did little to maintain confidence in the process, preferring to ignore the problem rather than call attention to it.

The UN failed in Angola and in Mozambique to ensure the neutrality of the police, with seriously detrimental effects for both peace processes. Monitoring the police was not an area in which the UN had a great deal of experience, and therefore its inadequacy might be understandable. Even in those areas in which it did have experience, such as humanitarian affairs, the result of the UN's efforts was still clearly inadequate.

Good Humanitarian Intentions and Bad Results

While ONUMOZ and UNAVEM II had similar tasks in some areas, such as monitoring the police, other aspects of the two PKOs were very different. ONUMOZ had a far more multidimensional mandate, and it was the first UN PKO to incorporate a large humanitarian component. The humanitarian challenge was considerable, given that there were two million Mozambican refugees in neighboring countries, about five million people internally displaced by the war, tens of thousands of demobilized soldiers to be reintegrated into civilian society, and, according to some estimates, a million land mines scattered throughout the country. UNAVEM II did not begin its efforts until after the peace process fell apart and the fighting resumed. Then it occupied itself mainly with trying to coordinate the efforts of the 102 NGOs working in Angola and attempting to ensure the delivery of food to those areas that needed it the most.[53]

In Mozambique, all of the humanitarian assistance efforts were supposed to be overseen by ONUMOZ's humanitarian component, the United Nations Office for Humanitarian Assistance Coordination (UNOHAC). The very concept of UNOHAC as a separate entity within a PKO was an innovation. So was the fact that it was headed by a former Assistant Administrator of the United Nations Development Program (UNDP).[54] UNOHAC needed high-level leadership because successful completion of its tasks was considered vital to the success of the peace process. As UNOHAC's wrap-up report recognized: "Mine clearance programmes and support for the demobilization of the armed forces and the subsequent reintegration of soldiers into civilian life were also viewed as critical to the pacification and normalization process."[55]

Despite the importance of its responsibilities, UNOHAC succeeded best where it did the least.[56] The return of the refugees and the displaced to their homes was one of the UN's major successes in Mozambique, in no small measure because UNOHAC had little to do with it. This task was undertaken by the traditional UN aid agencies, principally the High Commission for Refugees (UNHCR).[57] Where UNOHAC did play a major role, it became more an obstacle to progress than a means for achieving it. This was particularly true in demining and the reintegration of demobilized soldiers into civilian life. In both cases, UNOHAC's failures stemmed largely from bureaucratic obstacles. In demining, bureaucratic turf struggles in New York and cumbersome contracting policies hindered any progress until ONUMOZ was nearly over. In reintegration, the bureaucratic mindset of the UN caused things to happen too slowly if they happened at all. In both, it was the local donor community that seized the initiative and accomplished both tasks in a way that supported the peace process instead of delaying it.

Defusing a Time Bomb

With estimates ranging as high as 15 million and 3 million land mines respectively, Angola and Mozambique rank first and eighth among the countries in the world affected by mines.[58] These devices, together with light arms, have become the weapons of choice in the teacup wars. Each one costs only a few dollars to buy but thousands of dollars to remove. Since it is too expensive and impractical to remove them all, many of them remain where they were sown, ready to kill and maim until they biodegrade in a few decades. They impede peacekeeping by making the process much more dangerous for the peacekeepers and by making the movement of refugees, demobilized soldiers, and voters far more difficult. For progress to be made on a timely basis, the removal of land mines from key areas and roads is essential.

It is a task that the UN has yet to learn to do well, even though one would never learn this from reading UN documents. Aside from the dry and formulaic language of most UN reports, the rhetoric frequently bears little relation to reality. Diplomatic language and the self-protective nature of the UN bureaucracy seem to preclude frankness or critical introspection. There is perhaps no sharper contrast between the rhetoric and reality of the UN than in land mine clearance during ONUMOZ. With two million refugees and five million internally displaced, clearing mined roads was a key element in the peace process. It would allow these people and demobilized soldiers to return to their homes, vote in the elections, and rebuild their lives and the economy.

Writing in mid 1994, the Secretary General Boutros-Ghali asserted:

> The UN's chief objective is building indigenous capacity to clear mines. Within the UN the Department of Humanitarian Affairs has been assigned to coordinate mine clearance, working closely with the Department of Peacekeeping Operations. In Mozambique, about 300 mine clearers are deployed in a UN program overseen by a Norwegian non-governmental organization. A major road clearance project is now in progress. The UN demining headquarters in Mozambique also coordinates all non-UN mine clearance in the country.[59]

In reality, by mid-1994, when the Secretary General's article was written, ONUMOZ had been on the ground for 20 of its 26 months of existence. In that time the UN had not succeeded in lifting a single mine. With the end of the operation clearly in sight, the UN became desperate to accomplish something in demining. Hence the emphasis was switched from actual demining to establishing an "Accelerated Demining Programme" in order to have something tangible to which to point. The program's goal was therefore not the removal of mines but the creation of an indigenous demining capacity by training Mozambicans. Turning the task of demining over to the Mozambican government made sense only if it was accompanied by the hope that some donor country would eventually step forward to pay the salaries of the deminers and other costs of the program.

The UN blamed its failure to lift any mines on "the slow approval of the national mine clearance plan by the Cease-fire Commission as well as difficulties in identifying suitable contractors."[60] The real problem was that the two departments the Secretary General mentioned became involved from the outset in a bureaucratic turf fight that paralyzed progress in New York and in the field.[61] This, together with the UN's slow contracting practices and emphasis on building local capacity, meant that any mines lifted were removed despite, not because of, UN efforts.

Frustrated by UN inaction, aid agencies from individual countries went ahead with their own programs. Norwegian People's Aid, the NGO mentioned by the Secretary General, arrived on the scene early in the peace process but had to wait for over six months for UN approval to proceed. The US Agency for International Development (USAID) basically ignored the UN and contracted directly with an American firm, Ronco, that cleared thousands of kilometers of key roads.[62]

As for the local capacity that was to have been created, the UN kept trying after ONUMOZ had officially ended. Three years later, however, it still did not exist in any significant way. The government of Mozambique established the National Demining Commission (CND) to coordinate demining efforts. When the head of the CND did show up at his office, he was more an obstruction than a means of coordination. Donors had such little faith in the commission they refused to fund it, despite their considerable willingness to fund efforts to deal with the demining problem.[63]

While the UN has yet to alter its priorities, the need for local capacity also came into question as the scope of the problem in Mozambique became better understood. Instead of millions of mines, it gradually became clear that there were more on the order of 200,000 to 400,000. Since only four percent of Mozambique is arable land, it may make little sense to attempt to remove many of these mines. The debate among demining experts at the end of 1997 was over how soon the problem of mines would be effectively concluded.[64] Despite the lack of government capacity, NGOs continued their work and most felt that only five to seven more years were required.[65]

One official UN report did frankly raise the failure of the demining program, but it was not a report authored by the Secretary General or the Secretariat in New York. When the Security Council delegation visited

Mozambique in August 1994, its members heard so many complaints about demining that they included the following paragraph in their trip report:

> If there was one area of disappointment in an otherwise successful mission, it was that of mine clearance, which was late in starting and has made little progress. This must be rectified, with proper machinery put in place. There should be no attempt whatsoever to disrupt the programme, or to transfer existing resources to another operation. The Mission recommends that the mine-clearing equipment remain in the country.[66]

The mission's report at least identified the problem, but its recommendations had little impact on correcting it. Dealing with mines is made more difficult by the fact that the statistics are always suspect. The three million figure for the number of mines in Mozambique cited above was from a February 1997 magazine article.[67] The most common estimate used in Mozambique during ONUMOZ was two million. Even this number was criticized as grossly exaggerated by many including one of the most hard-line members of the government and a foreign human-rights organization.[68] The UN expert responsible for the figure admitted that he had made it up in November 1992, based on a nationwide survey. He defended the number by saying an accurate estimate was impossible given the variety of groups responsible for laying the mines and the lack of records.[69]

None of those involved in demining, including those interested in winning Nobel prizes, have any incentive to underestimate the number of mines. The UN and the parties to the conflict can attract more funds from the international community with a higher figure than a lower one. There were supposedly between 3 and 20 million landmines in Angola, although the wide range itself indicates the lack of precision in this case as well. Such estimates are at best based on surveys of the country, if not guesswork. Since the parties doing the mining almost never keep accurate records or share them with the UN if they do, there is no way to establish that figures are accurate. In both Angola and Mozambique, all of the combatants laid mines including the governments, rebel groups, Portuguese colonial forces, and troops from the other countries who fought there. The indiscriminate use of these weapons is a practice that began before independence, and new mines continue to be laid in Angola.[70]

Kuwait is a case that demonstrates the inaccuracy of the estimates for the numbers of mines planted. There demining was relatively easy given the desert terrain. Information was furnished by the armies that had only recently laid them, and funding was readily available. The estimates were that there were five to eight million mines, and yet only 1.7 million were found.[71] The tendency to overestimate is not surprising, since those making the estimates have a vested interest in seeing a higher number gain acceptance rather than a lower one. According to one expert: "Inflating the numbers is a standard ploy to get more donor funds. The estimates worldwide have doubled in recent years, without any commensurate increase in military activity or mine production."[72]

In Angola, demining was a semi-independent UN activity without any direct involvement under UNAVEM II (or subsequently UNAVEM III). Those in the UN responsible for demining suffered from the same desire to create local capacity as in Mozambique. This created a situation in which the UN had the funds, but Angolan officials had the decision-making authority. However, the Angolans lacked the skills to make or implement the necessary decisions. It was an operation one UN expert characterized as a car without a motor being pushed by the UN with the Angolans in the driver's seat.[73]

It was also an operation not interested in UNAVEM's priorities, targets, or timetables. Instead the UN, NGOs, and the parties all had their own ideas about what should or should not be demined. Negotiating between UNITA and the government slowed everything down, as both sides wanted to retain the mines in some areas because of their tactical importance. The government refused to allow any airfields to be demined, and UNITA denied the UN access to whole areas under its control. There is also ample evidence that mines were relaid in areas that had been cleared.[74]

Despite these difficulties, the demining program in Angola lifted more mines than in Mozambique. By mid–1996, over 80,000 mines and 115,000 pieces of unexploded ordnance had been removed.[75] Nonetheless land mines will be a problem in Angola for a long time to come. It took $750 million and two and a half years of intensive effort to remove the mines from the deserts of Kuwait. Only $15 to 20 million is being spent each year to eliminate them from Angola.

Getting the 300,000 Angolans who were refugees and the 1.2 million internally displaced back to their homes is obviously a serious humanitarian concern, one as important to the country's economic and political stability as it was in Mozambique. The number of amputees in Luanda is already estimated at five percent of the total population. Despite this, the demining process has gone much more slowly than it could have given the UN's willingness to defer to those who laid the mines in the first place and the unwillingness of the parties to give up the use of mines. That, plus the

UN's preference for creating local capacity rather than simply getting the job done, will ensure it remains a problem that generations of Angolans will face in the future.

Making Civilians Out of Soldiers

The reintegration of demobilized soldiers into civilian life was another responsibility that was given to ONUMOZ but not to UNAVEM II. While reintegration was a major success story in Mozambique, again the results occurred despite, rather than because of, UNOHAC's efforts.

The General Peace Agreement signed in Rome provided that a UN representative would chair the Commission for Reintegration (CORE). CORE was given the responsibility for planning, organizing, and monitoring the economic and social reintegration of demobilized soldiers.[76] Its chairman was the head of UNOHAC. As with demining, UNOHAC insisted on a long-term, developmental approach to the tasks assigned CORE, which was suppose to empower the government and create local capacity.[77] Ajello himself has described the problem this created, and he admitted that the criticisms by the donors were basically correct:

> The cooperation with the UN Agencies and the NGOs in the area of humanitarian aid became more difficult, and the love affair with the donor community came to an end. Increasingly, criticism was raised against UNOHAC's excessively bureaucratic rules and procedures, its tendency to build overly heavy structures at central and provincial levels, and its inclination to be involved in medium- and long-term programmes, where it had no mandate. The donor community began to question the very concept of an *ad hoc* Office for Humanitarian Assistance Coordination within ONUMOZ.[78]

Because of UNOHAC's bureaucratic and long-term approach, the donor community largely ignored it and went ahead with several programs to achieve what CORE was supposed to be doing. These were implemented by NGOs instead of the government. The most important element of the assistance for reintegration was monthly stipends paid to the demobilized soldiers, but other programs included a microenterprise fund and an information service for job referral and assistance with payment problems. All three programs added up to less than $50 million. When the monthly stipends ran out in the first half of 1996, an additional lump sum of $52 was provided in the first few months of 1997 for each of the 93,500 former soldiers who were eligible.[79] Even with this unforeseen payment, the program run by the donor community was seen as relatively cheap and effective.

Since demobilization in Angola came late, if at all, the lack of reintegration did not have an opportunity to become a major problem. The Angolan parties had created plans for reintegration but had grossly overestimated the donors' willingness to pay for them. When the Political Military Commission (CCPM) presented a proposal to the donors for $447 million, none of the donors reacted. As a result, none of the CCPM's projects were implemented, and only a few sporadic and inadequate vocational training programs were undertaken with foreign support.

In her discussion of this issue, Anstee asks rhetorically, "Might the outcome have been different had more satisfactory arrangements been made?"[80] The implication is that if the tight-fisted donors had simply come up with half a billion dollars for this specific purpose, things would have been different. However, the problem was not simply a lack of funds. In Mozambique, the reintegration programs were largely designed and implemented by the donors and NGOs. In Angola, the parties came up with the programs and the estimated price tag was nine times that of Mozambique, even though the number of men to be demobilized in Angola was only ten percent greater.

Poorly designed and wasteful programs often fail to attract donor support. However, some in the UN see the satisfaction of the host country as a higher priority than ensuring that contributions from developed nations are effectively spent. Perhaps this is because the UN seeks to avoid criticism and confrontation and the recipients of the aid are quicker to complain than those giving it.

Although this chapter concentrates on UNAVEM II as opposed to what followed it, UNAVEM III illustrates this point and shows how little had been learned from UNAVEM II or ONUMOZ. In the first half of 1996, the Angolan Armed Forces (FAA) were pushing a reintegration program that would have cost $800 million, of which the Angolans said they would contribute $364 million. Instead of providing assistance to individual soldiers, this program was to set up a "fourth branch" of the armed forces, which the demobilized would have to join. During their obligatory 24 months of service with the fourth branch, they would be organized in units to carry out reconstruction and civil works projects.

UNDP, the UN agency responsible for reintegration, did not want to get involved in the design of the program, preferring to let the Angolan government do it. What the FAA came up with was a program the military would administer because they believed the civilians in government incapable of organizing such an effort. Instead of reintegration, however, the program would have had three effects. It would have maximized the opportunities for corruption for the senior officers administering the $800 million program and minimized the effective reintegration into civilian life of those obliged to participate. It also would have provided ample opportunity for a repeat of the failure of UNAVEM II, since such construction battalions could easily be rearmed were fighting to break out again. Yet despite this, and a decided and justified lack of donor enthusiasm, the UN was unwilling to tell the Angolans the program was a nonstarter, let alone design a better one.[81]

Thus, both in Mozambique and Angola, the UN failed to come up with reintegration programs that made a contribution to the peace process. Another area in which the UN should have made major efforts to protect the process and preserve the peace in the future was in disarmament. There too, the UN was unable to achieve what was necessary.

Ten Guns For Every Soldier

Under the Rome accords, the Cease-fire Commission headed by ONU-MOZ was supposed to gather, register, and store arms, ammunition, explosives, equipment, uniforms, and documentation. The accords stipulated, however, that destroying or disposing of weapons, ammunition, explosives, equipment, uniforms, and documentation could be done only when agreed to by the parties.[82] Efforts at disarmament were also constrained by the fact that Chapter VI of the UN Charter, under which ONUMOZ was launched, specifies that actions by the Security Council to resolve a conflict may be undertaken only if all the parties to any dispute so request.[83]

Mozambique was awash with light weapons although, as with land mines, accurate figures were impossible to obtain and estimates varied widely. One study indicated there was more than one weapon for every adult. Another guessed that more than six million AK-47 assault rifles had entered the country (which is close to saying the same thing).[84]

It is probably only slightly easier to come up with an estimate for assault rifles than land mines, since the former are bigger and not buried. Accurate records rarely exist in such conflicts, and the numbers are at best guesses. As with land mines, they can also be fabrications designed to overdramatize the problem.

Even if the true figures were a fraction of the estimates, the problem would still be a serious one, with implications for the future of Mozambique's peace as well as regional stability. The Secretary General recognized this in one of his earliest reports on ONUMOZ and recommended that "All arms and ammunition not required for the new armed forces would be destroyed under close supervision of the United Nations."[85] However, this suggestion was not followed.

ONUMOZ did require each soldier who showed up at an assembly area to turn in a weapon. Collecting the remaining arms was left until after the completion of demobilization, when little time was left before ONUMOZ's mandate expired. At that point, neither party was fully cooperating, and both were reluctant to surrender what they had not turned in. As a result, progress was slow and time was running out.

During the demobilization process, ONUMOZ registered a total of 124,267 weapons, of which 117,342 were individual arms.[86] In addition, another 46,193 weapons, over 19,000 land mines, and over 2.7 million rounds of ammunition were found during the verification of declared and undeclared arms caches on both sides.[87]

In the end, all of this war material, with the exception of a minor amount of unstable ammunition, was turned over to the newly formed army in accordance with a decision of the Cease-fire Commission made at its meeting on November 11, 1994.[88] Thus the UN handed over in excess of 170,000 guns to an army that was supposed to consist of 30,000 men but that had at that point been able to attract only a little more than 12,000.

There was no enthusiasm for the destruction of the surplus weapons on the part of the Mozambican authorities, for an obvious reason. Even if they weren't needed should fighting break out again, the arms were a highly marketable commodity that could easily be sold in neighboring countries. One newspaper article asserted that an AK-47 could be bought for as little as $6 along the border between Mozambique and Zimbabwe. Another source cited a price of $14, which increased, however, as the weapon made its way to the townships of South Africa.[89] Corrupt police and army officers involved in the trafficking of arms were identified as a major source of the problem.[90]

In concluding his study of disarmament during the Mozambican peace process, Berman aptly summed up the situation:

It is rare when the UN and the international community have an opportunity to reduce significantly the threat that small weapons pose to law and order within a country as well as within a region. ONUMOZ presented such an opportunity, yet it was not appropriately exploited.[91]

In Angola, the parties were in control of disarmament, as they were with most of the peace process, and little was accomplished. When the CCPM did finally get around to establishing procedures for dealing with the weapons turned in by the assembled troops, they did not work well in practice. Weapons collected for the new army were to be stored in regional warehouses and the rest destroyed on the spot. There was a lack of both transport and secure storage facilities, however, and the process was far from complete by the time of elections. This happened, despite the fact that Anstee, "again going far beyond the mandate," authorized the use of UNAVEM planes and helicopters to carry the arms from the assembly areas to the warehouses. Even these inadequate arrangements, she pointed out, did nothing to deal with the problem of weapons "in private hands."[92] In contrast with what occurred in Mozambique, the UN in Angola did not even have the opportunity to bring about disarmament. Instead, the parties once again demonstrated their bad faith or inability to accomplish what tasks they had reserved to themselves—a characteristic failing even more pronounced when it came to demobilizing their individual armies and forming a united one.

Giving Up the Military Option

In both Angola and Mozambique, key elements of the peace process were the assembly of the government and rebel troops, the demobilization of many of them, and the formation of the remainder into a single unified army. In both cases, the parties delayed and resisted this process, since it required them to surrender a large part of their military power. Despite what had been negotiated and signed in the various peace accords, when it came to disarming and trusting that the other side would do so as well, when the time came, the parties were simply unwilling. In Mozambique, that reluctance was overcome, in large part due to pressure from the international community and its refusal to go ahead with elections without demobilization. In Angola, the international community neither forced the parties to live up to their commitments nor aborted the electoral process when they did not.

The peace accords signed in Rome in October 1992 by the Mozambican government and RENAMO called for the process of demobilization to begin immediately after "E day"—the day on which the cease-fire took effect. Sixty days later, the first 20 percent of the troops were to have been demobilized, with an additional 20 percent every 30 days thereafter. By E plus 120 days, therefore, the demobilization process was to have been completed.[93]

When the Secretary General visited Mozambique a year later, not only had no troops been demobilized, but the first assembly areas (AAs) had not even been opened to receive them. In addition, the elections had been delayed until October 1994, and although still a year away, they were already in danger of being postponed further. Boutros-Ghali's main concern on the trip was to convince President Chissano and Afonso Dhlakama, the head of RENAMO, that unless progress were made, the international community would seriously consider withdrawing ONUMOZ.[94] Whether the threat was real or not, by the end of the visit Boutros-Ghali was able to announce that there was a new momentum that would help him persuade the Security Council to give him a mandate to maintain the UN presence in Mozambique.[95]

Among other things agreed to during the Secretary General's stay was that the parties would start moving their troops to the AAs in November in order to ensure that demobilization could begin in January 1994 and finish by May. Despite these assurances to Boutros-Ghali from the parties, both sides were reluctant to give up their best units. They were unwilling or unable to provide the number of troops required to keep demobilization on schedule, and the process slipped further.[96]

Finally, demobilization formally commenced in March 1994. While RENAMO's troops began to move steadily into the assembly areas, the government's soldiers were showing up in fits and starts. Even though President Chissano and Dhlakama had agreed in early April to speed up the assembly and demobilization process, there were only marginal improvements. To complicate matters, the government presented a revised figure to the Cease-fire Commission that lowered the total numbers of its troops from 76,405 to 64,110.[97] Most international observers concluded that the discrepancy simply reflected the fact that the government had to admit that senior officers in the army had for years been collecting the pay for far more troops than existed. RENAMO refused to accept the figure, however, claiming it was a government attempt to hold back troops from the demobilization process. For its part, the government blamed ONUMOZ for the confusion in the government's figures. Finally a further revision was made, and the figure of 64,466 was agreed upon by all.[98]

Despite this agreement, the delays in getting the troops to the assembly areas continued. From March to May, the process slowed almost to a standstill, and the election timetable was put at risk once again.[99] With the time left to complete demobilization starting to run out, the choice was boiling down to going ahead with the voting as scheduled without demobilization completed or allowing the elections to be postponed again. The former risked a repeat of Angola's experience by going to the polls with the remnants of three armies—the former opposing forces and the unfinished unified military—still in the field. The alternative of further delay meant considerable expense, however, because the rainy season normally commences in November, making communications and travel difficult. Any postponement would have to last until the rains were over, and that would have extended ONUMOZ's presence for at least another five months at a cost of a million dollars a day.

Wishing to avoid such a Hobson's choice, the international community began to increase the pressure on the parties to live up to their commitments. As the UN's published assessment of ONUMOZ described it:

> On 5 May 1994, the Security Council adopted a resolution in which it urged the two parties to meet the target dates of 1 June for completion of the assembly of forces and 15 July for the end of demobilization. The Government responded that it could not achieve these dates, but said it would conclude assembly by 1 July and demobilization by 15 August. However, by 1 July, about 4,500 Government troops and 900 RENAMO troops had still not been assembled. The Government issued a statement protesting what it claimed to be partiality by ONUMOZ. The Government asserted that, while ONUMOZ had exerted considerable pressure on the Government for the cantonment of its troops, ONUMOZ had not done so with regard to RENAMO.[100]

As the government continued to produce more excuses than soldiers, the international community increased the pressure on it to live up to its commitments under the peace accords. On June 22, 1994, the international members on the CSC, the commission overseeing the peace process, issued what some called "an unprecedented statement attacking government delays in sending soldiers to the assembly areas."[101] The statement bluntly pointed out that at the current pace of 100 soldiers a day it would be impossible to assemble and demobilize the remaining men by August 15.

At the American Embassy's Fourth of July reception in Maputo where a speech by the ambassador was customary, I used the occasion to pressure the government to meet its commitments under the peace accord. My speech pointed out that Mozambicans, like voters everywhere, would be more inclined to vote for those who aided the peace process by fulfilling their obligations, such as demobilization. The speech also mentioned that voters were more likely to support those willing to share power than those who threatened peace by trying to monopolize it. Not surprisingly, the government and its supporters vigorously objected to my making such suggestions in public.[102]

The value of power sharing had just been demonstrated in South Africa and Malawi where the elections resulted in governments that included opposition parties. FRELIMO, however, was determined to ignore such examples in order to maintain its monopoly on power and was unwilling to surrender even a few cabinet seats to ensure that the peace was maintained. It believed firmly that elections would do politically what it had been unable to do militarily—eliminate RENAMO.

The central point of my speech, which was ignored by some analysts,[103] was that without progress on demobilization the election timetable and the whole peace process was at grave risk. Shortly after the speech, the government retracted a position paper it intended to table in the CSC, which offered only more excuses for its lack of compliance with the schedule to which it had agreed.

Instead, the government finally began to send the necessary troops to the assembly areas and the demobilization process got back on track. Ajello has acknowledged on more than one occasion that the speech demonstrated to the government that the international community would insist on moving ahead and that while my remarks were unwelcome to some, they were critical in getting the government to do so.[104]

On July 19, the Security Council reinforced the pressure when it again urged both sides to meet the August 15 deadline and stressed that the elections should be held on schedule on October 27 and 28.[105] The council pointed out that the mid-August date was critical because it was the last point at which demobilization could be completed and still allow the electoral campaign to begin and the elections to be held without delay.[106]

As international criticism of the government was mounting in an effort to overcome its foot dragging,[107] another factor came into play. The soldiers in the assembly areas (AAs) for both the government and RENAMO, many of whom had been there for months, began to riot and demand immediate demobilization. While accommodations in the AAs were minimal and the troops' reactions understandable, even those men in elite units, which the government had excluded from the assembly and demobilization process, began to riot and make the same demand. Whether it was international pressure or the internal meltdown of what remained of its army, these two factors did the trick and the process picked up speed. On August 15, 1994, all of the AAs were formally closed. Demobilization of those troops that were contained in other areas continued for some time, and by the end of November 57,540 Government and 20,538 RE-NAMO soldiers had become civilians.[108]

In Angola, the process of demobilization was also one of delays born of mistrust and the inability or unwillingness of the parties to meet their obligations. With only three weeks left before the elections, less than half of the government's troops had been demobilized, along with less than a quarter of UNITA's forces.[109] Lodico explains that UNITA's justification for its failure to demobilize was that "the government was really transforming its troops into the secret riot police." She also points out that "Despite United States reassurances that this allegation was not a serious threat, UNITA's presumption about the formation of a secret para-military force proved accurate."[110]

To help speed up the process, the United States deployed several C-130s to Luanda to move the troops from their assembly areas. The demobilization process continued even after the elections were held on September 29 and 30, 1992. By October 7, about 80 percent of the Government's troops, but a much lower proportion of UNITA's, had been demobilized.[111]

Given its mandate, there seemed to be little that Anstee and the others in UNAVEM II could do to ensure that the parties lived up to their commitments except cajole them politely. The international community did so largely without effect and then chose to ignore the obviously flimsy underpinnings of the peace process that resulted. In a joint declaration on September 27, 1992, the government and UNITA declared that their forces had been formally abolished, even though neither was fully disbanded. Nonetheless, Anstee notes that the peace process had survived yet another cliff-hanging experience and that a sense of relief heightened the euphoria that permeated the swearing-in of the first soldiers in the unified army.[112] That euphoria was neither based on reality nor long lasting, because the formation of the FAA was even more incomplete and inadequate than the demobilization had been.

Forming One Army or Simply Creating a Third

Under the Rome accords, RENAMO and the Government were supposed to contribute equally to a single, unified army of 30,000 soldiers.

The total number was the result of a political accommodation and not based on any threat assessment, nor on an analysis of how big a military Mozambique needed. During the peace talks in Rome, the government had argued for a larger force, given the large size of its military. RENAMO had pushed for a smaller one, knowing it would have greater difficulty producing its half of the recruits from a much smaller pool of men. The 30,000 figure represented nothing more than simply splitting the difference between the two sides.[113]

The commanders of the new unified Mozambican Defense Force (FADM) were also drawn from RENAMO and the government. They assumed their posts on April 6, 1994, in a ceremony presided over by Ajello. With the establishment of the FADM, the military structures of the government (FAM) and RENAMO were supposedly disbanded. The FADM initially existed mainly on paper, and both the government and REN-AMO tried to hold some of their forces in reserve. By July 1994, only 3,000 soldiers had completed the various training programs that were organized by the United Kingdom, Portugal, and France. By late August, after the AAs had been closed and the election campaigns begun, the FADM still numbered only 7,806 troops. By the end of ONUMOZ's mandate in December, it numbered fewer than 12,000 with about two thirds coming from the government and the remainder from REN-AMO.[114] It was a situation that both sides had to accept but neither one liked. The government had wanted a large military to provide jobs for its officer class, and RENAMO wanted to contribute half of the force to ensure it would not be used against them in the future.[115]

When ONUMOZ withdrew, the FADM consisted of a navy with no functioning ships, an air force with no planes that flew, and an army with almost no operable heavy weapons. With all of Mozambique's neighbors democratic countries vitally interested in its stability, the FADM had little reason to exist other than as a source for jobs and opportunities for corruption. But the parties were not worried about the external threat.

Despite the willingness throughout the peace process of the United Kingdom, France, and Portugal to provide military training, both parties failed to provide enough men and the government failed to furnish the necessary facilities in a timely fashion.[116] This was due to the desire of the parties to hold back their best troops and the unpopularity of serving in the FADM. The shortfall was so great that the UK was able to train only 6 of the 15 infantry battalions that had originally been planned.

Even that modest accomplishment was due not to the efforts of the parties but to the fact that the government and RENAMO, after delaying the process for months, asked the Secretary General to have Ajello take over the committee responsible for forming the FADM (CCFADM). Up to that point the CCFADM had included only the parties and the three countries doing the training. The Security Council agreed to the Secretary General's recommendation that Ajello take over the group, and the first meeting chaired by him was held on July 22, 1993.[117] Once in charge of the committee, Ajello was able to move its work ahead much faster. As the British Ambassador at the time observed:

> The exercise of establishing the FADM once again showed Ajello's qualities in the shape of his readiness to cut corners and slash through red tape. Without for example his willingness to provide transport for RENAMO to the training areas and to chair the CCFADM, the process of training (the FADM) would have at best have been much slower.[118]

Even after the training finally began in earnest, the government came up with only about half of the troops it was supposed to contribute to the FADM, and RENAMO only a little more than a quarter. It remained an option that the vast majority of the former combatants rejected, based on their experience. During the war, neither side had been able to properly equip, train, feed, or lead its troops, making a military resolution of the conflict impossible. Neither side had the resources to provide the military strength to win. The conditions of service, plus the open-ended nature of enlistments, made continued military service unpopular even though demobilization meant joining an economy in which 80 percent of the population survived by subsistence agriculture and jobs were few.

Mozambique's lack of resources may have worked to support the peace process by providing such little incentive to those who wanted to have the option of renewing the fighting. Thus, while ONUMOZ did its best to ensure the parties lived up to their obligations, in the end, the mutinies among the troops and lack of resources to keep them in uniform may have been more telling factors than international pressure. For whatever reason, demobilization was achieved and the elections went ahead with one army in existence, albeit only partially formed, instead of three.

In Angola, the inadequacy of the mandate given UNAVEM II was again demonstrated in the formation of the new Angolan armed forces (FAA). While the British, French, and Portuguese took on the task of training the new force, the UN peacekeepers were given neither a verification role nor even a seat on the committee in charge of the process (CCFA).[119] The failure to form the FAA also demonstrated the insincerity and incompetence of the parties and the willingness of the international community to ignore both and press ahead with elections.

In mid-May, with the elections only four and a half months away, the CCFA proposed selecting the 40,000 members of the FAA but to begin training only between 13,000 and 23,000 of them.[120] Immediately the lack of housing for the troops became a major problem, particularly since "The very idea of tents was repugnant to some of the Angolan military, who considered that barracks were a *sine qua non*."[121] The government never got around to submitting a formal request to the Secretary General for tents until early August, and the UN seems never to have come up with more than a token number before subsequent events made the issue irrelevant. The process continued to drift, and in his last report to the Security Council prior to the elections, the Secretary General noted that only 19 percent of the soldiers of the FAA had been chosen.[122]

In their joint declaration of September 27, in addition to announcing their respective armies disbanded, Savimbi and Dos Santos asserted that the FAA was the only unified armed force in Angola. The next day, the two Joint Chiefs of the General Staff of the unified Angolan armed forces (FAA) were sworn in just 14 hours before the polls were to due to open. Anstee describes a surreal scene:

> The reception that followed the [swearing-in] formalities was an occasion of great euphoria, with much back-slapping and mutual congratulation, and there was a very pervasive atmosphere of brotherliness and unity in a common purpose. None of us who were there could forget for one moment the intense precariousness of the situation. But one would not have been human had one not gone away at the end of the ceremony thinking, wishfully perhaps, that things might somehow work out, despite all one's misgivings, because in the final analysis, everyone wanted done with war.[123]

But the thinking *was* wishful, because neither side's army had been disbanded and the new, unified one hardly existed at all. The parties, who would continue to spend millions on weapons, could find neither the money for tents nor the will to make the FAA anything more than a wish. In the end, Savimbi had three times the military force at the time of the elections than the government. If he wanted to be done with war, he did not want it enough to accept the results of the voting, and the military option was not only available, it was attractive given his numerical advantage.[124]

Elections—Free, Fair, and Rejected

Nowhere are the differences in the peacekeeping experiences in Angola and Mozambique brought into sharper contrast than in the area of the elections. In both countries, the role of the PKO with respect to the holding of the elections, was similar and in both the voters turned out in very large numbers. Despite this grass-roots demonstration of a desire for democracy, in each case both the major candidates were sure they would win, and in both, the loser rejected the results. The two experiences were different, however, in that the local parties in one were far more successful in organizing the elections and in demobilizing the former combatants before the voting. As a result, the most tragic difference was that in Angola the parties returned to war, whereas in Mozambique they did not.

Both UNAVEM II and ONUMOZ were called upon to provide technical assistance, financial support, and verification of the elections. This element of the mission was supposed to be key to its success, since the peace process was designed to culminate in the countries' first elections. It was felt that a democratically chosen government would have the legitimacy to bring a definitive end to the civil war. With a government in power that had been legitimized by an election victory, the necessary stability would have been established to enable the peacekeepers to consider their job done and depart. Unfortunately, in both cases, the system was to be winner-take-all, leaving the loser with no share of political power and little incentive to accept the outcome.

In both cases, the actual organization and conduct of the elections was handled by the parties, not by the UN. The logistical challenge of bringing off the first elections in countries with few roads and little infrastructure was enormous. Both countries are huge—Mozambique is nearly twice the size of California, with 15 million people. While Angola has only about half as many people, it is even larger geographically. In Mozambique there was simultaneous voting in over 7,000 polling stations, and there were over 4,000 polling places in Angola. The situation in Angola was made even more difficult by the fact that nearly 70 percent of the roads were unusable because of land mines and destroyed bridges.[125] Therefore the logistical problems alone in both countries presented huge obstacles, even if there had been the political will to see the elections successfully held.

The main differences between the UN's role in the elections in the two countries was that in Angola it was an afterthought and done on the cheap. This was to prove critical to the manner in which the outcome was received. The Protocol of Estoril did not specifically designate the UN as technical advisor for the Angolan elections or even as an observer body.[126] After a government request in December 1991, the Secretary General recommended the enlargement of UNAVEM II's mandate to include observation of the elections.[127] However, the UN assistance provided to help organize the elections was still minimal. As Lodico points out: "A mere 89 civil servants were deployed for all electoral activities in the six regional centers and 18 provincial centers throughout the country."[128]

In addition to the thin UN presence, the parties themselves did little to contribute to a successful electoral outcome. The National Electoral Council (NEC) was not sworn in until May 11, 1992, barely four and a half months before the elections. Although UNAVEM developed and urged the adoption of an electoral code of conduct, the NEC never saw fit to use it.[129] Despite serious gaps in the coverage of its efforts, the NEC refused to extend the period for registration, saying it could not do so simply because of UN or international pressure.[130] The government then rejected critical logistical support offered by the South Africans and later by the American government, arguing that its sovereignty would be abridged by accepting such offers.

As the military and police functions of the UNAVEM II faltered and failed to reach their objectives, the efforts of peacekeepers were increasingly directed at helping the electoral process and hoping it would succeed.[131] Yet the parties continued to refuse to carry out essential elements of what they had insisted on reserving for themselves. As each side traded threats and little was achieved, Anstee was powerless to avert the disaster she feared was coming. She said she simply did her best to exert steady and, she hoped, diplomatic pressure wherever and whenever she could.[132] Clearly such subtle tactics did not work.

She had no luck in getting the parties to ensure the integrity of the elections and not much more success with the international community. When the voting took place in Angola, there were only about 800 international observers, of which half were supplied by the UN.[133] In contrast, in Namibia, a country with only 12 percent of the population of Angola and good roads and other infrastructure, there had been 1,758 UN electoral and 1,035 UN police observers supervising 358 polling stations.[134] But as Anstee was reminded by New York when she pointed out this difference, in Angola the parties had limited the UN's job to simply observing the elections, not supervising and controlling them.[135] Despite the lack of international oversight, Angolans still flocked to the polls hoping, like the UN, that the elections would bring peace. About 92 percent of the 4.4 million registered voters cast their ballots.[136]

In Mozambique, the UN also played only a supporting role in the elections. It was a much more extensive one, however. One lesson learned by the international community in Angola was that it made little sense to try to save money on oversight of the elections if they were supposed to be the crowning element of the peace process and the guarantee of future stability. Mozambique also benefited from two other factors. It had a very generous and supportive group of donors, chaired by the local UNDP representative, and a National Elections Commission (CNE) composed of Mozambicans who did their job very well.

The donors were a key part of the electoral process because they contributed $55 million of the total of $60 million required for the elections. The Mozambican government came up with the remaining $5 million in the budget and several ideas to make the process more expensive. The government insisted, for instance, on an expensive photo identification document for each voter. Perhaps the authorities saw it as an opportunity for greater control over their own citizens, since the police began to ask for this form of identification when questioning people. For whatever reason, cheaper, equally effective methods of voter identification were available but rejected.

The budget was driven up by the need for 350 vehicles, 30 helicopters, and 3 planes in addition to the voter identification system used. The vehicles were purchased new instead of leased for the few months they were needed. The UN did not recover any of this cost as the vehicles were donated to the government, wrecked, or simply disappeared. In the end, the elections cost an average of $11.30 per voter in a country that spends far less than that, per capita, each year on health care and education combined.[137]

While the cost of the elections could be questioned, the quality of the work done by the key Mozambicans responsible for bringing them off could not. The CNE was headed by Dr. Brazao Mazula, who turned out to be a brilliant choice. He, like Ajello, was credited with having been one of the main reasons for the success of the peace process in Mozambique.

The peace accords signed in Rome in October 1992 called for elections within a year. It quickly became clear that this would be impossible to achieve, given the delays in the deployment of ONUMOZ and in troop demobilization. These delays, plus the lack of agreement on an electoral law, caused the elections to be postponed for a year.

When the CNE members (ten from the government, seven from RE-NAMO, and three from other political parties) were sworn in on January 21, 1994, most observers thought a further postponement might be necessary. Mazula was a consensus builder, however, who was viewed as genuinely nonpartisan. He was able to persuade his colleagues on the CNE to rise above petty party politics and make the necessary decisions.[138] That, plus generous financial assistance and occasional pressure from the UN and the key donors, kept the elections on track.

When the elections were held, there were 52,000 polling officers at 7,244 voting sites being monitored by 2,300 international observers, and 35,000 representatives from all of the 14 contending political parties.[139] The latter group of observers was especially important to the process and was organized virtually at the last moment. Using USAID funds, the International Republican Institute, the International Organization for Migration, and CARE provided training, transport, food, and pay to these volunteers.[140] The program was almost too successful, as many more people than were needed tried to sign up for the benefits, even if they were to last for only a few days. Nonetheless, they were of tremendous importance in building the necessary level of confidence in the electoral process and in its outcome. The opinion of international observers counts for little if the people whose future is being determined by the elections have no confidence that they were free and fair. In addition, local officials cost far less than those from abroad. Each international observer cost hundreds of dollars a day, whereas the local monitors were hired for only a few dollars apiece.

The voting in Mozambique was nearly thrown into turmoil when, just a few hours before the polls were to open, Dhlakama claimed FRELIMO was rigging the election and instructed his followers to boycott it. Only after intense international pressure and assurances that any irregularities would be investigated did he agree to reverse himself and allow RENAMO to participate in the elections.

As with getting the government to move ahead with demobilization, the American role in helping to overcome this last-minute hitch is often underestimated.[141] The afternoon of the first day of voting, when RENAMO's participation was still in doubt, I met with Dhlakama's top advisors and delivered a simple message—the elections were going to be held as scheduled, with or without RENAMO. That evening I met alone with Dhlakama for over an hour and repeated that message. I also assured him that any claims of electoral fraud would be investigated seriously. Shortly after we met, and I was virtually the only visitor he received that evening, he instructed his supporters to participate in the elections. A third day of voting was added to ensure that everyone had an opportunity to cast their ballots. The elections were concluded successfully with a very high turnout.

After the votes were counted in both countries, the UN and virtually all of the international observers declared both elections to have been free and fair. In both instances, the loser rejected this judgment. The Mozambicans had done the work of organizing the elections far better than the Angolans had, however, and the international efforts to monitor and verify had been far more extensive in Mozambique than in Angola. As a result, Dhlakama's claims of fraud were investigated and found to have little credibility. Savimbi's assertions were more difficult to disprove, although most believed them to be equally groundless. More importantly and tragically, Savimbi still had an army with which to renew the fighting, and Dhlakama did not.

Thus, while the UN tried in both Angola and Mozambique to ensure that the peace process succeeded, it had decidedly varying degrees of success in carrying out tasks that were critically important. This was due to both bureaucratic inability and the failure to get the parties to live up to their commitments. While the UN struggled to manage those factors that should have been under its control, the factors external to the PKO, which the UN could at best only influence, had an even more important and negative impact on the outcome.

Chapter Six

The External Factors

In addition to the internal factors, there are important external factors outside the scope of the PKO that can have a critical impact on the chances for success of peacekeeping. These factors can be influenced by the UN but cannot be completely controlled by it. First and foremost among them are the parties to the conflict and the degree to which they are committed to the peace process. The parties in a civil war may have spent years negotiating a peace treaty but are unlikely to trust each other. Reaching permanent peace requires them to surrender, or at least put at risk, real power. Political, economic, and military power are given up, or at least suspended, through demobilization, elections, and other elements of the peace process.

At various points in time, the parties (or hardline elements among them) will argue against continuing to go forward. The argument will be made that the other side cannot be trusted or that the UN has not adequately verified their compliance. The motivation for putting the process on hold, nonetheless, will be unwillingness to either surrender power or to run the risk of losing it.

Also, the parties may have reserved for themselves obligations and responsibilities that they are incapable or unwilling to fulfil when the time comes to do so. National pride or irrationality, as well as insincerity, may preclude admitting this and asking the UN to take on greater responsibilities. Simple logistical problems may be beyond the capacity of the parties to solve and can easily become major obstacles that bring the whole process to a halt. While the UN can attempt to resolve the problem at that point if asked by the parties, delays might have been avoided if the UN had been given the responsibility in the first place. As discussed in the previous chapter, the UN tends to take the mandate that the parties allow it to have, rather than to insist on one that has greater chances for success. If the parties falter, a weak mandate affords little opportunity for the UN to try to keep the peace process from failing.

The more the parties control the peace process, the more they can retard its progress when it suits their purposes. The parties should, but often won't, be willing to cede to the UN sufficient responsibility and authority to ensure that the PKO stands some chance of adhering to the agreed timetable. This requires, in the case of the government, surrendering a significant measure of sovereignty, which it will always be reluctant to do. Governments will use the sovereignty argument selectively, asserting it when it is in their interest and ignoring it when it is not.

A party may agree to a peace process that leads to voting but will work to ensure that the results of that vote are an outcome it finds acceptable. This can include hindering the efforts of the UN to bring about elections that are free and fair. In Morocco, for instance, "once the cease-fire took effect, the Government began to hamper the referendum's implementation. Morocco blocked deployment of many of the UN peacekeepers and refused to allow UN-chartered supply ships to unload at the Moroccan port of Agadir."[1]

The degree of cooperation of the parties can be greatly affected by a second external factor—the resources of the country itself. Resources can fuel the conflict and provide much to fight over. When they are plentiful and easily marketable, they can be used to buy more arms and ammunition. Conversely, a country's lack of resources can bring considerable pressure to bear on the combatants to bring the fighting to an end and provide an incentive for it not to break out again.

Resources can also motivate another external factor—the outside actors. These can be countries or organizations. While civil wars are intrastate conflicts, they always have interstate implications, and a wide range of other nations will be interested in the war's outcome. They can include the neighboring states, major or regional powers, and donor nations. The latter, along with their degree of willingness to underwrite the peace process and postwar reconstruction, can play an important role.

Participants in that reconstruction will include the humanitarian groups trying to alleviate the human suffering caused by the conflict. Often the desire to provide humanitarian assistance in a situation where suffering is widespread and life-threatening can alone provide the impetus to launch a PKO. At other times, it is an important component of a multidimensional effort. In either case, the provision of such aid has inescapable political and military implications. There will be some who wish to ignore this fact and treat humanitarian action as totally neutral, which can make it more difficult for peacekeeping to succeed. Since humanitarian assistance can be provided by UN organizations or by NGOs, it does not fall neatly into either category of factors, internal or external. Since it has great potential for affecting the outcome of the mission, the interplay between humanitarian action and peacekeeping will be addressed in the next chapter.

While the UN can be faulted on occasion for not managing the elements of a peacekeeping operation better, there are other important factors that affect the chances for peace. While these factors are beyond the UN's control, the UN can attempt to influence them, if it is willing to recognize the need to do so. The principal external factors are the parties themselves, the country's internal resources, and the external actors.

The Real Culprits—The Parties Themselves

If there is a single key element to the success of peacekeeping, it is the cooperation of the parties. If they are determined to continue fighting, there is no peace to keep. Unless the UN is willing to use force, its efforts will amount to little. Even if it is prepared to use force, the UN's tolerance for casualties will likely be lower than that of the parties, as was demonstrated in Somalia. When it cannot protect innocent civilians, or even its own peacekeepers, the UN looks not only incompetent but ineffectual as well.

While the need for the parties to cooperate may seem obvious, they rarely make their lack of cooperation evident. In addition, the UN is slow to acknowledge publicly that cooperation is being withheld and loath to pull out when it is. Diplomatic norms seem to require a high tolerance on the part of the UN for insincerity by the parties. Nor is there any shortage of other culprits who can be blamed for the failures of the peace process by the parties and the UN: colonial legacies, foreign influences, a PKO's weak mandate or insufficient resources, lack of international attention (be it from the media or governments). All can be offered as reasons for why a PKO is not working. These factors play a part but are unlikely to have as deciding a role as the conduct of the parties.

The fundamental, and often missing, factor is a true interest by the parties in a lasting peace if it does not provide a means to attaining their goals. While the parties will always maintain they want peace, it will be a peace on their terms, with neither costs nor risks to their claim on power. Peacekeeping can be used by either party in a conflict for its own purposes. A

PKO is seen as a no-cost option that requires only a change in tactics, at least for a while, without changing one's ultimate goals. The parties can therefore readily agree to a peace arrangement more out of tactical necessity than because of any significant commitment to peace. They can hold back the forces needed to resume the war if they don't like the outcome of the peace process, and its failure is thereby assured.

Angola illustrates this case well. As one writer observed:

> The Government alleged that UNITA maintained hidden reserves and UNITA charged that the Government's mobilization of riot police was a ruse for a parallel army. In fact, both parties' allegations proved correct after the elections. [2]

A cease-fire and a PKO can therefore mean to one or both parties simply the opportunity to regroup and rearm; consenting to a peace agreement and calling for peacekeepers has little political and no economic cost to the parties. They know they can always return to fighting if necessary, and the peacekeepers will be able to do little to stop them.

The potential for fighting to break out again is significant because the parties to a "teacup" war will usually see things only in winner-take-all terms. The peace agreements that the parties sign can reinforce that impression. In both Angola and Mozambique, no provisions were made for power-sharing with the losing side in the elections. A 1993 State Department assessment attributed the failure of UNAVEM II to the fact that Angola had a winner-take-all system in place. The study cautioned that Mozambique resembled Angola in key aspects and might fail for the same reason.[3]

Interstate wars are usually fought over territory that is easily defined and divided. Intrastate wars, which give rise to the vast majority of today's peacekeeping situations, are about political power. The parties know that whoever controls the government controls the economic resources, given the degree of state intervention in the third world countries where such wars are usually fought. They also know that there is little value in second place. The elections that crown some peace processes are often designed to select a winner with legitimacy and not as a means to share power. (Such was the case in both Angola and Mozambique.) With limited economies and weak institutions, the losers will have little representation in government and few possibilities for finding economic or political power outside it. Having little stake in the resulting political structures provides the loser little incentive to preserve them.

But if the parties do not fulfill their obligations and commitments, the PKO inevitably fails; and neither the UN nor any other outside party will be able to keep the peace process on track. In Angola and Mozambique, the process was to start with the assembly of troops, the demobilization of most of them and the formation of the rest into a single army. This was to be followed by elections to select democratically a government with enough legitimacy to rule the country without a military challenge from those who lost the elections. Each step in such a process requires the parties to surrender, or at least put at risk, power—military, political, or economic. When these points are reached, peace accords, no matter how carefully and laboriously negotiated, can begin to lose their appeal. In addition, the parties can simply be logistically incapable of completing their part of the bargain and unwilling to let the UN do it for them.

The first PKO in Angola achieved its limited goals with very limited resources precisely because the parties cooperated and wanted the UN to succeed in its mission. Established by the Security Council in December 1988, UNAVEM I consisted of 70 military observers whose task it was to verify the withdrawal of Cuban forces from Angola. After the last of the 50,000 Cuban troops departed in May 1991, the Secretary General attributed the success of UNAVEM I to the full cooperation of the parties involved.[4] Verifying the exit of foreign troops was achievable because all of the parties wanted it to happen.

Verifying free and fair elections and ushering in an era of permanent peace was a far more complex task requiring much more of UNAVEM II but also much more of the parties. If one had to identify a single cause for the unsuccessful outcome of UNAVEM II, it would have to be the failure of the government and UNITA to implement the obligations and commitments that they had agreed to in the Bicesse Accords. The kind of behavior Anstee describes over and over again as she attempted to carry out UNAVEM II's mandate makes it clear that the Angolan parties were interested in peace only if it came at no cost to their political, military, or economic power. Yet she places the blame for the return to war on the lack of attention and resources devoted to the problem by the international community. She also attempts to exonerate the UN by making the case that with sufficient funds and manpower the PKO could have succeeded.

Without the cooperation of the parties, however, additional resources would have resulted only in a much bigger PKO that was ultimately as unsuccessful as the one she presided over. As one foreign military observer, who was present when the war in Angola resumed, noted: "With the resources available, Anstee was not prepared to handle the situation, but she could not have succeeded with 10,000 peacekeepers given the absence of political will on the part of the Angolans on both sides."[5]

Political will begins with the leadership of the groups involved. Both major candidates in Angola and in Mozambique were convinced they were going to win. The losers in both countries asserted that the elections were not free and fair, even though there were hundreds of international observers who certified to the contrary.

Despite these similarities, the leadership factor was a significant difference in the experience of both countries. Anstee vividly described the leadership situation in Angola and it was not a pretty picture:

> Dr. Savimbi and President Dos Santos did not have a de Klerk-Mandela relationship. Theirs was not a close association where personal and political rivalry was suppressed for the overriding national interest. These two men were prepared to fight out their political destinies to the end. Pride was involved too. Savimbi's pride in himself was very evident, to the point of resembling arrogance. Some thought it even approached megalomania. He was a man with a mission and a messianic view of his role in history: he saw himself as the man born to govern Angola and to lead the people out of the wilderness.[6]

Anstee's opinion was not unique, and little changed after she left Angola. According to a columnist in *The New York Times* writing in early 1996: "The two things keeping this war going now are the ego of Jonas Savimbi and diamonds."[7] One diplomat described Savimbi to *The Economist* as "a megalomaniac who has run out of options."[8] That view was expressed in mid-1995; over two years later Savimbi was still playing the same options by refusing to join a government of national unity and reserving a portion of his military forces.[9] A report in early 1997 noted that the outlines of a stable political settlement in Angola were still unclear because "Jonas Savimbi has demanded that the question of his role be at the top of the agenda."[10] And it is likely he will keep it there until satisfied. In a March 1996 speech he said: "I have not known of any historic leader who disarmed his forces and stayed in power."[11]

Savimbi is at least consistent. In April 1997, UNITA deputies were sworn in at the National Assembly in Luanda, and the Government of National Unity and Reconciliation was established. Savimbi was absent, however, despite having been granted the special status as leader of the largest opposition party, which he had insisted on. He claimed that the capital was too unsafe for him to visit. A newspaper article describing the events quoted one diplomat as saying, "Make no mistake, UNITA is a one-man show. If Savimbi does not get what he wants, if things are not going his way, then he will stop the whole process." Other sources in the same article noted that UNITA still retained the bulk of its military might, having turned in unserviceable weapons and forced farmers to go to demobilization camps to meet UN targets.[12]

Such descriptions of Savimbi's behavior stand in sharp contrast to what occurred in Mozambique. Moments before RENAMO President Afonso Dhlakama signed the General Peace Accord with the Mozambican government in Rome, he told a UN official that he "was not a Savimbi" and that he would not take up arms again.[13] He has repeated this reassurance often, and while he protested that the elections were not free and fair, he has been true to his word thus far. To be sure, Dhlakama lacked the internal resources and external actors that aided Savimbi's return to war, but he also apparently lacks Savimbi's megalomania. For his part, Mozambican President Chissano has shown "that while he was not Mandela as he rejected any notion of a government of national unity, he nonetheless remained committed to the peace process."[14]

Leadership that provides the political will to assure that peacekeeping can succeed is essential, but it is not enough by itself. A lack of discipline or control can threaten the peacekeepers and the success of the mission. Lodico points out:

> From the time the observers (military, police and civilians) were deployed until the elections, UNAVEM personnel were subject to intimidation and, in some regions, they were fired upon while in their camps. During the political campaign period, UNAVEM personnel were forbidden to have cameras.[15]

Assuming that this harassment was not conducted under instruction from Luanda or Jamba, such conduct would be due to the inability of either headquarters to control their troops. The leadership may also be precluded from respecting the peace agreement by the inability to control factions among its followers. One diplomat with a long history of involvement in Angola stated that Savimbi feared he would be killed by his generals if he accepted the outcome of the elections.[16]

While UN reports are not known for their candor, occasionally the blame gets laid clearly and squarely where it belongs. As the President of the Cease-fire Commission (CCF), Colonel Segala pulled no punches when he noted in his final report that:

> Among the difficulties faced [by ONUMOZ in Mozambique] it is worth-
> while to highlight the following:
>   —the political game of the parties
>   —the lack of trust between the parties
>   —the lack of basic infrastructure in the country.[17]

Segala, a colonel in the Italian army, at least had the advantage of chair-
ing the CCF and therefore had some degree of influence over its work.
UN representatives also chaired the commission that oversaw the whole
peace process (CSC), one that organized the reintegration of demobilized
soldiers (CORE) and another that formed the new army (CCFADM).
While these achieved varying degrees of success, they all vastly outper-
formed the three other commissions composed exclusively of Mozambican members that were responsible for assuring the neutrality of the police
(COMPOL), monitoring the government intelligence service (COM-
INFO), and unifying under a single public administration the territory
controlled by the government and RENAMO (the Commission for Territorial Administration.)[18] In all three of these latter entities, the parties
were rarely able to overcome their mutual mistrust and make the body
function in a way that would allow it to achieve its objectives. In all three
cases, the UN could do little to accomplish what the parties had reserved
to themselves but refused to do.

All the News That's Fit to Invent

Another area in which the parties often play a negative role and prevent
the UN from playing a positive one is in the information provided the
public. During the conflict, the government, and frequently the rebels, will
have their means of communicating their point of view to the local populace. Both sides will continue to use these means after the fighting is suspended, usually to the detriment of the peace process. The parties are
usually unconstrained by democratic institutions or principles and have
few, if any, other sources of information against which they have to compete. In such circumstances, the parties will often resort to propaganda or
even disinformation.

The government will probably control most of the media and will have
the right to license others. Frequently this governmental licensing power
will be used to deny the opposition a voice and to prevent more objective
parties, including the UN, from having access to media outlets of their

own. The UN may argue for its own ability to disseminate information but will defer to the government if it asserts this version of the national sovereignty argument.

If a rebel group has sufficient economic resources, it may also have its own means of mass communication. It will control access to those means just as tightly, and use them for partisan purposes just as ruthlessly, as the government. There will not be enough sustained interest from the international media to provide a consistent and steady outside source of objective information. When the media is used in this way, it will sow the seeds of distrust, place the peace process at greater risk, and make the peacekeepers' job that much more difficult.

In Angola, both sides had formidable propaganda machines, which, when they were not attacking each other, often attacked UNAVEM and Anstee personally. Both the government and UNITA had their own newspaper and radio and television stations.[19] There were no resources or mandate for UNAVEM II to operate its own radio station, as was done in Cambodia. As Anstee notes, it was desperately needed to provide unbiased information to an electorate that was being bombarded by propaganda.[20]

UNAVEM II was never able to fill that desperate need effectively. In the end, all Anstee could do was rationalize: "One of the lessons of almost all peacekeeping operations is that, if you truly strive to be impartial, you must expect to be reviled, at various times, by both sides. An ultra-thick skin is an essential item of equipment for such assignments."[21] While such a stiff upper lip is admirable, it did nothing to lessen the poisonous atmosphere that was created by the propaganda generated by both sides. Such an atmosphere fueled the distrust between the parties and made the return to war more possible.

In Mozambique, the government's strangle hold on the media was nearly complete. RENAMO did not have the resources to support its own media outlets. Late in the electoral process, the German government provided equipment for an FM station for RENAMO, which broadcast for only a short time and with very limited range before closing for lack of funds. With that brief exception, the government or its supporters owned all of the electronic media and virtually all the print media.

Next to word of mouth, the most common source of information for Mozambicans is radio. Living mainly in rural areas and predominantly illiterate, the people had to rely on the only AM station in the country, which was owned by the government. In addition, the government owned one of the two TV stations, which broadcast only in the three largest cities. The other was far from independent, however, since it belonged to a member of

FRELIMO's central committee. The government also owned the country's two daily newspapers (one in Maputo and the other in Beira), the only Sunday newspaper, and the only weekly news magazine. It also owned the only news agency—the Mozambican Information Agency (AIM), which it used to produce stories for its newspapers and to disseminate its one-sided version of events abroad. In order to support all of these entities, the Ministry of Information had a budget that was larger than those of almost all of the other ministries.[22]

Because of the limited ability to distribute newspapers and transmit television, the media, with the exception of radio, served a mainly urban audience. This may partially explain why FRELIMO won a majority of the urban vote and RENAMO had a majority in rural areas. While control of the media certainly helped FRELIMO win votes in the urban areas, the exodus during the war of its supporters from the RENAMO-controlled countryside undoubtedly added to its strength in the cities.

The government used the media to portray its actions in the best light and to denigrate RENAMO. The kind of crude and vicious propaganda that Anstee and UNAVEM had to endure in Angola were not directed at Ajello and ONUMOZ in Mozambique. Nonetheless, the media probably prolonged the war and certainly threatened the peace. A number of the participants in the peace process cited the lack of trust between the parties as one of the principal obstacles to progress. With the media firmly in the hands of the government, and constantly trying to demonize RENAMO, this lack of trust could only be reinforced.

One of the most blatant examples of this manipulation of the media took place shortly after the votes were cast in the elections on October 27, 28, and 29, 1994. Because of the lack of communications and transportation infrastructure, it took several days for the official results to filter in from the various parts of the country. The partial returns, to which the UN and the parties had access, demonstrated several clear trends. These trends were also fully evident in the UN's "quick count," which projected nationwide results on the basis of a small sample of the voting districts. According to these indicators, Chissano would win the presidency by a narrow majority with Dhlakama a distant but respectable second; FRELIMO would do significantly worse and might not gain a majority in parliament; and finally the other 10 presidential candidates and 12 parties would each earn not more than 1 or 2 percent of the votes.

It became obvious to the FRELIMO leadership that such results would be likely to generate renewed calls for power-sharing, including arguments that RENAMO be given seats in the cabinet. Earlier in the peace process, the government and its media had adamantly rejected any suggestion of a government of national unity, as had just been installed in South Africa and in Malawi. When asked about the possibility, Chissano diplomatically stated that he would select only the most qualified people for his government if he were elected. It was clear, however, that FRELIMO wanted to preserve a winner-take-all situation. Having failed to defeat RENAMO on the battlefield, FRELIMO was confident of winning at the polls and saw no reason to surrender cabinet positions to its former enemies.

As the partial returns continued to confirm the initial trends, the FRELIMO leadership decided to launch a preemptive strike against any suggestion of power-sharing. On November 13, 1994, during the height of this period of uncertainty and tension, the government newspaper *Domingo* published a front-page story that asserted that RENAMO was planning to go back to war, assisted by American diplomats and foreign businessmen. The paper claimed it based its report on a RENAMO document that had come into its possession. Yet the paper never attempted to verify the authenticity of the document or to ask those accused for their reaction.[23] This transparent effort at disinformation was denounced the next day by Ajello and the CSC ambassadors at a press conference.

When the final results were announced on November 19, the initial trends were all confirmed. One minor party did just exceed the 5 percent minimum required to gain seats in parliament. Most observers credited this to the fact that it was at the bottom of the ballot for the parties, just as Chissano was in the last position on the ballot for the presidential candidates. Enough of the largely illiterate, first-time voters simply marked the bottom slot on both ballots to put the party over the 5 percent threshold. In the end, Chissano won a bare majority while FRELIMO gained a bare plurality. Because only three parties had made the 5 percent cutoff, FRELIMO nevertheless won a slight majority of the 250 seats in parliament. Its attempt to demonize RENAMO the week before, however, demonstrated that FRELIMO was willing to risk a return to war to avoid sharing power.

Control of the media is therefore a weapon that will not be readily surrendered in the peace process, and it will be available for use at any point. It is also a weapon the UN feels powerless to remove from the parties' arsenal, no matter how disruptive it may be to the creation of an environment in which the peace has a chance to last. The UN may try to offer an alternative, unbiased source of information, but it will be deterred easily if the parties seek to prevent it from doing so.

Enough Resources for War but Not for Peace

The media is one resource in a country that can hamper peacekeeping considerably. Other resources may also have the capacity to undermine lasting peace, especially if they take a form that is easily transported and converted to cash, such as diamonds. A country's resources can constitute an incentive for war because peace will usually result in one side in power, with control over those resources. The losing side winds up not only without political power but also denied the economic power that the spoils of war offer. Since the "teacup" wars are usually fought in countries with underdeveloped economies, there are few alternative avenues to political or economic power available to the losers of elections. Political power translates into a monopoly on economic power and there are no think tanks or businesses that are sufficiently independent of the government to provide an opportunity for the losers to find a place where they can bide their time until the next election.

Angola's blessings in resources have also been its curse. The country's oil and diamond deposits are easily exploited and generate huge revenues, giving Angolans and foreigners much to fight over. Oil revenues for 1996 exceeded $4 billion, and diamond sales were more than $850 million.[24] As the State Department's human rights report on Angola notes, "most of the country's wealth is concentrated in the hands of the small political, military and business elite."[25]

By using current income or mortgaging future revenue, the warring parties used much of this wealth to sustain their militaries. According to one study, Angola imported just under $11 billion in arms between 1984 and 1994.[26] These figures are probably low, since neither the government nor UNITA is willing to make public data on precisely how much each spends on arms. These weapons acquisitions undoubtedly prolonged the war, endangered the peace, and left very little in the way of funds for social or government services to the civilian population. In a country with the world's highest infant mortality rate, an estimated 40 to 50 percent of the Government's revenues went to the military, while just 2 percent of the budget was spent on health.[27] In a country where human rights abuses by security forces are common, the budget of the Justice Ministry, including salaries, was $60,000 a year.[28]

These huge military expenditures provided not only the means to continue the war but also a strong incentive for making sure that peace did not take hold. Besides those government resources that are stolen outright, arms purchases provide a lucrative opportunity for a major portion of these expenditures to end up in the pockets of generals and ministers. According to one source, the kickback on arms purchases can be anywhere from 10 to 40 percent.[29] Using that as a rule of thumb shows just how good a business war can be for the participants. With the Angolan government estimated to have spent $3.5 billion on arms imports in 1993 and 1994 alone,[30] the "commissions" pocketed by those making the decisions on such purchases could have ranged anywhere from $350 million to $1.4 billion.

While the government fueled its war machine mainly with oil revenue, diamonds provided the source of income for UNITA. Angola is the world's third-largest producer of gems, and their value and easy transportability make them the ideal resource for sustaining a guerrilla movement. UNITA held much of the diamond diggings in northeastern Angola, while generals in the government's army held concessions in other diamond areas.[31] The diamonds dug in UNITA-held territory are estimated to be worth $1 million a day. Because of this, one magazine article observed that "until Angola's diamond wealth is divvied up to UNITA's satisfaction, the country has no assurance of peace."[32] It may be even more complicated than that. Individual generals are given their own concessions on both sides. Until all of the most powerful among them are satisfied with their take, both in absolute terms and relative to the others, peace may not be possible.[33]

In contrast to Angola's resources, half of Mozambique's annual gross domestic product and 90 percent of its exports were generated by agriculture.[34] In Angola, agriculture accounts for only 15 percent of the economy while oil contributes 60 percent. Mozambique's principal exports are shrimp, cashew nuts and other agricultural products. They do not generate huge wealth and are neither easily transported nor geographically concentrated. Since RENAMO had no navy, it could never threaten economic activity in offshore fisheries. It did control great parts of rural Mozambique, however, and was able to deny the government much of the country's agricultural wealth.

Because Mozambique has far fewer resources than Angola, the combatants in its civil war had far less to spend on weapons. For the period 1984 to 1994, arms imports for Mozambique were estimated to be $1.4 billion, or about 13 percent of what Angola spent during those years.[35] Without resources that were worth fighting over or that could sustain huge arms expenditures and generate opportunities for kickbacks, Mozambique's elite had less of an incentive to avoid peace than in Angola, where the stakes were enormous.

It does not take a great many resources, however, to provide a disincentive for peace in a civil war. Liberia's assets are chiefly iron ore, rubber, and timber, which are incapable of generating huge wealth in the midst of a conflict. Yet, as Reno describes it: "Ultimately conflicts like the one in Liberia are not about ideology or political programs: they are about looting resources and controlling people to make rebel leaders rich."[36]

Outside Actors—For Good or Ill

The opportunity for looting a country's resources will often attract outsiders who can inadvertently help to prolong the fighting. If they have interests that would be threatened by an end to the war, they can actively work to prevent peace. While civil wars are internal conflicts, the involvement of outside actors is inevitable, and they can make peace more possible or much more difficult to achieve.

Most important among these outside actors are countries such as world or regional powers, donors, neighbors, or any other state with an interest in the outcome of the conflict. If all of these actors are willing to support the objectives of the peacekeeping mission, its chances for success will be greatly enhanced. Such unanimity of purpose is rare, however. As each of these countries pursues its own interests, the country in conflict will often suffer the consequences. In the "teacup" wars, even a little outside aid to one of the armed factions can ensure that the war will be protracted.

Even when all of these countries endorse peace and are sincere, they may not be able to control events within their own borders sufficiently to help make it happen. Another type of outside actor is the international organizations that provide humanitarian assistance to the victims of the war. Their special role and the impact of humanitarian assistance will be considered in the next chapter.

The involvement of the superpowers was far more important in Angola than in Mozambique. During the Cold War, the superpowers played out their confrontation through surrogates in the third world in places like Central America, Afghanistan, and Africa. In the post–Cold War era, the collaboration between Russia and the United States has made peacekeeping more possible. Nowhere has this been more true than in Angola. For years, both superpowers funneled arms to their respective sides. In his December 7, 1988 speech to the UN General Assembly, Gorbachev articulated the change in Soviet perceptions and attitudes that had made peacekeeping more possible and the UN more effective. As early as April of that year, Secretary of State Shultz had perceived this shift with regard to Angola and had been working to get Soviet support for a Cuban troop withdrawal and the plan to bring about the independence of Namibia.[37] From promoting the war in Angola, the superpowers shifted to attempting to preserve the peace. The U.S. and Russia, together with Portugal, the former colonial power, became the troika working to keep the Angolan parties on the road to a lasting settlement.

The role of the superpowers in Mozambique also underwent a transition during this same period, but it was far less dramatic since neither country was involved in Mozambique's civil war to the extent that both were in Angola's. Perhaps because it lacked the resources or the tens of thousands of Cuban troops that were stationed in Angola, Mozambique was never considered of sufficient concern to merit more direct American involvement.

There were those in Washington who believed differently, however, and saw all anti-Communist guerrillas as deserving support. They viewed Mozambique as a place where the "Reagan Doctrine" should be applied and the antigovernment forces supported. As Secretary Shultz described it in his memoirs:

> President Reagan could be led to agree with the proposition that all freedom fighters—UNITA and RENAMO alike—deserved unquestioned support. South Africa, with [CIA Director] Bill Casey's encouragement, was particularly vigorous in supporting South Africa's surrogate force, RENAMO, against Machel's government. In late August 1985, Casey's CIA briefers were showing their audiences in the administration and Congress a map of Mozambique colored to indicate—falsely—that RENAMO controlled virtually the entire country.[38]

Such arguments did not carry the day, in part because of the success of the personal diplomacy of Mozambique's president. Samora Machel made an official visit to Washington in July 1985, much to the consternation of pro-RENAMO elements in the Reagan administration. In his White House meeting, Machel impressed Reagan and won him over with a medley of anti-Soviet and other jokes. By the end of their talk, the danger of the Reagan Doctrine being applied to Mozambique was over.[39] Thus the conflict in Mozambique was never elevated to the level that it was in Angola, and the outside support came from elsewhere. The other superpower, the Soviet Union, went from being the main source of FRELIMO's arms to a largely passive supporter of the peace process. While Washington had at times cool but correct relations with Maputo during the war, it worked diligently for the success of the peace process.

A far more dramatic transformation than that of the superpowers was the role of the regional powers, who went from being the main external supporters of the war in both countries to some of the most effective advocates for peace. In Mozambique, Rhodesia had a great deal to do with RENAMO's creation and external support (although there is some debate as to whether this rebel movement would have come into existence and survived were it not for Rhodesian assistance). When the white-ruled Rhodesian government was replaced by the democratically elected government of Zimbabwe, the main source of RENAMO's support became South Africa. In Rhodesia and in South Africa during apartheid, both regimes wanted to prevent Mozambique from being used as a platform for liberation movements. All of Mozambique's neighbors, including South Africa and Zimbabwe, rely to varying degrees on its transportation routes and ports, which could not be used effectively without peace. Thus these countries, but particularly South Africa and Zimbabwe once they became democratic, worked to support the peace process and ONUMOZ.

The Secretary General recognized the importance of this fact to the outcome of ONUMOZ when he noted that:

> The regional dimension was another crucial factor in the Mozambique peace process. The improved political environment in southern Africa from the end of the 1980s, which coincided with the end of the cold war, made possible the successful search for peace in Mozambique. A key element in this success was the active participation of governments in the region in bringing peace negotiations to a fruitful conclusion in Rome. Their involvement, along with that of other members of the international community, throughout the implementation of the General Peace Agreement was equally vital to the success of ONUMOZ.[40]

The change to democracy in South Africa also brought a similar change in its approach to Angola. During the war, it had supplied arms and its own troops to fight alongside UNITA against the Cubans and the Angolan Communists. With the end of apartheid, South Africa tried to use its influence to help keep the peace process on track. During South Africa's transition to democracy, however, its policy toward Angola was also in transition and not always as helpful as it could have been.

Anstee describes at length the tense situation immediately following the Angolan elections. Even before the results were announced, Savimbi had rejected them. Foreign Minister Pik Botha arrived on the scene and attempted to help avert a return to war. In between one "large glass of whiskey"[41] after another, however, he became convinced there had been fraud in the voting. In the end, he only added to the confusion and probably encouraged Savimbi's recalcitrance rather than calmed the situation. While the South African government's intentions were good, the inability to resist siding with its former client prevented it from making a more positive contribution at that critical juncture.

Powerful countries, be they superpowers or regional ones, that have an interest in the outcome of a civil war can fuel that war or encourage the peace that ends it. They can make peace and peacekeeping possible, and it would be hard to imagine a situation in which a major player could not prevent both if it wanted to do so.

Less powerful countries can, because of their location, also greatly affect the prospects for peace. Based on the influence of Zimbabwe and South Africa on the situations in Mozambique and Angola, one might conclude that the chances for peacekeeping to succeed in a country increase if its neighbors and the regional powers are democratic. Zaire is another example of an undemocratic neighbor that contributed significantly to the failure of peacekeeping. Because Mobutu's regime saw its interests served by undermining the Luanda government, UNITA had no trouble obtaining its war material through Zaire long after any American and South African aid ceased. Zaire had a long history of providing a covert conduit for arms to UNITA. Secretary Shultz opposed overt U.S. assistance to UNITA and insisted such aid should be covert because it had to pass through Zaire or Zambia, and he did not want to embarrass these countries by making their role public.[42]

When American support for UNITA ceased, the Zaire channel stayed open. Given the corruption there, everything could be bought. It was so widespread that even in early 1997, as Zaire struggled with its own insurgency and rebels seized control of the eastern third of the country, the flow of arms to Angola continued. Relatives and aides of Mobutu were so interested in making a profit that they sold hundreds of tons of weapons to UNITA. In so doing they not only rearmed UNITA and increased the likelihood of renewed civil war in Angola, but they contributed to the collapse of their own military. In the end, Mobutu fell because his army was unable or unwilling to stop the rebels.[43]

Ironically, while Zaire had played such a major role in Angola's internal conflict, Angola in early 1997 was making significant contributions to the civil war in Zaire. The Luanda government sent aid to the rebels attempting to overthrow Mobutu, and UNITA sent similar assistance to the Zairian government to help prop him up.[44] The Angolan government was so interested in retribution against Mobutu that it provided the rebels heavy support in men, money, and material. Western intelligence reports also showed "Angolan army units poised to intervene directly in the conflict to tip the balance against Mobutu if necessary."[45] Liberia also demonstrates the negative impact that neighboring countries can have on a peacekeeping situation. Most of the weapons and ammunition that Charles Taylor's rebels received came from Libya via Burkina Faso and the Ivory Coast. Libya presumably saw in Taylor a low-cost way to strike at American interests in Liberia. The leaders in Burkina Faso and the Ivory Coast had no great love for the Liberian president, Samuel Doe. Even after Doe's demise in September 1990, they were unwilling or unable to stem the flow of arms through their countries, even if the weapons did fuel the war next door.

While neighboring countries can pursue their interests and thereby make a positive or negative contribution to the peace process, the motivation of the donor countries is more clear-cut and their impact generally helpful. Naturally, the extent of the generosity of the international community is important, but equally so is the latitude allowed in the use of funds. A multidimensional PKO has various elements that need extensive financial support, and being able to respond to funding needs in a flexible manner can make a significant contribution to its success.

Countries within the donor community may be generous for reasons that have little to do with the merits of the particular case in question. A country may underwrite a PKO because of a historic relationship with the country in which it is being conducted or because the donor country has invested some of its prestige in the peace process. The Scandinavian countries and the Netherlands were among Mozambique's biggest donors out of solidarity with an African experiment in socialism, and because Mozambique was on the front line in the struggle against apartheid.[46] They were also major supporters of the peace process. They gave generously to underwrite the budget for elections and programs for reintegration and demining, as well as to traditional development activities.

Italy became a major supporter of the process in Mozambique for another reason. It was drawn into the process when the Catholic lay society, Sant'Egidio, began mediating the peace talks between RENAMO and the government in Rome. The Italian government quickly became the main financial support for the negotiations. The importance of that contribution was explained by an American observer of the process, who noted that the dialogue between the two parties "wouldn't have gotten anyplace unless the Italian Government hadn't bankrolled the operation. This is something that is easy to ignore, but it was absolutely essential. Somebody had to pay the hotel bills for people staying in Rome."[47]

While some governments would have found it relatively easy to fund food and lodging for a time, the Italians supported the process for two years and did so in other, less conventional ways. For instance, most of the RENAMO delegates had come to the talks directly from years in the bush but wanted to feel respected and on a par with the government delegation. About three days before the end of the negotiations, when the outcome was still in doubt, the RENAMO delegates appeared in new dark suits paid for by the Italians. At that point the American observer noted the new suits and observed:

> We knew RENAMO had really made a commitment to getting through to that signing ceremony. But this is something that, without the assistance that the Italian Government put into it, it wouldn't have happened; something the American Government would find pretty difficult to do.[48]

Other donor contributions were also important to the successful outcome in Mozambique. Britain, France, and Portugal provided military training and some equipment to the new army to make it a force worthy of the name. Over 20 countries contributed to the two trust funds. One assisted RENAMO to convert itself to a political party, while the other allowed the minor parties to compete in the elections with at least a minimum level of resources. Ajello was given the discretion to dole out some of the funds to RENAMO without having to require receipts for every dollar spent. While few democratic governments could tolerate such loose bookkeeping in their own accounts, this flexibility was important in allowing RENAMO to participate in the political process.

In making an overall comparison of the factors that were beyond the control of the UN, it is immediately clear that Angola suffered from multiple problems that Mozambique did not have. Neither side in Angola was willing to accept losing in a winner-take-all situation. The country had ample resources to fight over which could fuel indefinitely the war. While most outside actors eventually became strong supporters of peace in Angola, the impact of having Zaire as a neighbor was decidedly and continually negative. The difficulty posed by the PKO's weak mandate and few resources was greatly compounded by the unwillingness of the parties to let the UN do the job or to admit they were incapable of doing it themselves.

In Mozambique, on the other hand, some key conditions (as well as the outcome) were quite different from those in Angola. Although the country also had a winner-take-all system, at least one side in Mozambique could accept losing, albeit grudgingly, without returning to war. This attitude was reinforced by the fact that the country lacked the internal resources to sustain renewed fighting. It was also supported by neighboring countries that had all become democratic and were therefore very interested in seeing the peace maintained. That peace was also nurtured by a PKO that, despite its failings, had ample resources, a strong mandate, and strong leadership. While that PKO did not succeed in all its tasks, it did accomplish the key functions of demobilization, reintegration, and verification of the elections.

Over the long term, the question remains whether Angola can achieve peace and whether stability will be permanent in Mozambique. How the UN concludes a PKO and what it leaves behind have an important impact on a country's future prospects for peace. After the chapter seven considers how humanitarian assistance affects the conduct of a PKO, chapter eight will discuss the postdeployment phase of peacekeeping and whether the money spent on the effort by the international community is likely to be a good investment in the long run.

Chapter Seven

Humanitarian Aid and Peacekeeping Failure

Given the nature and victims of today's intrastate conflicts, providing humanitarian relief is often an integral component of many peacekeeping operations. In a large, multidimensional PKO, it is usually one of the key elements. In a protective engagement mission, permitting the aid workers to provide assistance is the primary objective. Humanitarian assistance is usually considered to be unquestionably beneficial, because it is designed to alleviate the suffering of innocent noncombatants. Some consider humanitarian action to be, and perceived by all to be, impartial, neutral, and independent from political, religious, or other extraneous bias.[1]

However, humanitarian assistance has inescapable political and military consequences. It will not be seen as neutral and impartial by the combatants in a civil war, because it is not. Providing aid to some, or even to all, will always alter the balance of power because the ability of some of the warring factions to pursue a military resolution of the conflict is strengthened. In Somalia, Liberia, and Rwanda, the contribution of humanitarian action was far from universally positive. In Mozambique, the failure to distribute food aid in some areas actually hastened the end of the conflict and contributed to the subsequent success of the peacekeepers. Given the complexity, difficulty, and track record of multidimensional PKOs, humanitarian assistance is often the only response the international community is willing to apply in some situations. Alone it cannot be a substitute for political and military action however. Because of this, the interaction of aid and peacekeeping should be carefully considered, as the former can contribute to the failure of the latter.

Even the most ardent proponents of humanitarian aid admit that neutrality is difficult to achieve. In writing about Liberia, Scott points out:

Experience has not demonstrated a clear formula for isolating humanitarian action from political engagements. At the same time, however, the experience has shown that a realistic mandate carried out by skilled professionals can yield positive humanitarian benefits.[2]

That the provision of humanitarian aid yields humanitarian benefits is hardly a surprising conclusion. But neither is it a conclusive argument. Liberia does offer some useful lessons, even though it is not the most typical case study. It is not typical because while the UN and NGOs organized the humanitarian relief efforts, the bulk of the peacekeeping forces was provided by the nations of the Economic Community of West African States (ECOWAS) and not the UN. This regional peacekeeping force was both corrupt and at times militarily incompetent. It was not neutral and was never perceived as such by the warring parties.[3] Its prowess at looting was such that Liberians began to say, only half in jest, that ECOMOG stood for "Every Car Or Movable Object Gone" instead of the Economic Community of West African States Monitoring Group.[4] Because the UN and the NGOs distributing aid were rightly or wrongly identified with ECOMOG, they were not considered impartial. In addition, in a tribal conflict such as Liberia's, any aid not given to one's own ethnic group was seen as going to strengthen the enemies of one's group.

While in Liberia humanitarian aid failed to be neutral, this fact has broader applicability to circumstances other than Liberia's. Neutrality will prove elusive under any conditions. Even if those administering and distributing the aid are totally impartial, they will not be seen to be so by the warring parties. In reality, the warring parties are simply recognizing what some proponents of humanitarian assistance refuse to acknowledge. The total separation of humanitarian aid from political factors is simply not possible, because the provision of aid in a civil war situation has inescapable military and political implications.

Humanitarian assistance has military implications because soldiers, be they government or rebel, will always eat before the civilians. No armed group is going to go hungry while unarmed relief workers distribute food aid to noncombatants in areas under its control. The theft and sale of food also provides funds to sustain armies by providing the cash to buy arms, ammunition, and other essentials of war or simply to enrich the combatants.

In Somalia, relief officials quickly learned that they had to switch from providing high value, marketable foodstuffs to items that had a lower value in relation to their bulk. In addition, an attempt was made to flood the country with food. Both tactics were designed to make the value of the food so low that it would not be worth the time of the warring factions to steal it.[5]

Food is not the only military and economic resource that the international humanitarian groups, whether UN or NGOs, unwillingly or unwittingly provide the combatants. Aid workers are also a ready source of transportation and communications assets that are always there for the taking. The warring parties, no matter how impartial the Red Cross or other humanitarian organizations try to be, will accuse aid groups of favoring their enemies. Thus there will always be a ready excuse for the combatants to seize the relief organizations' vehicles, radios, and satellite telephones. Such items are always in short supply among armies and rebel groups in civil wars, and the temptation to appropriate them from the well-supplied aid workers is rarely resisted for long.[6] In April 1996, when fighting broke out anew in Liberia, gunmen from several factions ransacked the offices of relief organizations. In addition to stealing office equipment and furniture, they seized almost 500 vehicles valued at $8 million.[7]

NGOs carrying out humanitarian assistance operations can also be forced by the various warring factions to pay for protection. Like the Mafia, these factions provide protection or, if an organization refuses to pay, a source of trouble. What they charge will depend on how much they think the market will bear, even though the aid organizations are there to assist their countrymen.

Humanitarian aid is also a source of political power for both sides in a civil war because it gives to both the government and the guerrilla group opposing it the appearance of being able to do things for the civilian populations under their control that neither may have the capacity or interest to do. Most if not all of the funding and organization will come from the international community, yet there will be officials of the armed groups with whom access must be negotiated and who will want to "supervise" aid distributions. Someone with the title of Minister will appear and his or her permission will be needed.

In addition, the local population will be very unlikely to perceive that aid is being given by the international community in the hopes of being politically neutral. They will understand only that they have to be thankful for such help to whoever controls the territory they are in. Even if they are perceptive enough to recognize the aid does not come from the warring faction in control of their area, such assistance will tie the noncombatants to this territory and to whoever controls it. This population base provides a source of recruits and other advantages to whoever is in charge.

As one Reuters story about the Great Lakes conflict in Central Africa put it: "Refugees are the pawns and at times the prize."[8]

The peace process designed to put an end to an intrastate conflict is often designed to culminate in elections to choose a government with sufficient legitimacy to govern. Military leaders turned presidential candidates under such circumstances will often attempt to use humanitarian aid to buy votes. To the extent that there is a government in place, it will have the advantage in this regard, since it will generally have better established relationships with the aid agencies and be in a better position to control the flow of assistance.

Aid's Negative Effects—The Case of Zaire

There is no better example of some of the perverse effects of humanitarian aid, and the international community's inability to avoid them, than the Rwandan conflict. Rieff described the situation regarding Rwandan refugees in Zaire in late 1996 as follows:

> Until quite recently, it was generally assumed by both aid workers and the public at large that humanitarian aid, deployed in situations where the need was great and the suffering genuine, would always be a force for good. It is becoming increasingly clear that humanitarian aid alone is not just powerless to resolve crises. It can, in fact, make them worse. The movement of 2 million Hutus out of Rwanda was as much an organized effort on the part of the old genocidal regime to preserve its power base as it was the result of mass panic or intimidation. For aid workers, the goal was simply to feed as many people as possible, to organize sanitation and to get the public health crisis under control. They made a crucial mistake by carrying these tasks out with the help of the community structures carried over intact from the old regime. The UNHCR and the aid workers were, in effect, trapped by their wish to help people in need and their belief that continuing this mission superseded any other consideration. The camps were full of armed soldiers, and no foreign power was willing to send troops into eastern Zaire to disarm them.[9]

The Rwandan government saw the military threat posed by the camps in Zaire. It was also angered by humanitarian assistance from the international community to the refugees unaccompanied by any action to solve the political problem posed by them. As a result, the Rwandans armed and aided the Banyamulenge, a group of ethnic Tutsis of Rwandan origin, who attacked the camps and drove the Zairian army from the area. As hundreds of thousands of Hutu refugees fled in fear, television screens in the first world filled with the scenes of this latest humanitarian crisis. Pressure quickly rose for an international response to avert disaster, because nearly a million people were at risk.

The form of that response became as fluid as the situation on the ground. On November 13, 1996, after intense pressure from Canada, France, and the UN Secretary General, the White House announced that U.S. troops would participate in an international relief effort. The White House press secretary noted that the force was approved by the Security Council and would have robust rules of engagement, as provided for under Chapter VII of the UN Charter. In other words, the peacekeepers could use all necessary force to carry out their mission. At the same time, he also stressed it would not be a UN blue-helmet mission and would not be equipped or prepared to fight its way into a hostile environment.[10]

How such an armed force could avoid hostilities and provide the aid required in the midst of a multifaceted tribal conflict where hundreds of thousands had already died was never put to the test. The refugees, with the incentive provided by the Rwandan government, solved the problem themselves. As one UN official stated: "Refugees move or don't move for one reason and one reason only: fear."[11] To the consternation of aid officials, the refugees' fear of becoming casualties in the fighting apparently outweighed the fear of what would happen when they returned home. As a result, the bulk of them began to make their way back into Rwanda.

Nonetheless, there were still many people in danger of starvation, and pressure continued to mount an operation to help those still left in Zaire. Defense Secretary Perry, on November 27, 1996, ruled out any participation by U.S. combat forces but said Washington was ready to take part in a Canadian proposal to parachute food in. How such an airlift could meet the logistical challenge of feeding a group that was estimated at anywhere from 200,000 to over 500,000 and was now scattered over an undefined area was never put to the test.[12]

In the end, instead of a force of 15,000 or a massive operation mounted to parachute huge quantities of food into the country, only 300 Canadians and liaison officers from 6 other countries arrived on the scene to help ongoing aid efforts. Even they left by the end of December, as the success of the Rwandan government in forcing the refugees to return made extraordinary international relief efforts both unnecessary and futile.

The Tanzanian government, not wanting to replace Zaire as the long-term haven for the Hutus who were responsible for genocide, apparently decided to follow the example of the Rwandan government. Tanzania ordered the 540,000 Rwandan refugees in Tanzania to return home by December 31 and used its army to help ensure the refugees left. The vast majority of these refugees complied and crossed the border, heading home well before the deadline.[13]

Even after the international community had spent a million dollars a day for two years to feed the Rwandans in Zaire, it could come up with no better strategy, in the face of the crisis, than to propose sending more food aid escorted by armed soldiers who could do no more than protect themselves if attacked. Not surprisingly, the Rwandan government did not wait for this plan to be attempted and decided to bring about its own solution to the problem.

Ironically, many of the Hutu extremists slipped back into Rwanda after the Rwandan government had forced them out of their camps in Zaire. These extremists, who had been protected and fed by international aid workers, are believed to have started targeting them once back in Rwanda. Between January 18 and February 7, 1997, six expatriate aid workers were brutally murdered, causing senior UN and other international aid officials to wonder whether Rwanda had suddenly become too dangerous to work in.[14]

The international community made repeated attempts at a diplomatic solution to the Great Lakes problem. In early 1996, Aldo Ajello, who had been so successful as the UN Special Representative in Mozambique, became the European Commission's envoy to the region. A plan, based in part on the proposals of Ajello, was put forward to solve the dilemma. Had it been successfully implemented, it would have resulted in the closing of only some of the camps in Zaire. Even this limited objective would have taken some time, and it depended on Zaire to provide the troops to enforce it. No other country wanted to commit troops to the task, even though Zairian officials were widely assumed to have been selling arms to the Hutus in the camps.[15]

The situation of the Rwandan refugees in Zaire was therefore one in which diplomacy failed to find a political solution, and no government except Rwanda's was willing to invest the troops to find a military solution, even though anything less would have failed. The international community's response was limited to humanitarian action, despite the fact that it continued to provide a base of support for those responsible for the Rwandan genocide and planning to repeat it. As one aid worker put it: "Humanitarian assistance was a fig leaf to cover the international community's failure to act."[16]

Peace Enforcement—No Easy Answers

Because of the continuing unrest in the Great Lakes region, for the first time in UN history, representatives of several aid organizations briefed Security Council members and urged them to act to provide protection for aid workers and refugees in the area. One of the NGO officials, noting the CNN effect, stated: "There is a need for coherence. The efforts cannot stop and start. We have the feeling that when the camps are on TV screens, we get attention; when they come off we lose political backing."[17]

Even with political backing, the question remains: what could peacekeeping troops do if they were to be inserted into such a situation? Would they be limited to a protective engagement operation designed only to make sure aid was delivered? Under such conditions the best that could have been hoped for was maintenance of the status quo indefinitely. Unless some country was willing to send in troops to do much more than protect refugees and aid workers, there would be no readily apparent source for the political solution necessary to end the crisis.

Solarz and O'Hanlon suggest that, following outside military intervention, long-term peace building should have been attempted:

> The outside forces might have sought ultimately to pass along authority to a new coalition government of moderates, probably including a number of members of the Rwandan Patriotic Front as well as other individuals. Even if doing so required years of military presence, or fell short of stopping all ethnic tension and violence, that would have been preferable to the hundreds of thousands of deaths that were the consequence of international indifference. Even if the presence of the UN peacekeepers was required for a prolonged period of time, the experiences of the United Nations in Cyprus and Kashmir and of the United States in Korea and Europe suggest that it is possible to sustain support for such deployments if the consequences of withdrawal would be severe.[18]

It wasn't international indifference that led to international inaction as the tragedy in Rwanda unfolded. It was the complexity of the situation. The classical peacekeeping efforts in Cyprus and Kashmir have almost nothing to do with what would have been required in Rwanda. To suggest that the RPF and its backers would accept a minor role in a coalition government is to ignore the depth of the animosity between the ethnic factions. To assume that public and congressional support for a large military presence in Rwanda would be sustainable indefinitely is to assume the peacekeepers would suffer no casualties. For that to happen, the Hutu extremists responsible for genocide would have to be willing to march quietly off to their war-crimes trials without putting up resistance. Solarz and O'Hanlon acknowledge almost as an afterthought, "Admittedly, it would be difficult to ensure through outside military intervention that large-scale ethnic killings would never recur in Rwanda."[19]

The problem is that the situation in Rwanda offered no easy solutions, not even long-term ones. Short of what was required in Bosnia, the international community has yet to find a formula that is acceptable for sending troops into a civil war in which they have to kill some people to save others.

The Contrast Between Liberia and Mozambique

Rwanda is not unique in presenting a humanitarian disaster in which the options the international community are willing to consider are few and unpalatable. While humanitarian aid did not play a role in the war in Angola because the combatants had the resources to feed themselves if necessary, it was a different story in Liberia. Scott describes Liberia as a situation in which "the international community, principally the United States and the European Union, chose to respond to the war and attendant human suffering through humanitarian aid rather than diplomacy."[20] Such a comment completely ignores the fact that with a great deal of diplomatic assistance from the international community, the warring parties in Liberia negotiated 14 peace agreements. The first 13 failed, however, mainly because of a lack of good faith among the warring factions. Although the fourteenth resulted in the election of a president, whether this will yield a long-term solution to Liberia's problems remains to be seen.[21] A large number of those Liberians who voted for Charles Taylor did so knowing that if he lost he would label the elections fraudulent and return to war.

In Liberia, humanitarian aid was provided impartially, allowing the various rebel groups to sustain themselves. During this time Nigeria was unwilling to admit defeat even though ECOMOG was incapable of either impartial peacekeeping or a military solution. The absence of democracy in Nigeria allowed its government to absorb hundreds of casualties among the peacekeepers without ever having to explain why it was in the national interest to do so.

After seven years of war, the Liberian people elected Charles Taylor, the leader of the strongest armed faction. Liberia has never had a popularly elected government before. Prior to Doe the presidency was the exclusive preserve of those 5 percent of Liberians who were the descendants of freed American slaves. Doe took power in 1980 after he and 16 other noncommissioned officers jumped the wall of the presidential mansion and murdered President Tolbert in his pajamas. Doe won the elections held in 1985, but they were widely believed to have been rigged. While Taylor may be Liberia's first democratically chosen president, his character and background give little hope that his administration will be an improvement over the past.[22]

While humanitarian aid sustained Taylor on his way to the presidency, it had a different effect in Mozambique, where humanitarian aid was deliberately not provided on an impartial basis. While this lack of impartiality diminished with the arrival of the peacekeepers, the policy contributed to their ultimate success. Such a policy resulted from a consensus among nearly all of the donors and aid organizations that helping RENAMO would be wrong given its record of human rights abuses.[23] The policy was reinforced by the government, which, unlike the anarchy in Liberia, continued to function. Barnes explains and justifies the lack of impartiality as follows:

> While the concern for impartiality is important, it is difficult to encounter a case where the humanitarian relief assistance provided within a conflict situation was not used for political and often military ends by at least one party to the conflict. At the same time, impartiality can imply that the parties in conflict are equally legitimate or just, negating the historical and political context or important human rights considerations.[24]

Barnes cites a small booklet published in 1988 by Christian Aid (UK), which recommends:

> No support or recognition should be given to RENAMO. It is only a military organization. It has no political programme which might allow it to be an alternative to FRELIMO nor has it a civilian arm. Its object is destruction. Its method is massacre, mutilation and other atrocities against the civil population.[25]

Most organizations seem to have agreed with this advice. As Barnes notes:

> Almost all humanitarian assistance to civilian populations during the conflict period was destined for government controlled areas. Only one organization, the International Committee of the Red Cross (ICRC), was

providing humanitarian assistance to civilians in RENAMO-controlled areas. It was only towards the end of the negotiation process in mid-1992, that UN agencies began to consider assistance to RENAMO areas.[26]

As a result, when drought struck in southern Africa, RENAMO began losing its population, including its soldiers, according to one source cited by Barnes.[27] Some observers believe the drought was the major incentive for peace, as without the humanitarian aid that was available in the government areas, RENAMO simply could not sustain itself.

Had that aid been provided impartially prior to the conclusion of the peace accord, it could have sustained RENAMO and prolonged the conflict. UN operations in Liberia were considered a success because humanitarian assistance was delivered in sufficient quantities in Monrovia (where ECOMOG was in charge) although less adequately up-country, where a variety of rebel groups held sway.[28] Had aid in Liberia been distributed less impartially, the 13 peace agreements that failed might have had a better chance of success and the war would have been shortened.

The potential for humanitarian relief having a negative effect seems more likely in those situations of anarchy in which the opposing sides are war lords vying for power, such as in Liberia and Somalia, or where there is only a very weak and/or corrupt government, such as in Zaire. Perhaps this is the case because if there is a relatively strong government, the international community feels compelled to pay some respect to its wishes and can use it to create the conditions in which aid can be provided. The first thing any government that is being threatened in a civil war would do is attempt to limit the amount of humanitarian assistance to those areas under the control of the rebels trying to overthrow it.

Avoiding Unintended Consequences

In a multidimensional PKO, humanitarian aid can threaten the chances for a successful outcome by having unintended political and military effects. When the objective of the peacekeeping mission is solely to provide that aid, the peacekeepers are given the task of doing nothing to help correct the political and military conditions that brought about the humanitarian disaster that made the aid necessary. In any event, it should be recognized that despite the best of humanitarian intentions, aid always has a political and military impact. It will inevitably have profound effects on the chances of success for peacekeeping, whether the operation is multifunctional or limited to protective engagement. While designed to save lives, humanitarian aid can, if it fuels the conflict and prolongs the war, ultimately cost more lives than it saves. It would be better to admit that humanitarian assistance without political effects is impossible so that the impacts of these effects can be more carefully considered.

As Prendergast observed in his book on humanitarian aid and conflict in Africa:

> Humanitarian aid will continue to be utilized as an instrument of war and will continue to fuel conflict. It is incumbent upon those providing the aid to minimize this phenomenon and to consciously and strategically enhance aid's role in the peace-building process.[29]

How then can such aid efforts be organized to do no harm? Natsios describes part of the problem:

> NGOs, some of which have developed philosophical approaches to relief and development, guard their autonomy with such energy that they sometimes seem to be suggesting that autonomy is a form of strategy. It is not. In fact, it is one reason why international responses to emergencies have been so chaotic.[30]

His solution is a unified strategy:

> If we are to change the behavior of the participants in a conflict in order to reduce the level of violence and return their society to normalcy and marginal-level self-sufficiency, we must use every lever of influence available to policy makers to encourage more responsible behavior. Absent a coherent strategy, the contestants will manipulate the outside stakeholders working in the crisis, playing one off against another, to achieve their political and military objectives.[31]

Such a strategy is necessary to avoid unintended consequences, which Natsios points out are frequently pernicious, with bad "political, economic, military and social outcomes."[32] A unified strategy must be designed and implemented in a coherent manner, but who can undertake this responsibility? Natsios believes that while the UN has some claim to carry out this function, it is "probably unsuited to this role as it lacks the diplomatic influence, military power, organizational discipline, and financial resources needed to implement what it designs."[33] He also sees the NGOs as having a major part to play, but as being incapable of formulating the policy necessary. For him, there is only one viable answer to this question—the Great Powers. In his view, "Only they have the political, military and financial clout to design and implement strategy."[34] While this may be true, it may not be realistic. The great powers seem to be reluctant to commit themselves in the Contraction Period unless their interests are directly involved.

Others see the lead role in humanitarian assistance efforts as best played by the UN. One NGO, Save the Children, maintained in a position paper that "the world's humanitarian needs can best be met by the UN, with appropriate reforms, but . . . the need for reform is urgent."[35] As the last chapter will discuss, reform of the UN means different things to different people and may be difficult, if not impossible, to accomplish.

Even if the UN was reformed, the task of coordinating humanitarian assistance sufficiently to reduce its political impact would not be easy. In fact, it may be well beyond the ability of the UN to accomplish. As Durch points out:

> Part of the inherent complexity of humanitarian intervention stems from the presence of multiple national, international, or nongovernmental relief groups whose activities on the scene may predate the UN's intervention and whose protection may have been the proximate cause of that intervention. These organizations, even those nominally part of the UN system, have their own policy priorities, field objectives, and sources of funding. The peace force must interact with these groups to coordinate activities and share information. Moreover, they may need direct assistance with transportation and communications, in addition to intelligence briefings and medical support. But while they may need the military for security of supply depots and relief convoys, aid providers are often reluctant to cooperate, out of concern that such cooperation will damage their image of neutrality and thus their effectiveness, and make them even more prominent targets of local factions. They may also have preexisting security arrangements with local "protectors" who may prove reluctant to give up their (extorted) incomes.[36]

Chapter Eight

Getting Out and Afterwards

Given the variety of conditions and challenges that confront peacekeepers, there is no standard definition of success. Diehl notes that one way to define success is the fulfillment of the PKO's mandate. He points out, however, that mandates are vague and focusing on them exclusively ignores the common purposes of PKOs and limits comparisons between them. He believes better indicators of success are whether the PKO limited or prevented hostilities and succeeded at conflict resolution.[1]

A multidimensional peacekeeping mission has multiple goals designed to deal with the different effects of a "teacup" war, such as humanitarian needs and land mines. In attempting to ensure that the fighting has ended and the conflict that started it is resolved peacefully and permanently, the PKO is often charged with encouraging a political process that is supposed to result in leaders accepted by all.

Elections are normally the route chosen because they provide a claim to legitimacy and the mandate the new leaders will need to govern. To do this, the multidimensional PKO must assist the parties to get to and through the elections. The installation of the new government is considered the culmination of the political process, and the UN declares the PKO a success if the peacekeepers can depart without the country returning to war. But can a PKO be considered a success if it simply avoids obvious failure for as long as the peacekeepers are on the ground? If, after they depart, the peace proves unsustainable, the international community will have little to show for its investment. At a cost that can run into the billions of dollars, PKOs should be expected to achieve more than a temporary respite from the conflict. The international community should therefore have an interest in ensuring that all that has been accomplished does not begin to unravel as soon as the peacekeepers have left.

A distinction can be drawn between today's multidimensional PKOs designed to end a civil war and the classical peacekeeping operations more common in the past. In the latter, permanent peace is usually achieved through a division of the territory in dispute between the two contending states. Such a division, and adequate safeguards to ensure it is permanent, are often difficult to achieve. Unlike multidimensional PKOs, however, the pressure to get out in these cases does not outweigh the concern for what subsequently happens. To understand why this is so, it is worth considering how PKOs end, since that will affect what comes afterwards.

There are essentially three possible outcomes for a peacekeeping operation—outright failure, indefinite extension, and a declaration of success. Under the first outcome, the peacekeepers leave voluntarily, or are forced out, after they fail to achieve all of their objectives, as happened in Somalia and Rwanda. The second outcome could be termed a nonexit strategy, as it describes a situation in which a PKO is simply not terminated. A variation of this second outcome is one in which the PKO continues but with a new name, mandate, and level of resources. The third outcome occurs when the UN declares victory and departs after having shepherded the peace process through certain specific events, such as elections and the installation of a new government.

The first outcome—outright failure—obviously damages the image of the UN and support for peacekeeping. In addition, the international community does not like to admit defeat. In Angola, when the peace fell apart in late 1988 the government decided to blame the peacekeepers and seek a military solution to the problem. It therefore refused to consider an extension of MONUA, and the UN and the Security Council had little alternative but to recognize the failure of the peacekeepers' efforts and withdraw them.

The second outcome—staying on indefinitely—does not always help the UN's reputation, but it can do less damage than renewed hostilities. If, under the third outcome, the UN departs and war breaks out again, few will fail to recall the cost of a PKO that was declared a success at its conclusion but proved impossible to sustain over the long term.

The first outcome, in which the UN falls short of its goals and leaves or is forced out of a country, is rare. The parties don't often insist that the UN leave, and as long as they don't, the UN will be reluctant to admit defeat. When faced with a situation in which the peacekeepers cannot succeed, the international community will often opt for the second outcome over the first. If it is a classical PKO, it will simply be extended. If it is a multidimensional PKO with multiple tasks, its name may be changed and it may given a more achievable mandate. In either case, the goal may be to maintain a presence that will allow the UN to have some positive effect while waiting for conditions to improve.

One of the rare instances in which the UN did not opt for the second outcome when faced with the first became one of its earliest peacekeeping "failures." In the Sinai in 1967, after a decade of successful peacekeeping, UNEF I was brought to an end at the request of one of the parties. Having received false Soviet intelligence reports that Israel was planning to attack Syria, the Egyptians asked for the removal of the peacekeepers, and Secretary General U Thant ordered them to withdraw.[2]

U Thant was subsequently criticized from various quarters for having done so. Some suggested that he should have consulted the General Assembly before acting. Both of the parties to the conflict attempted to blame the UN for the renewed conflict that followed the peacekeepers' departure. The Israelis argued that the peacekeepers should have been more steadfast. Egyptian officials maintained that their request was for a limited and temporary withdrawal of the peacekeepers despite considerable evidence to the contrary. Regardless of where the blame should have been placed, the UN's reputation as a peacekeeper was seriously tarnished by the whole affair.[3]

Whether it was this early experience in Sinai or the consistent triumph of hope over experience, when the UN cannot declare victory and depart, it often prefers the second outcome to the first. By continuing the PKO, perhaps under a new name with a modified mandate, the UN can avoid admitting failure. But in using this tactic instead of putting the blame on the parties and pulling out, the UN and its continued presence can prolong the conflict. As one writer described the situation in Somalia:

> The UN's peacemaking machine was cursed with a built-in flaw: it desperately needed to succeed. When the only way to bring peace to Somalia might have been to walk away, the bureaucracy was compelled to stay and find a peace for which it could take credit. As the UN stayed in Somalia it continued to supply the raw material of the conflict—loot.[4]

Somalia actually contained elements of all three outcomes. The initial PKO, UNITAF, was originally given the mandate of guaranteeing a safe environment for the distribution of food. UNOSOM II was subsequently created and given the mission of using peace enforcement to lessen the humanitarian catastrophe that the civil war continued to create. When this mandate became a disaster for the peacekeepers instead, the UN forces were restricted to keeping the roads open to ensure that food aid could be delivered to the interior. When peace still proved elusive, the Security Council finally called for the withdrawal of all of the peacekeepers by the end of March 1995.[5] Thus, while the UN's initial response was to modify the mandate and carry on, it was eventually forced to give up and withdraw. When continuation (the second outcome) proved unsustainable and something that could be called victory (the third outcome) proved unattainable, failure (the first outcome) became inevitable.

The tragic situation in Rwanda also produced variations of all three outcomes. Initially, the UN became involved when it sent a small group of military observers in August 1993 to monitor a portion of the border between Uganda and Rwanda. The 81 observers who comprised the mission (UNOMUR) were supposed to verify that no military assistance was crossing into the border area controlled by the Rwandan rebels, the RPF. Another mission, UNAMIR, was established in October to help the Rwandan parties to implement the Arusha peace accords. Demining, disarmament, demobilization, and the formation of a new army and police were all supposed to be accomplished with the aid of the peacekeepers prior to elections and the installation of a new government by the end of 1995.

After the April 6, 1994 plane crash that killed the presidents of Rwanda and Burundi, full-scale civil war broke out. As the RPF expanded the area under its control, the Secretary General, in a June 16, 1994 progress report to the Security Council, noted that it made little sense to monitor one of Rwanda's borders and not the others. He nonetheless asserted that UNOMUR was "a factor of stability in the area and had been particularly critical in recent months as UNAMIR had sought to defuse tensions resulting from the resumption of hostilities."[6]

On July 18, the RPF, now in control of most of the country, declared a unilateral cease-fire, effectively ending the civil war. The Secretary General informed the Security Council on September 19, 1994, that UNOMUR would be officially closed two days later. He also stated:

> While the tragic turn of events in Rwanda prevented UNOMUR from fully implementing its mandate, the Observer Mission had played a useful role as a confidence-building mechanism in the months following the conclusion of the Arusha peace agreement and during UNAMIR's initial efforts to defuse tensions between the Rwandese parties and to facilitate the implementation of that agreement.[7]

However, declaring victory, even a partial one, and departing was not an option for UNAMIR. After the civil war eliminated the opportunity for UNAMIR to accomplish any of its original goals, it shrank from 2,165 peacekeepers to 444 by May 1994. As the humanitarian situation worsened, the Secretary General proposed that UNAMIR II be initiated, with 5,500 troops. Their task would be to provide safe conditions for displaced persons and to help with the provision of assistance by humanitarian organizations. UNAMIR II did not reach its authorized strength until November, and was able to do little to stop the bloodletting. As the UN's assessment of the operation acknowledged:

> The speed and ferocity of these events taxed to the utmost the attempts of the international community to respond and virtually invalidated the mandate of UNAMIR. Over the succeeding months, the Security Council revised UNAMIR's mandate in an effort to enable the force to help stabilize the situation, promote national reconciliation and adjust to a rapidly changing situation.[8]

In late 1995, the new Rwandan government refused to agree to another extension of UNAMIR II's mission, saying that "it did not respond to the country's priorities,"[9] and the PKO was officially brought to an end in March 1996. The government was angered by the level of international aid for Rwandan refugees in Zaire, which it saw as providing a base of support to its former enemies. Thus while the UN tried to extend the mission and find something it could accomplish, in the end it was asked to go without having achieved very much. The best the UN could do was note that UNAMIR had disabled 1,420 mines, rebuilt 4 bridges, helped restore operations at the Kigali airport, reestablished the phone service, and provided medical aid and humanitarian assistance.[10]

Classical Peacekeeping and the Endless PKO

Classical peacekeeping does not entail the multidimensional challenges that the UN had to face in Somalia and Rwanda. However, the interstate conflicts that have resulted in classical peacekeeping operations do seem to challenge the UN's ability to bring these PKOs to a close. Of the 17 PKOs in operation in early 1997, 6 resulted from interstate conflicts, if one considers the 4 underway in the remnants of the former Yugoslavia to be the result of an intrastate conflict. These 6 are the oldest of the 17 PKOs, with an average of almost 30 years in existence.[11]

These PKOs are so long-lived because the traditional tasks of monitoring a peace between two countries can go on successfully for an indefinite period without a permanent resolution of the conflict. A geographical accommodation is reached that neither side accepts as permanent, but with which each can nonetheless live indefinitely. The UN, in its classical peacekeeping mode, can provide a buffer to help maintain the status quo. Paradoxically, it can at the same time contribute to making itself a permanent feature and a disincentive to finding a permanent peace. As one writer observed:

> By maintaining a status of peaceful coexistence between two or more hostile countries (or factions), and by eliminating the sense of urgency that crises impart, a peacekeeping force may subvert the search for a more permanent solution to the hostility.[12] ✳

Arriving at a permanent solution would require one side or the other to surrender part, or all, of its territorial claims and accept a compromise. Given that this could entail considerable domestic political risk, for many governments the status quo is often preferable to a permanent solution. The absence of war is an acceptable alternative to the absence of real peace, especially since the UN is paying the bill for maintaining the peacekeepers.

Despite occasional questions about its duration, for a PKO engaged in classical peacekeeping the absence of war is considered an accomplishment. It can help maintain a military stalemate that provides an acceptable status quo between two countries but often not the elements necessary for a permanent solution to the conflict. The lack of real peace is considered secondary to the avoidance of a new war, given the costs of renewed conflict.

This policy of "containment," although resulting in indefinite PKOs without permanent peace, seems to be the preferred option of the conventional PKOs in Cyprus and the Middle East. UNFICYP in Cyprus was begun in 1964, UNMOGIP in India and Pakistan in 1949, and UNTSO in Israel in 1948, and all continue to this day. These missions help maintain the status quo, and no one wants to risk seeing fighting break out again by withdrawing the peacekeepers. Since these PKOs involve only a few hundred military personnel, their costs are relatively low and they carry on year after year with the international community generally content with the outcome.

Declaring Victory Prematurely

The older, traditional PKOs engaged in classical peacekeeping are smaller and less expensive and involve far less complex tasks than the multidimensional PKO required to deal with today's "teacup" war. Because of its size and expense and the notable record of failure in places like Bosnia, Somalia, and Rwanda, a multidimensional PKO is under considerable pressure to arrive at a declaration of victory and proceed with withdrawal rather than indefinite extension. The multidimensional PKO designed to help bring to a permanent end a civil war is bigger, more expensive, and more complex, because it deals with the humanitarian nightmares caused by today's intrastate conflicts and because of its nation-building aspects. It must also help the parties to find a permanent solution to the conflict, and that requires a political as well as a military accommodation.

Nation-building and the establishment of even a minimum level of trust between two former warring parties takes time, however. It is not only the lack of enthusiasm in the international community for difficult and expensive multidimensional mandates that brings pressure for withdrawal. The parties themselves are often interested in seeing the UN depart quickly. Since the mandate of a multidimensional PKO involves a degree of interference in the internal affairs of the country, this type of PKO will often be tolerated by all the parties only for the shortest time possible.

The end point of these PKOs is therefore usually tied to the holding of elections, the installation of a new government, or some other specific event. Once that event happens, the peacekeepers pack up and leave. The problem is that the country is left with little changed except, on occasion, those in power. The weak institutional structures that failed to resolve the conflict over political power in time to prevent a civil war are probably still inadequate. Rarely will they have been strengthened sufficiently during the time the peacekeepers are on the ground, even if the PKO had a nation-building mandate. Nonetheless, after having invested a billion dollars or more, the UN is unwilling or unable to use its influence and leverage to push for a more permanent remedy to these institutional inadequacies.

It is this third outcome, therefore, that is of most interest for the purposes of this book. In the first outcome, in which one or more of the parties forces the UN out, there is little the international community can do, unless it is willing to issue a mandate under Chapter VII rules of engagement. In such a case, the peacekeepers can employ "all necessary means" to achieve the PKO's goals. As Somalia demonstrated, that is no guarantee of success. If the parties are more willing to take casualties than the international community is, the UN can still be forced out. Other than resisting the inclination to become involved in the first place, there may be little that the UN can do to avoid failure. The UN could analyze objectively the parties, the resources, and the external actors to see where it could use its

influence to improve the chances of an acceptable outcome before deciding to get involved with a PKO. Why this is difficult in practice will be
considered in the next chapter.

The second outcome has even fewer implications than the first for considering how peacekeeping fails. In the second outcome, the lack of an
endpoint is acceptable, even though success must be defined as the absence
of failure and the costs of the PKO must be borne indefinitely. It is the
third outcome that poses the most questions and uncertainties. At what
point should the UN leave, and what can its role be in a country following the departure of the peacekeepers are questions that will be critical to
the sustainability of the peace that the UN has helped create. What the UN
can do to help make the peace permanent and how long it should do it
are not decisions that should simply be left to the parties themselves. This
is basically what the UN does, however, as it sets national sovereignty
ahead of the preservation of the peace, just as it often puts it ahead of creating the peace during the predeployment and deployment phases. As the
former Secretary General noted in his "Supplement to Agenda for Peace":

> The timing and modalities of the departure of the peacekeeping operation
> and the transfer of its peace-building functions to others must therefore be
> carefully managed in the fullest possible consultation with the government
> concerned. The latter's wishes must be paramount; but the UN having in-
> vested much effort in helping to end the conflict, can legitimately express
> views and offer advice about actions the government could take to reduce
> the danger of losing what has been achieved.[13]

Even in the most ambitious of PKOs, however, the political structure
that emerges from the peace process will still be fragile at best. Nation-
building takes generations, especially in a country that has just undergone
a civil war. Nonetheless, because of the expense of the PKO and because
of the national sovereignty argument, the UN prefers to declare victory
and withdraw after the installation of the new government. Cambodia has
recently demonstrated the bankruptcy of this approach. There a multidimensional PKO was ended without the UN continuing its efforts to
strengthen the democratic and civil institutions necessary to ensure the
country's long-term stability.

UNTAC, the peacekeeping mission in Cambodia, was considered by
some to be the UN's "high point in multidimensional peacekeeping."[14]
UNTAC was designed to implement a peace agreement that "sought to
deal with a conflict comprehensively, in its military, social, and political di-

mensions."[15] It was not only the UN's most comprehensive multidimensional PKO, but at a cost of $2 billion, one of its most expensive. As Schear has pointed out, however, "Even at the time, many worried about the impermanence of UNTAC's numerous accomplishments, and subsequent events have served only to heighten that concern."[16] At UNTAC's conclusion, the UN considered it a major success story. Schear notes:

> By the end of UNTAC's mandate, the prospects for Cambodia's transition looked brighter than at any time since the signing of the Paris Accords. When [SRSG] Akashi bid a final farewell to Phnom Penh on September 26, 1993, the key questions for Cambodia were how durable its new governing coalition would be and what role the international community would play in assisting its post-transition recovery.[17]

The UN's "success" did not endure long. The elections that UNTAC oversaw resulted in a coalition government in which Prince Norodom Ranariddh and Hun Sen agreed to share power. Writing in November 1996, Shawcross described the fragility and inadequacy of this arrangement: "What is clear is that the new [Cambodian] government that emerged in 1993 from the UN's most ambitious peacekeeping effort has become mired in corruption, violence and deception."[18]

By June 1997, preparations for a new national election the next year were on hold, the coalition government had ceased to function, and the two faction leaders were instead making preparations for renewed armed conflict.[19] In one newspaper article, a Western diplomat summed up the situation by saying:

> What is happening now is a fundamental crisis. We thought we could build a new laboratory of multiparty democracy in Asia. But all our hopes have been destroyed. We were too ambitious and pretentious. Violence is something inside the Cambodians and those in power now have no long-term vision of how to bring stability and prosperity to their citizens.[20]

Another diplomat quoted in the article described the situation more succinctly: "It's basically two rival mafias competing for territory and assets. No one works for the government *per se;* they just work for one party or the other."[21]

This unstable situation did not hold together much longer. Brief but intense fighting in early July left Hun Sen firmly in control after ousting Ranariddh.[22] Ranariddh went into exile as Hun Sen's troops embarked on a "reign of terror," summarily executing political opponents.[23] One of those killed was Ho Sok, a government official who was threatened by Hun Sen after Ho Sok prepared arrest papers for a prominent businessman and ally of Hun Sen on drug charges. According to sources quoted in the *Washington Post*, "Hun Sen has surrounded himself with suspected drug traffickers who bankroll his projects, lavish gifts on him and other leaders and seem bent on turning Cambodia into an Asian narco-state."[24]

The billions of dollars invested in UNTAC therefore bought fewer than four years of peace and led to government by a murderous autocrat with links to drug trafficking. The money spent on UNTAC was not the only aid the international community poured into Cambodia in recent years. The country received 57 percent of its national budget from foreign donors, and 39 percent of that, or some $216 million a year, was in the form of direct cash subsidies to the government.[25] As some foreign donors suspended aid following Hun Sen's takeover, his spokesman defiantly asserted: "We will not die, and development will continue, though it might be slow."[26] But a government that gets over half of its budget from the international community cannot afford to ignore pressure from abroad. Not all of the donors suspended aid to Cambodia, however, and pressure is hard to bring to bear uniformly without donor consensus, even when a country's future is at stake. Whatever that future holds for Cambodia, no one will again claim UNTAC was a success.

After Sales Service

What the international community can do to ensure that peace lasts after the fighting has stopped has been called post-conflict peace-building (PCPB). This is a process that ought to be initiated well before the UN has declared victory under the third outcome and the peacekeepers begin to depart. They will have to turn the bulk of this task over to others who are going to have a longer-term presence and a development mission, but the peacekeepers can start to lay the groundwork if it is included in their mandate. In fact if measures to ensure PCPB are not negotiated into the peace accords, it will be far less likely to happen. The winner of the elections designed to end the conflict will rarely be magnanimous or far-sighted enough to strengthen the peace by ceding any degree of political power unless required to do so.

PCPB has not suffered from lack of attention in academic circles and in the UN itself.[27] The War-torn Societies Project of the UN Research Institute for Social Development (UNRISD), for instance, was designed to address this specific question. While these efforts have identified many of the problems of PCPB, solutions have been harder to come by. The problems identified defy easy remedy, in part because they have much to do with the way the UN and the international community operate.

A major difficulty is posed by the fact that the UN is not institutionally organized to deal with PCPB, even though it may be the only body with a mandate broad enough to address such situations. As del Castillo notes:

> Only the UN has the capacity to integrate the many political, humanitarian, military and socio-economic activities relating to peace and development. In practice, however, the potential of the UN to carry out an integrated approach has not yet been fully developed, either within the UN itself or with the agencies.[28]

Del Castillo suggests three steps be taken to ensure that PCPB is given the importance it deserves. First, peace negotiators should begin to think about and plan for the requirements and constraints of PCPB. Second, multidimensional PKOs with PCPB responsibilities should have a unit to deal solely with such matters. Third, PCPB responsibilities need to be clearly assigned in New York, since, given the UN Secretariat's structure, there is no self-evident place for such a task to be assigned.[29]

Each of these suggestions would be difficult to put into practice. Peace negotiators concern themselves with reaching a deal acceptable to the parties and rarely consider post-peace process problems. Multidimensional PKOs have had little in the way of PCPB responsibilities as the third outcome dictates speedy withdrawal without follow-on once the new government takes office and begins to assert its sovereignty.

The third suggestion of a designated place in the Secretariat that would have responsibility for PCPB has been implemented in theory though it remains to be seen how effective it will be in practice. At the same time he announced his major reform proposals in July 1997, Secretary General Annan designated the Department of Political Affairs, in its capacity as convener of the Executive Committee on Peace and Security, as the focal point within the UN for PCPB. The Executive Committee was given the responsibility for the design and implementation of PCPB initiatives including the definition of objectives, criteria and operational guidelines for PCPB by the organizations of the UN system.[30]

Since this step did not require General Assembly or Security Council approval, the Secretary General was able to implement it immediately.

However, there is more to reform than bureaucratic reorganization. A consistent and purposeful PCPB effort would require considerable commonality of purpose and political will on the part of the international community. In addition, there is the question of how the coordination among donors would be carried out on the ground. Another element of Annan's reform would bring the UN agencies in the field together under one roof in each country, but this is neither a new proposal nor a vehicle that ensures effective coordination.

Aggressive PCPB would also rapidly come into confrontation with the national sovereignty described as paramount by Secretary General Annan's predecessor. Outside academic study and traditional development aid, the UN appears unwilling and unable to pursue PCPB activities that involve much more than appeals to reason and conferences. There may be peace, but after years of war the former antagonists are not always willing to treat each other with mutual respect. Instead of resolving the differences between the parties, elections can exacerbate them since they establish winners and losers in a way that the military conflict was not able to accomplish.

The problem of keeping pressure on the parties to maintain the spirit as well as the letter of a peace agreement is not unique to the UN. The international community in general has similar problems. Getting a country shattered by war to accept and follow through a peace process provides a goal on which most can agree and work jointly to achieve. In the post-war, post-peace process period, as various countries revert to the pursuit of their own interests, that unity of purpose dissipates quickly.

There is a debate, for instance, within the NGO community as to which values should be encouraged in the peace-building phase. Some argue that economic liberalization is not a valid goal in economies that they maintain are prone to criminalization as a consequence of war and international involvement. This argument misses two points. First, the conflict may have arisen because of the concentration of political and economic power, and liberalization is one way to give the "losers" in the peace process a stake in the system and less incentive to return to war. Second, attributing the causes of corruption to war and international involvement will be popular among the corrupt since they can shift the responsibility for their actions to others. The best safeguards against such criminalization, however, are economic and political liberalization and a free press. Whatever the position one takes in such debates, that there can be disagreement on such issues implies little likelihood that the international community can act with unity of purpose. Without governments and NGOs working to together to ensure that peace is really built and that the underlying political problems are not simply papered over, it will often be only a question of time until the next round of fighting.

There are at least three fundamental policy areas in which UNRISD has identified a lack of clarity that contributes to this lack of unity. There is confusion as to the policy mix with which the international community should intervene in post-conflict situations. Because there are so many different agents of international assistance and cooperation (different departments and agencies of the UN, other multilateral bodies, bilateral actors, and the NGO community), there is no clear idea of where the responsibilities for PCPB lie on the institutional and operational level. Also there is no clear agreement on the nature of the relations between the international community and what remains of state and local authorities, local NGOs, and civil society. As a result, "the international response to conflict and reconstruction has increasingly veered to short-term and spectacular measures at the expense of assistance in the political and development fields."[31] Such confusion is a problem in Mozambique, and it will be in Angola if the destruction ever ends and the reconstruction begins.

Leaving Mozambique Completely

When the UN does declare victory and the peacekeepers leave, there is hardly a look back, let alone any sustained effort to sustain the peace. Mozambique, from which the last peacekeepers departed in December 1994, still both poses major PCPB challenges. The peace has held in Mozambique, but not because of attention from or efforts by the UN. After the Secretary General filed his final report on ONUMOZ on December 23, 1994, the Security Council held a final meeting on Mozambique on January 27, 1995. In that meeting the foreign minister of Mozambique repeated the words of his predecessor, who at the forty-ninth General Assembly said: "Where there is a government, even with weak institutions, peace-keeping missions should work in close cooperation . . . with the local authorities and respect and strengthen those institutions, rather than try to weaken or undermine them."[32]

An official who sees a PKO as a threat to the institutions of government is not likely to be interested in forceful and effective PCPB. The minister should not have worried. Since that final meeting, the Security Council has not discussed Mozambique, passed any resolutions on it, or received any reports concerning it. However, the institutions in the country remain weak and the peace fragile. Despite statements that he would appoint the most qualified people to government positions, President Chissano named only FRELIMO supporters to all of the posts including the governorships of the five central provinces in which RENAMO won a majority. Although FRELIMO has only a narrow majority, the legislature remains a rubber stamp. Individual parliamentarians have no offices, no staff, not even a secretary, telephone, or desk to call their own.[33] The judicial system is neither independent nor effective, and the media remain "largely owned by the Government and manipulated by a retrograde faction within the ruling party."[34]

The country's first local elections were repeatedly postponed but eventually held in 1998. Virtually all the opposition political parties refused to participate claiming the government was manipulating the electoral process. Fewer than 15 percent of the registered voters bothered to cast their ballots, and the FRELIMO candidates won all 33 mayoral seats at stake. The voting was also plagued by major logistical problems and was so poorly run that even the government-owned media harshly criticized the effort.[35]

Even if the process had been more credible, the Mozambican people would be entitled to be skeptical about their first exercise in democracy at the municipal level. The end result has been the creation of a large number of local officials who will have a salary but very few resources that are not distributed from and controlled by the central government. How Mozambicans will come to view a newly elected political class with a paycheck but no power will remain to be seen.

As the boycott of the local elections indicates, the quality of the dialogue between the government and the opposition does not seem to have improved in the years since the 1994 elections. As one news report put it: "Mozambique still has a long way to go to learn about democracy. Verbal attacks and mutual accusations about insignificant issues are still at the top of the politician's routine."[36] RENAMO's attempts to organize demonstrations have ended in violence, with both sides blaming each other. Police arrested 30 RENAMO supporters after violent demonstrations in Nampula in May 1997. In response, party leader Afonso Dhlakama instructed his colleagues to ignore a summons issued by the district court, saying it was harassment on behalf of FRELIMO.[37]

Some progress has been made. After Chissano made an official visit to Washington, the parliament accepted the opposition's proposals for a new electoral law. The measure was adopted by a unanimous vote and will govern the general elections that are scheduled to be held on December 3–4, 1999. The major candidates for president and the outcome may be the same, but at least it will be movement in the right direction if the process is seen as free and fair.

Whether all this is simply the rougher edges of a very young political process or a long interlude prior to a return to widespread violence remains to be seen. Mozambique does not have diamonds to fuel its conflict or outside actors interested in a return to war. Those factors will weigh more heavily in the country's future than any others.

The principle PCPB activity in Mozambique has been to make it one of the case studies of the War-torn Societies Project. The project's stated objectives are: first, to aid postwar Mozambican society in preventing violent conflicts in the future; second, to encourage national and foreign actors to provide the resources necessary for the development of the country; and third, to cultivate, through joint action, the necessity of maintaining peace and a democratic culture in a multiparty system.[38] The project attempts to accomplish these goals by encouraging dialogue between the parties and by looking for "entry points." These *pontos chave* are described as those problems whose resolution is essential for the process of reconciliation.[39]

The problem with this approach is that it takes time to promote such understanding, and it assumes the cooperation and collaboration of the domestic actors. The former combatants in a civil war are not likely to have developed trust and confidence in one another just because the UN was on the scene for a time. If the elections resulted in the winner taking all, as they did in Mozambique and would have in Angola, there is far less incentive to cooperate. As Cambodia has demonstrated, even where there is power-sharing, the result may not be good governance or a situation in which future conflicts are avoided. If the international community funds economic reconstruction but does little to encourage political reconciliation, the outcome will not always ensure continued peace.

Even when there is peace within a country, the lack of serious PCPB can have negative regional repercussions. As Berman noted:

> There are two problems, therefore, with the international community's approach to post-conflict processes: on the one hand, the international community, under pressure to react to increasingly violent internal conflict, has put a higher value on peace in the short-term than on development and stability in the long-term; and, on the other hand, those who do focus on long-term stability have put a higher value on the societal and economic elements of development than on the management of the primary tools of violence, i.e., weapons.[40]

When it comes to the most basic underpinnings of democracy and the peacekeepers are still on the ground, the UN is reluctant or powerless to insist that the parties respect in practice what they have endorsed in principle. In Angola, after the failure of UNAVEM II, the UN decided to set up its own radio station to combat the propaganda from both sides. The Security Council, in the resolution authorizing UNAVEM III, endorsed the Secretary General's view that there was a need for the PKO to have an effective information capability, including a UN radio station that would be established in consultation with the government of Angola.[41] The government refused to let the UN do so, however. Instead, UNAVEM III had to obtain time on the government's TV and radio station.

Although the Angolan constitution provides for freedom of expression and of the press, the government does not respect these rights in practice, according to the 1996 human rights report on the country by the Department of State:

> The Government runs and tightly controls the only daily newspaper, the only television station and the major radio station. It tightly restricts opposition leaders' access to these media. While two commercial radio stations and three private weekly and biweekly newspapers all practice self-censorship, several occasional newsletters are published that are openly critical of government officials and policy. UNITA runs a tightly controlled radio station whose broadcasts of often inflammatory material are heard throughout Angola.[42]

The practice of self-censorship by Angolan journalists is more than an exercise in economic survival. Criticism of the government could result in dismissal or worse. The murders of the editor of an independent newsletter and a state-television reporter in 1996 remain unsolved.

In Mozambique too, following the departure of ONUMOZ, little has changed with regard to the press. According to the U.S. Department of State during 1996, "The Government continued to restrict press freedom; the media remained largely owned by the Government and state enterprises and manipulated by factions within the ruling party."[43] This despite the fact that one of the conclusions of the Mozambican case study of the War-torn Societies Project was:

> A large part of the national information organs are perceived by political actors, by civil society and by donors as being politically tendentious, exacerbating national political tensions and consequently putting at risk national reconciliation. One of the causes of this situation is generally attributed to the fact there exist organs of information in the public sector, that it is alleged, are easily manipulated by the Government. On the other hand, the

so-called independent organs of information are accused of exercising their independence through opposition to the Government.[44]

As in Cambodia, in Mozambique well over half of the government's budget comes from the international community. There was good donor unity leading up to the elections in 1993, as everyone focused on that goal and UNDP provided strong leadership. Following the installation of the elected government, there was a general feeling at the first Consultative Group (CG) meeting of the donors that economic reform measures postponed by the war should now be taken, including a shift from military expenditures to greater support for health and education. (The Consultative Group meeting is an annual exercise in Paris at which donors indicate what level of support they are going to provide a government during the year. The World Bank chairs the meeting and totals the pledges to see if the country's estimated economic needs will be met.)

This push for significant policy reform was strongly resisted by the government and initially not supported by all the donors. Reform was put at the top of the agenda only because several weeks before the elections I wrote to the World Bank representative in Maputo. My letter pointed out that the new government that would emerge from the elections would not have time to come up with a strategy for reform by early December when the CG meeting was normally held. My letter also noted that a new government might not even be in office, particularly if a runoff election was required due to the absence of a majority in the first round. I stressed that since more time was needed to develop the new policies required, the meeting should be delayed until well into the new year since it made far more sense to postpone the meeting than to postpone the reforms necessary for a year. I added that the United States might not attend a meeting that came too early or that refused to deal with such important issues.

With the support of a few other key donors, the American point of view prevailed despite the government's reluctance to deal with reform on an urgent basis and its efforts to avoid any delay in holding the meeting. By the next Consultative Group meeting a year later, however, donor unity and willingness to force the pace of change was already dissipating. Development specialists from some capitals demonstrated they were uncomfortable pushing the government to reform further either economically or politically. The Canadian delegate insisted "It's time to put the Mozambicans in the driver's seat."[45]

While one could not argue the Mozambicans should not be in charge, it was unrealistic to assume the right thing would happen by itself. Emerging from a civil war with weak institutions, no checks and balances, and having no previous experience in practicing democracy, how could they be expected to make all the right decisions without assistance, and in some cases pressure, from the international community? Getting into the back seat and going to sleep, in other words, doesn't assure that the driver steers the vehicle to the right destination—that is, that development assistance will be wisely spent and the peace maintained.

As was noted earlier, a French anthropologist concluded that even if Rhodesia and South Africa had not organized and aided RENAMO, civil war would probably have occurred, given FRELIMO's governing style. It remains to be seen whether that style has changed enough to make a recurrence of war less likely. Getting unity among the international community to ensure that style has changed for the better does not seem likely based on the attitudes taken at the CG. Whether the success of ONU-MOZ will be sustained over time is therefore open to question.

Leaving Angola Reluctantly

While the UN has done little to ensure the peace in Mozambique is sustained, at least peace was achieved. In Angola, one can only speculate about what will happen when the war finally ends. The four successive PKOs in Angola went through variations of all three possible outcomes—continuing indefinitely, declaring victory and withdrawing, and failure—before the mandate lapsed on February 26, 1999, and the peacekeepers began to withdraw.

UNAVEM I was successful in fulfilling its limited mandate of helping oversee the withdrawal of Cuban forces because of the cooperation of the parties. UNAVEM II had neither adequate resources nor the authority to help the parties find peace, even if they had been sincere about wanting it. UNAVEM III, which had the mandate and the resources that UNAVEM II lacked, was scaled back and finally closed out despite the fact that the relative peace it achieved was built on the shakiest of foundations. Perhaps because of that, and because of the reduced scope of its mandate, its successor was not called UNAVEM IV. Instead MONUA, with 2,000 military, police, and civilian personnel, was asked to accomplish in a few months what 8,000 peacekeepers could not do in over two years during UNAVEM III.

On April 16, 1997, the Security Council passed Resolution 1106 approving the final extension of UNAVEM III's mandate. The resolution expressed satisfaction with the recent progress in the peace process and instructed the Secretary General to "proceed with the transition towards an observer mission." It also asked for his recommendations regarding the structure, specific goals, and cost implications of such a mission.[46] A week later, in hearings before the Subcommittee on Africa of the U.S. House of Representatives, Assistant Secretary of State for African Affairs George Moose asserted, "When one looks at what has been accomplished over the past two and a half years in establishing peace and a national unity government in Angola, the level of progress that has been achieved thus far has been extraordinary."[47]

While the progress may have been extraordinary in some areas, it was not uniform in all. Two particular areas in which the Lusaka Protocol was not being implemented in which the demobilization of UNITA's military forces and the extension of the government's administrative authority throughout the country.[48] The deteriorating situation in neighboring Zaire combined with this lack of progress to threaten all that had been accomplished and to demonstrate the weakness of the foundation on which the peace was based.

As the rebel forces in Zaire fought to overthrow President Mobutu Sese Seko, the media noted the presence of foreign forces on both sides of the conflict. Thousands of UNITA soldiers were supporting Mobutu, and troops sent by the Luanda government, backed up by armored vehicles and heavy artillery, aided the rebels.[49] After Mobutu fled Zaire on May 16, Laurent Kabila's forces took over, and Zaire became the Democratic Republic of Congo. The effect on Angola was not long in coming. For UNITA, Mobutu's overthrow represented the loss of its principal foreign ally. For the Angolan government, it represented an opportunity to wrest control of the diamond-rich, northeastern part of the country that was producing revenue for UNITA estimated at anywhere from $500 million to $660 million a year.[50]

By the end of the first week in June, the media was reporting that fighting in northern Angola had been under way for a fortnight and by mid-month they were describing a state of near-war and frantic efforts to save the peace process.[51] Despite what one publication called "the highest military tension since the signing of the Lusaka Protocol" and "the serious threat of a return to full-scale war," the UN pressed ahead with the drawdown of UNAVEM III and the transition to MONUA.[52] The intensity of the fighting demonstrated not only that UNITA still controlled major portions of the country but that it had hidden a major military capacity from the UN. One UNITA colonel who defected claimed that Savimbi still had 60,000 men at his disposal.[53] Subsequently, Savimbi admitted to having 4,500 troops in his "presidential guard" and his "mining police." Sources cited in media reports called such figures preposterous, however, and estimated his strength at anywhere from 15,000 to 35,000 soldiers.[54]

On June 30, 1997, the Security Council brought UNAVEM III to an end with Resolution 1118, which recognized the PKO's "successful contribution to the restoration of peace and the process of national reconciliation." At the same time it expressed concern "about the increase in tensions, especially in the northeastern provinces, and the attacks by UNITA on UNAVEM III posts and personnel."[55] Despite this inconsistency, the Resolution established the United Nations Observer Mission in Angola (MONUA) and urged the parties to cooperate with the new mission, which was expected to be completed by February 1, 1998.

While Resolution 1118 brought UNAVEM III to an official end, the operation had been in the process of being reduced for some time. By June 1, 1997, the number of military personnel in the PKO stood at 4,700, down from a peak of over 7,000 in 1995.[56] MONUA was designed to be a much more modest operation. It was authorized a strength of 193 military contingent personnel, 86 military observers, 345 police monitors, 310 international civilian staff, 250 Angolan employees, and 60 UN volunteers, together with a budget of $64.5 million for its projected seven-month existence.[57]

Despite its limited size, the mandate of MONUA was nonetheless broad. The Secretary General pointed out that "the delays observed in the fulfillment of certain aspects of the Lusaka Protocol will require the new mission to undertake additional responsibilities." He described the overall mandate of the follow-on mission as assisting "the Angolan parties in consolidating peace and national reconciliation, enhancing confidence-building and creating an environment conducive to long-term stability, democratic development and rehabilitation of the country."[58]

As the Secretary General was making this report to the Security Council on June 5, 1997, the situation in Angola was rapidly deteriorating. By the time the Security Council passed Resolution 1118 at the end of that month, the prospect of a new war in Angola was growing by the day, and the failure of the UN's efforts to prevent one was increasingly evident to anyone willing to compare the resolution with reality.

The situation in Angola unraveled quickly in the second quarter of 1997 despite the optimism of a few weeks before. On April 11, over 30 heads of state from around the world came to Luanda to witness the installation of the Government of National Unity and Reconciliation (GURN), which was to incorporate UNITA members and make permanent peace possible. It had taken months of pressure by the international community and a visit to Angola by Secretary General Annan to persuade the parties to make enough progress on implementation of the 1994 Lusaka Protocol to permit the ceremony to take place.[59] The event was not a total success. Despite being given special status as the president of the largest opposition party, UNITA leader Jonas Savimbi refused to attend, fearing for his safety.

Four UNITA ministers and seven vice ministers nonetheless joined the government. Seven new ministries had been created to make room for representatives of UNITA and all the other parties in the parliament, swelling the cabinet to 29 ministers and 56 vice ministers in order to ensure there were enough high-level positions to go around.[60] Since the entire Justice Ministry had an overall budget of $60,000[61] and other ministries (except defense) were presumably equally short of funds, it is unclear what all of these officials with impressive titles and few resources would be able to accomplish. Perhaps that was not the point, however, since the goal may have been simply to co-opt as many key people as possible. In fact, subsequent reports indicate that the level of cooperation within the GURN was good. Integration of UNITA followers was taking place below the cabinet level as well. Over 11,000 former UNITA soldiers were incorporated into the Angolan Armed Forces.[62]

As peace once again fell apart, MONUA's efforts to deal with the situation were largely unsuccessful as both sides refused to cooperate. A team of five military observers sent to the border to investigate allegations of UNITA attacks were detained for three days by UNITA. The UN also protested the fact that the government had prevented MONUA personnel from visiting an area that the government took journalists to a day or two later.[63]

The UN was determined to scale back, however, and wanted to be able to declare victory and depart. The threat of a return to war did at least slow the pace of withdrawal. In his August 13, 1997 report to the Security Council, Secretary General Annan noted that "The peace process in Angola is experiencing some of the most serious difficulties since the signing of the Lusaka Protocol."[64] He recommended postponing further withdrawals of UN personnel from Angola and retaining 2,650 military personnel but only until the end of October 1997.

Historically UNITA tried to do just enough to give the Security Council an excuse for not imposing sanctions. UNITA turned over the key northern town of Negage to the government, just before a deadline of September 29, 1997, for a decision on sanctions was reached.[65] While doing the minimum, however, it was not about to disarm. UNITA's claims that it had only 6,052 troops left to demobilize was dismissed by the UN as "unconvincing," and the quality and quantity of weapons turned over were termed "insignificant."[66]

Finally the patience of the international community ran out and new sanctions were imposed on October 29, 1997. These included an international ban on the travel of UNITA officials, the closing of its offices abroad, and a prohibition against flights into its territory without the approval of the Angolan government.[67] The international community always found imposition of the sanctions difficult, however, even with simple measures like shutting UNITA's offices abroad.[68]

For its part, the Angolan government used its military might to weaken support for Savimbi even when that meant destabilizing a neighbor. The overthrow of the democratically elected government in the Congo Republic was attributed to an injection of Angolan troops and air power in the battle for Brazzaville.[69]

With neither side seeming to have changed its attitudes or tactics, MONUA had little chance of success. In a 1993 report to the Security Council, the Secretary General described the breakdown of the Abidjan talks as "a major and tragic setback to the peace process," but added that it would be unthinkable for the United Nations to abandon Angola at this critical juncture. He instead recommended a further interim extension of UNAVEM II on a reduced basis.[70] As the situation deteriorated once again, what had been unthinkable in 1993 became plausible in 1997 and inevitable in 1999.

Diamonds are Forever, and Maybe War Too

If one had to summarize the problem of finding permanent peace in Angola in a single word, that word would be "diamonds." They provide the funds that allow Savimbi to maintain his military forces. Such funds, instead of prolonging the conflict, could be used to help end it if an accommodation can be reached between the government and UNITA as to how to divide them. Diamonds could provide the funds for Savimbi to sustain a security force to ensure his own protection and at the same time finance the conversion of UNITA to a political party. One such plan to mine and market the diamonds and divide the proceeds between the Government and UNITA was floated by Maurice Tempelsman. An international businessman like Tempelsman could provide needed confidence to both sides and better exploit a resource that some experts estimate could generate a billion dollars annually for the next half century.[71] If marketed properly, the diamonds could probably generate far more than they do now, making it possible for the government to gain additional revenue without UNITA's having to lose too much.

Tempelsman's proposal was front-page news in the *Washington Post*, which highlighted his contributions to the Democratic Party. Given the interest in campaign financing scandals in the U.S. media at the time, it was clearly his status as a major political contributor that earned the story such prominence. An article merely about a plan to help end the war in Angola would have been relegated to the inside pages at best.

Tempelsman's proposal could help provide a basis to end the conflict by devising a means to divide the spoils. Any such accommodation would require the cooperation of both parties, which is not likely in the current climate. Both sides have failed to demonstrate the will to implement either the spirit or the letter of the agreements they have signed. The Secretary General's August 13, 1997 report stated in uncharacteristically blunt language that UNITA had submitted data on troops and weapons that were neither complete nor credible. The report also pointed out that UNITA had prevented the normalization of the government's administration throughout Angola, continued to use its radio station to make anti-government and anti-UN broadcasts, contributed only 10,899 of the planned 26,300 troops to the army, and engaged in laying new mines in areas that had been cleared. For its part, while the government professed to have no intention of resorting to military action, it was described as having repeatedly deployed some of its 5,450 rapid reaction police without notifying MONUA, and as threatening to terminate their being quartered in 13 agreed-upon locations.[72]

Thus, the parties distrust each other with good reason and prefer to fight over the country's resources rather than entertain proposals on how to share them. One thing the parties will probably agree upon is that the international community should bear the responsibility of the resumption of the fighting because of the failure of peacekeeping. There should be little doubt about where the blame should really lie. If war does return to Angola, the parties will no doubt blame the UN for what happens, even though they are responsible for the fact that the UN has little to show for its years of effort in attempting to secure a permanent peace in Angola. An August 1997 editorial in the *Washington Post* remains true:

> There won't be much argument about what went wrong in this phase. The bulk of the responsibility will fall on the Angolan faction led by Jonas Savimbi.

Not that his arch-rival over the decades, President Jose Eduardo dos Santos, does not deserve a share of the blame, especially now if he launches the sort of premature attack that could destroy the lingering possibilities of a political rescue operation.[73]

There are therefore many pitfalls that can contribute to the failure of peacekeeping in the predeployment, deployment, and postdeployment phases. Regardless of how well the peacekeepers do their job, external actors, internal resources, and the parties themselves can conspire to make success impossible to achieve. The next chapter will consider what the international community and the UN might do to improve the chances for permanent peace and why those steps might not be taken. It will also discuss why some reforms, even if implemented, might not work.

Chapter Nine

"Inconclusion"—Why Real Reform Might Not Be Possible

As described in chapter one, today peacekeeping is more necessary, more desired, and more possible than ever before. Because of the change in the nature of the world's conflicts, it has also become much harder to do. In its early years, the UN was most often confronted with interstate wars. Classical peacekeeping in such situations meant the UN simply had to separate two conventional armies belonging to two states along well-defined battle lines in a specific area. The UN then had only to monitor a cease-fire until the parties could negotiate a permanent peace.

In the post–Cold War era, the UN has had to deal almost exclusively with intrastate conflicts in which the battle lines were as blurred as the distinction between soldiers and noncombatants. The opposing troops were almost always lightly armed, poorly trained, and rarely disciplined. To make peace possible after a civil war of this type required rebuilding the country through a PKO with multiple goals. This involved operations that were much larger, much more expensive, and far more complex than classical peacekeeping. The inability of the UN and the international community to deal with this complexity and to achieve the many intended goals led to peacekeeping failures and a loss of both confidence and the willingness to take risks and casualties.

As a result, peacekeeping has fallen into disfavor when compared with just a few years ago. The scenes of suffering on CNN now provoke concern and debate about what level of suffering warrants international intervention but not the dispatching of blue-helmeted troops.[1] In this latest period of peacekeeping, the international community seems interested only in limited commitments of limited duration. The operations undertaken are mainly small, observer missions. There are exceptions, but these occasional larger efforts have been initiated because the interests of at least one of the Great Powers are directly involved.

The UN's annual review of peacekeeping described this present era in the following terms:

> As 1996 ended, some 26,000 military personnel and civilians were serving in 16 UN peace-keeping operations at a total annual cost of about $1.6 billion. Clearly, the pendulum has swung away from the heady days of what some have referred to as peace-keeping overstretch. Only a year before, in 1995, some 60,000 personnel were serving in 17 UN peacekeeping missions—including three in the former Yugoslavia—at an annual cost of some $3.5 billion.[2]

Certainly one way to avoid one's reach from exceeding one's grasp is not to aim to achieve very much. How long the international community will continue to impose its own self-limiting constraints on peacekeeping's application will depend in part on whether the causes of failure that brought about the current era can be corrected.

Whether this situation can be corrected is a question without an easy answer. Chapters three, four and five discussed how peacekeeping can fail before, during, or after the peacekeepers are deployed. The problem having been described, together with its causes and the implications of the current trend for the future, it is appropriate to draw some conclusions and tentatively suggest some solutions.

The current situation exists, however, not because there has been a lack of assessments of what is wrong and how to remedy it, but because there is always resistance to change, and "solutions" to this problem are not easily adopted. Even though reform might improve the chances for peacekeeping to succeed, the status quo serves someone's interest and that someone will see change as detrimental to those interests. Protectors of the status quo can include the member states of the UN, the UN bureaucracy, or NGOs.

One might begin by asking whether reform is possible, and who and what should be changed. Because the UN is both a bureaucracy and an organization made up of 185 member states, there are many different attitudes toward and definitions of reform. Improving the efficiency of the bureaucracy will amount to little if it is not accompanied by changes in the actions of the member states, including what they ask of the organization. Some are skeptical that changes can be made. Applebaum in 1993 wrote:

Reform is a constant topic among the UN's top bureaucrats. Yet from year to year little seems to change. In a bureaucracy which is responsible to everyone and no one, even press scrutiny has had little impact. Individuals who try to reform the system from within risk ostracism and loss of their jobs.[3]

The new Secretary General did announce a much-heralded set of proposals for overall reform of the UN in July 1997, however. While the official U.S. Government reaction was cautiously positive,[4] U.S. congressional leaders and others expressed disappointment that the proposals did not go farther.[5] The skeptics questioned how a reform proposal that cut neither jobs nor programs could have much effect. Others questioned whether the first Secretary General to have risen up through the ranks of the UN bureaucracy could implement the reforms necessary. In fact, when briefing his fellow UN employees, Secretary General Annan is reported to have said that he would be bringing in outside management experts to review work practices but that "It is not their reform. It is our reform."[6]

Others questioned how he could implement real change while balancing the competing interests of UN employees, the bloc of third-world countries that form a majority of the member states, and the various fiefdoms that each UN agency has become.[7] Despite the skepticism from some quarters, the General Assembly the reforms and Deputy Secretary General Frechette was appointed to implement them.

Everyone seems to agree that reform is necessary, but no one agrees on what that means. One UN ambassador, in commenting on the issue, observed:

> No one in this assembly can seriously question the need for reform. Unfortunately it appears from working groups it has different connotations for different states, and different groups' failure to make reform efforts has generated tension and mistrust among ourselves that we must endeavor to diffuse.[8]

The ambassador was not the first to remark that reform in the UN means different things to different people. In 1992, Muller pointed out:

> Reform has acquired a particular meaning at the UN and is viewed in at least four different ways: first, as a response to new challenges or emerging concerns of member states; second, as an attempt to undermine the interests and concerns of member states which consequently react to preserve the status quo; third, as a process through which economies can be achieved by

cutting activities often without concern for substance; and fourth, as a conspiracy on the part of the secretariat to enhance its position or on the part of some member states to promote their interests at the expense of others resulting in stalemate and an exchange of accusations.[9]

The inherent resistance to reform within the organization has not precluded some attempts to improve its ability to perform peacekeeping. Several institutional changes have been made to improve the technical capacity of those elements of the organization involved in peacekeeping. A Mission Planning Service within the Department of Peace-Keeping Operations was established to design plans for multidimensional operations and to coordinate with other departments. A Situation Centre was set up to provide 24–hour contact with peacekeepers around the world. A Policy and Analysis Unit, a Training Unit, and a Civilian Police Unit were created to deal with those aspects of PKOs.

In addition, the UN established a Lessons Learned Unit in April 1995, which was supposed to help the organization avoid repeating the same mistakes from one PKO to the next.[10] This attempt to create an institutional memory that could be applied to future operations consisted of an office of eight people. The unit has put out four reports since its creation and is gathering material for assessments of the efforts in Yugoslavia and Angola.[11]

Ironically, at the same time the UN was making these efforts to improve its peacekeeping capacity, the political will of the organization to use that capacity was waning. Compounding the lack of political will is a continuing lack of confidence in the UN's ability to undertake peacekeeping despite the organizational changes. The lack of confidence reflects, in part, the fact that reform is easier to announce than to implement. Despite the establishment of a Lessons Learned Unit, it is unclear to what degree the organization has been able to incorporate what has been learned. Even with the experience of ONUMOZ in demining, the Security Council in August 1996 felt it necessary to point out that operational demining should be an integral part of peacekeeping mandates. It also called for improved coordination and a clear delineation of responsibilities between the Department of Peacekeeping Operations and the Department of Humanitarian Affairs—the same two departments whose bureaucratic squabbling prevented ONUMOZ from lifting any mines for so long.[12]

Even if organizational changes were successfully implemented, it is clear that correcting the flaws in the bureaucracy alone is not likely to be sufficient to make peacekeeping a more effective instrument. As one UN document noted:

No amount of tinkering with procedures and machinery is enough. Only agreement on the scope of UN operations and a commitment by member states to support them politically with feasible mandates and financially with the resources necessary will allow the UN to respond effectively to future distress calls.[13]

The Kind of Peacekeeping Now Possible

Given the five different types of peacekeeping operations, as defined by Lewis and described in the first chapter, one might ask what kind of distress calls the UN will answer in the future and to what degree each of these five types of operations need reform. Peace-making, often called preventive diplomacy, will continue because it requires few people and little risk or expense. The biggest challenge of this kind of peacekeeping is to pick a special envoy who can play well the UN's limited role in helping to broker a peace. That role is limited by the constraints on the UN's capacity to be an effective mediator as described by Touval in chapter three. It will also be limited by the degree to which the international community is reluctant to backup the special envoy with punitive economic, political, or military measures against those who prevent peace and those who support them. Nonetheless, this should continue to be a type of peacekeeping that the UN can and will carry out.

Peacekeeping in Lewis's definition is classical peacekeeping, and the UN has shown that it has the experience and capacity to carry that function out as well. The only difficulty is that with the change in the nature of the world's conflicts, classical peacekeeping is rarely necessary because interstate wars have become the rare exception rather than the rule. The endless, classical PKOs the UN is currently engaged in are therefore unlikely to increase in number.

One recommendation for reform that need not be made is with regard to peace enforcement operations. If the UN has learned anything, it is that those types of distress calls should be answered by others. While the former Secretary General expressed the wish to create such a capacity within the UN in the long term, he recognized that neither he nor the Security Council had the ability to deploy, command, or control operations for enforcement purposes.[14] Talk of creating such a capacity is still heard but not acted upon.

There seems to be general agreement, in the wake of Bosnia and Somalia, that peace enforcement operations should be left to military coalitions that have the blessing of the UN but are not under direct UN control. As Daniel observed:

> When the UN is in the direct chain-of-command, the prospects for success seem to be generally limited only to consensual peacekeeping, whether traditional or multi-functional. Peace enforcement under UN control simply runs too much against the grain of what the organization and its members can or are willing to support administratively, financially, or politically.[15]

The remaining categories of operations—protective engagement and peace-building—unlike peace enforcement are still within the realm of the possible for the UN. They nonetheless have an uncertain future because they still pose difficult challenges to the UN.

A UN Special Committee that was charged with reviewing peace-keeping operations stressed in its report to the General Assembly that for peacekeeping to succeed the consent of the parties, impartiality, and the nonuse of force except in self-defense were essential.[16] Protective engagement is unnecessary if all the parties consent. Furthermore, if the peace-keepers are allowed to use their arms to defend only aid workers and themselves, they will be reduced to mere observers as innocent civilians are attacked.

Given the nature of today's conflicts and the humanitarian disasters that they cause, situations requiring protective engagement are sure to arise. CNN will be there to cover them, and the NGOs and others with an interest in humanitarian assistance will pressure the UN to act. The UN does not appear to have a response to these situations at the present and it is clear technical reform won't provide one. For protective engagement to become possible, political will, not simple administrative or logistical efficiency, is required.

The last of the five types of PKOs, peace-building, presents another dilemma to which the UN in the Contraction Period does not have a ready answer. To be effective, peace-building would have to encompass both the deployment and postdeployment phases. A multidimensional PKO would normally incorporate peace-building measures as it strives to rebuild institutions that make a lasting peace possible. Peace-building in the postdeployment phase is what has previously been referred to as PCPB (post-conflict peace-building). Given that the international community is presently interested in limited commitments of limited duration, multidimensional PKOs are unlikely to be undertaken, especially if the expectation is that the peacekeepers will stay indefinitely. By their nature multidimensional PKOs are large affairs with several goals. While their termination may be tied to certain events, such as elections, because such events are so often delayed, these PKOs can be of uncertain duration. Once the peacekeepers do depart, there will always be much in the way of PCPB left to do. It is at that moment, however, that the international community begins to lose what unity of purpose it may have had while still tying to end the conflict.

Only in cases like Haiti and Albania, where the interests of a major power are directly affected, does there seem to be sufficient support for major operations in the Contraction Period and even those are of decidedly limited length. In Haiti, after landing 20,000 troops in September 1994 to restore President Aristide to power, "The United Nations mandate that made the intervention possible has been allowed to expire, a casualty of international exasperation with a lack of progress here."[17]

In Albania, as noted earlier, the peacekeepers departed rapidly after the elections. Because of its quick, albeit limited, success, some have suggested that Operation Alba (as the PKO was called) may become a model for the large PKOs that might take place during the Contraction Period. The Secretary General, in his final report to the Security Council, concluded: "Operation Alba has been a good example of how a political and military operation of international stabilization can be undertaken with responsibility and solidarity."[18] In the Security Council's meeting to review the operation upon its termination, several speakers praised the regional cooperation involved in the initiative, as well as its success.[19]

In his comments, the Egyptian delegate struck a much more cautionary note. He said that the operation's success could not be viewed as a substitute for the UN role in containing a variety of world crises, particularly in Africa.[20] His point is an important one, as there will be no African Albania. Operation Alba was unique in several respects. It involved the troops of 11 European nations (9 of which were from Western Europe) in helping another European country. Over half of the 7,215 troops deployed were Italian. The operation benefited from the assistance of an alphabet soup of European organizations, including the OSCE, WEU, EU, NATO, and the Council of Europe.[21] They made major contributions to the organization and monitoring of the elections and other objectives of the mission.

The operation accomplished its limited goals quickly (from April 15 to August 11, 1997), successfully, and without having a single peacekeeper killed or even attacked. It also helped that Albania was a small, poor country with only 3.5 million people and that the conflict was not an ethnic one. Even though President Berisha would have liked to use the PKO to help him cling to power, he was so thoroughly repudiated by his people that he was left with no other option but to step down.

Several speakers in the Security Council session mentioned another factor in Operation Alba's success:

> Strict compliance with the three golden rules of updated peacekeeping operations: the request and consent of the legitimate government; absolute impartiality of the peacekeepers; and no recourse to weapons by the peacekeepers except in self-defense.[22]

None of these factors are likely to be present in an African context, in much of the rest of the third world, or in the former Soviet Union where today's PKOs take place. The troops will not be predominantly first-world soldiers who are well-trained and come with their own logistics, communications, and transport. No single major power is likely to contribute over half of the troops and lead the operation. The distances involved, area covered, and population to be assisted will all be much larger. There won't be a host of well-funded organizations looking for an opportunity to prove their relevance and ability to assist. The loser of the elections will probably not go quietly. The conflict will be a civil war with ethnic overtones in which the legitimacy of the government will be a fundamental question. The warring factions, when not attacking each others' civilians, will not hesitate to attack the peacekeepers if they see doing so as in their interests or if they lose control of their troops. The obstacles to a lasting peace will not be quickly or easily resolved, allowing the peacekeepers to depart rapidly and leave the country to its own devices.

The use of peacekeeping will therefore continue to be very constrained, with little likelihood that it will be used as frequently as it has in the past. Were the UN to improve its ability to conduct peacekeeping, it might be applied more frequently. This presupposes that real reform is possible and that should not be an easily-made assumption.

The Kind of Reform That Is Possible

The desire for "reform" has prompted changes within the bureaucratic structures of the UN and the addition of units designed to deal with specific aspects of conducting peacekeeping where the UN was weak in the past. Because of the limitations on the operations that the international community is willing to undertake, these may be solutions to a problem that no longer exists. If protective engagement and peace-building are unlikely to be attempted, the UN's ability to carry out such operations is a moot point. If the UN is to conduct more than small observer missions, more than administrative changes will be necessary. Changes in the attitudes of the member states and particularly those on the Security Council are a more important, but still missing, element of reform.

A lack of political will to undertake more ambitious operations and the inability to carry them out effectively are mutually reinforcing. If this situation is to be changed, success of peacekeeping has to become the overriding objective. While successful peacekeeping may seem an obvious goal, capability and realism seem to take a back seat to other considerations.

For instance, in recent UN debates on peacekeeping, much has been made of the problem of gratis personnel on loan to the Department of Peacekeeping Operations.[23] Of the Department's 400 staff members, only 55 are paid for from the UN's regular budget with the rest being loaned from, and paid for, by governments. Over 80 percent of these 345 personnel on loan came from developed countries. The General Assembly, with the support of the Non-Aligned Movement (NAM), asked the Secretary General to reduce the number of gratis personnel, saying the practice undermined the equitable geographical representation and international character of the department's staff.

The concern voiced in the argument was not that the practice reduced the department's capability, just that it reduced its representation from the third world. While the UN Charter speaks of the principle of geographic equity, PKOs are neither distributed nor paid for on an equitable geographic basis. The troops that participate in them are volunteered by member states, not drafted on an equitable geographic one. It is unlikely that an equitable geographic distribution of the peacekeeping troops would have improved the chances for success in Somalia, Rwanda, or Bosnia. Yet when the issue is well-paid employment in New York, many believe the principle of geographic equity should prevail even it means less capability and higher cost to the organization.

One of the main functions of government is to provide jobs to a country's elites, especially where the local economy has trouble absorbing them. Perhaps for some, the UN should do the same. Viewing the UN primarily as a source of patronage jobs, or simply a mechanism for transferring resources from the developed to the underdeveloped world, will continue to weaken its capacity to carry out important responsibilities such as peacekeeping.

Capacity may be undervalued at the UN because the organization suffers from a lack of accountability and difficulty in measuring its own performance. The UN spent the first 49 years of its existence without a serious internal audit capability. Although an Office of Internal Oversight Services was finally established in September 1994, its initial efforts were criticized as lacking vigor.[24] The corruption and waste the office has uncovered have not been enough to threaten the success of a PKO, but they do nothing to build the image of an institution that can conduct one efficiently. In its annual report, the office noted:

> In Angola, acceptance of delayed defective and short supplies from a vendor resulted in excess payments of $288,000 and losses of $980,000. There was also serious irregularities noted in the contracting of an aircraft. Internal control weaknesses resulted in extensive abuse of communications facilities.[25]

The effectiveness of the organization is hard to gauge because the tasks it performs usually defy easy measurement, the exception being UNHCR, where mortality rates among refugees give clear indications of when its efforts are inadequate. In addition, the UN bureaucracy resists measurement and accountability because it answers to 185 members who all pursue their own national goals, leaving the UN civil servants potentially open to criticism from every direction. The lack of accountability minimizes the risk of criticism but creates a culture in which accomplishment is equated with the absence of criticism. This often gets translated into keeping the government happy in the country in which a program is being conducted even if it affects the effectiveness of that program.

Some may find that judgment harsh, but demining in Mozambique provides an example of the phenomenon. The UN's assessment of its efforts on this problem asserted:

> It is not the number of square meters cleared which has been the measure of success of the Accelerated Demining Program (ADP) to date, it is more the development of the Mozambican staff from the headquarters to the field.[26]

In other words, the number of mines lifted is not an important measure of the success of a demining program in the UN's view. It is the capacity created within the local government. While creating capacity is a worthwhile goal, pursuing it may not accomplish much unless the objectives are simply to give the UN a program to administer and the local government access to jobs and other resources. As noted earlier, the UN's demining efforts neither supported the peace process in Mozambique nor contributed to the success of ONUMOZ.

Even if one accepted the idea that capacity-building within the local government is the most important goal, the demining program in Mozambique fails even by this measure of performance. After ONUMOZ was brought to a conclusion, the UN's efforts at demining continued after the departure of the peacekeepers. Demining experts agree, however, that the Mozambican government's demining organization after five years of UN effort is still in complete disarray and anything that accomplished in demining has been due to the work of NGOs.[27]

Despite this track record, some still see capacity-building as a critical element of a PKO. Synge concludes his history of ONUMOZ by suggesting six elements for successful peacekeeping and includes capacity building among them. He reasons: "A general policy of support for key government structures, rather than one of displacement, should help to provide sustainable management capacity for the political and administrative authorities at the end of the process."[28] That is a nice thought, but like much of Synge's study, it unfortunately bears little relation to reality. Capacity-building takes decades and today's peacekeeping mandates don't afford the luxury of staying that long. If capacity is to be created, it will have to be part of post-conflict, peace-building measures.

Another feature of the UN that limits its effectiveness is the fact that the vast majority of the member states make little financial contribution to the UN's budget. This is certainly justifiable to a degree, since poorer countries with underdeveloped economies have little ability to pay to support the organization. It creates, however, an expense-is-no-object attitude on the part of those who don't have to pay the bills but who often receive the benefits. For that reason, NAM representatives can argue that gratis personnel should not be accepted, and budgetary constraints should be no excuse for the lack of greater employment opportunities in the Department of Peacekeeping Operations.

The linkages between those paying the bills (generally the taxpayers of the first world), those spending the money (the UN bureaucracy), and those receiving the benefits (in peacekeeping, those in underdeveloped countries) are sufficiently weak to have a negative effect on both the efficiency and the accountability of the organization. The UN has no legislature closely monitoring its efforts, little close scrutiny from the press, and no outraged taxpayers demanding an end to waste when they observe it. An organization that serves everyone in reality answers to no one.

The UN's Office of Oversight Services is beginning to uncover some of the organization's faults and attempt to deal with them. According to one article, the office's third annual report released in October 1997 revealed:

> . . . a pattern of sloppy management in which contracts are awarded and money disbursed without reference to the organization's financial regulations or accepted rules of accounting. It describes a world of petty criminality, where cash sometimes seems to be sitting around for the taking. In this freewheeling atmosphere, diverting money is relatively easy.[29]

The article also indicated one of the reasons why real reform of the situation is hard to achieve:

> Furthermore, national governments put pressure on UN officials to hire or promote—but never dismiss—citizens of their countries who clamor for the prestige of jobs in the organization, and then find ways to enhance their incomes by manipulating travel allowances or salary advances. UN employees have provided numerous accounts of officials being transferred rather than dismissed after being caught breaking the rules.[30]

This lack of accountability and measurable performance has been compounded by peacekeeping's failures, which brought additional focus on the need for reform of the UN. If the reform required for improving the chances for successful peacekeeping is perceived at the UN in any of the last three of Muller's definitions, it will be difficult if not impossible to achieve. If instead it is taken to be a way to better respond to the new challenges posed by the situations created by today's intrastate conflicts, it may have some chance of being implemented.

Assuming the latter case, the three phases of peacekeeping—predeployment, deployment, and postdeployment—can be reconsidered to see where improvements might be made and also speculate why they might not be. Whether at this point in its history the UN (in the form of its bureaucracy or of its member states) is ready to respond to new challenges or is only intent on not repeating the failures of the past is an open question.

Avoiding Failure Before Starting

The chances of success in peacekeeping depend in no small measure on what kind of peace there is to keep. As described in chapter three, peace can come in a variety of ways—when one side defeats the other; when it is negotiated, but both sides continue to seek victory; when it is imposed by an outside party; or when an agreement is reached that is accepted by both parties and supported by the important external actors.

An imposed solution won't work, according to the British Ambassador at the UN in 1982, Sir Anthony Parsons. In his judgement the UN is not an instrument for providing collective security, but an instrument of persuasion. According to Parsons:

> The UN is not, and should not try to be, a forum for the solution of disputes. If I have learned anything from my experience, it is that problems can ultimately be resolved peacefully only through direct negotiations between the parties themselves. It is no use expecting outside bodies, including the UN, to draw up detailed blueprints and to impose them on recalcitrant parties to a dispute. It simply does not work.[31]

If direct negotiations between the parties are necessary, does the UN have a role? The UN Charter permits the Secretary General to bring to the Security Council's attention any matter that may threaten international peace and security. The Secretary General can use the council's attention and his own to attempt to get the parties to negotiate. He may have difficulty getting the parties to an agreement however. As Touval has pointed out, the UN is not the best mediator because it lacks many of the tools necessary.

To say someone else should play the role of mediator assumes that there is someone willing who is willing and able to do the job. Durch (1993) listed three requirements for successful peacekeeping: the consent of the parties, their desisting from attempts to win everything, and the support of the Great Powers. Ideally at least one of the Great Powers should take up the task of mediator and be willing to invest its time, prestige, and resources in seeing the process through until the right outcome is achieved.

Whoever is the mediator should strive for an outcome that is durable and that often implies a peace agreement that results in power-sharing. As one African expert explained: "One should ask do the parties have a deal, at least an implicit one, giving the loser a stake in the outcome and hope in the future."[32] As was seen in Angola and may yet be seen in Mozambique, a winner-take-all scenario provides little incentive for the loser to resist the impulse to return to war.

When the UN becomes involved in implementing a peace agreement it did not design, it finds it difficult to insist on the changes even if they are necessary to prevent the agreement's failure. It could develop a checklist to see that the agreement contains the critical elements essential for successful implementation. This would also put the parties and any mediators on notice that such elements are necessary for the UN to consider becoming involved.

These elements should include provisions to give the UN sufficient authority and responsibility and to keep the cost of the operation down. Such provisions can be spelled out in the status of forces agreement (SOFA), which the UN concludes with the government of the country to which the peacekeepers are being dispatched. Negotiating this agreement can take time and can delay the arrival of the peacekeepers. If the UN feels a greater sense of urgency to conclude the SOFA than the government, it will be under pressure to make concessions to government demands. The Secretary General's July 1997 reform proposal describes the problem and suggests a solution:

> Considerable difficulties are also at times encountered in negotiating and properly implementing a SOFA. Amendments proposed by certain host governments sometimes constitute fundamental departures from the customary practices and principles applicable to UN peacekeeping operations, and negotiating on such a basis delays the conclusion of an acceptable agreement. A time frame prescribed by the Security Council for the conclusion of the SOFA and an inclusion in the resolution establishing the operation of a provision to the effect that the model SOFA shall apply provisionally, pending the conclusion of such an agreement, would contribute to expediting its conclusion.[33]

This attempt to shift to the Security Council the responsibility for putting pressure on the host government demonstrates that the Secretary General feels himself in a weak bargaining position when it comes to negotiating a SOFA with a country about to receive a PKO. If a government is more interested in a SOFA that it finds acceptable than in the welfare of its citizens, even the Security Council may not have enough leverage to bring the negotiations to a conclusion so that the peacekeepers can be dispatched. What happens when the time period established by the Security Council runs out without an agreement is not clear. The UN could deploy the peacekeepers without a SOFA and assume the host government will honor the model one, even though the government has not agreed to it. Or the Security Council could extend the time period for concluding the SOFA, draw another line in the sand, and agree to remain seized of the matter. When under pressure to do something to alleviate the situation, the UN finds it easier to make concessions than to resist the urgings that it become immediately involved.

One element of a SOFA should be that the PKO is exempt from any local levies or taxes. The host government will often see the PKO as an economic opportunity and a revenue source. In Mozambique, for instance, civil aviation authorities attempted to insist that planes carrying election materials pay exorbitant landing fees. A PKO's chances for success will be improved if the parties to the conflict not only do not make money from it but pay a portion of its costs. Shifting the costs of the PKO to the parties to the conflict is difficult, however, especially since the "teacup" wars tend to take place in underdeveloped countries in which the parties are busy destroying what few resources there are. Nonetheless, some of the billions that Angola earned from oil and diamonds and spent on weapons or sent to bank accounts abroad could have been used to reimburse the UN. It would have provided an incentive to the parties to help keep the costs of the operation down and its duration short.

The peace agreement and the mandate given the PKO must unequivocally put the UN in charge, with all the power necessary to accomplish whatever tasks are required and to minimize the obstructionism that the parties will occasionally display. The UN should also have the authority to destroy any weapons that are in excess of the needs of the army and to destroy all land mines. Effective disarmament could be the key to sustaining the peace, not only in the country in question but in the region.

Giving such discretion to the UN may become a problem for the host government, which will use the sovereignty argument to protect its prerogatives. However, the UN should not accept the responsibility for a peace process without the authority to ensure that it succeeds to the maximum extent possible.

The UN must also have the ability to communicate directly with the people of the country via radio to explain its actions and counteract the propaganda that the parties will be intent on distributing. This is not a role that the UN has always been comfortable with, as was pointed out by one participant in UNTAC: "I do not believe that anyone could now deny the criticality of Radio UNTAC to the whole process. In my view, this was obvious from the start and only the UN bureaucracy delayed it."[34]

Boutros-Ghali also recognized in his "Supplement to an Agenda for Peace" the need for a PKO to have its own information capacity.[35] It was also called for in UNAVEM III's mandate. And yet, despite the propaganda war that both sides in Angola continue to engage in, the UN never overcame the resistance of the parties or its own inertia to set up such a capacity of its own. Whether it wanted to keep its costs down or simply yielded to the government's intransigence, by not having its own communication capability the UN did not improve its chances for success.

One of the easiest criticisms when a PKO encounters problems once it does become operational is that there was a lack of planning. The UN has improved its ability to plan, as indicated by the expansion of the number of personnel, albeit most of them gratis, in the Department of Peacekeeping Operations. One aspect of planning that is not likely to change is the suggestion that was made by the general in charge of UNTAC's military component: "Regrettably, for almost everyone in UNTAC, the process was one of on-the-job training, while implementing plans prepared by someone else. Plans need to be prepared by the people who will be responsible for their execution."[36] There is no indication that the planners in New York stand in any danger of having to become the implementers in the field, even if there were enough of them. The general had good reason to complain about the plans for UNTAC. Righter points out: "As for the UN's tiny peacekeeping department, suffice it to say that the Cambodia operation was sketched out by a Nigerian desk officer in an afternoon."[37]

Another simple suggestion that is difficult to implement is that the right people should be picked to do the job. This applies to the SRSG, the civilian staff, and the military units. Such decisions, more often than not, seem to be subordinate to other considerations such as bureaucratic politics, interests of key member states, and a desire to avoid embarrassing anyone. The UNTAC military commander again provides an example of this:

> The UN Secretariat alone reserves the right, in the light of the views of the Permanent Five, to decide which troops come from which countries. This is done in accordance with the Secretariat's priorities, which in the case of UNTAC, were not always consistent with the needs of the mission.[38]

While the right military units are important, the key personnel decision lies in choosing the right SRSG. This is often the most political of all the appointments. That person needs to be given the power to select key staff members and should have the responsibility, authority, and resources to achieve the mandate of the mission. This should include authority not only over the members of the PKO but over the staff of the UN agencies that are operating in the country as well. Coordination of the humanitarian relief efforts of NGOs should also be part of the SRSG's responsibilities. This is again more easily asserted than accomplished. UN agencies tend to act as fiefdoms free from the direct supervision of the Secretary General. Their field offices are therefore unlikely to take orders from an SRSG. The many NGOs that are typically present have diverse agendas and funding sources and are even more resistant to control or even coordination.

Another suggestion that is more difficult than it sounds to put into practice is for the SRSG to be replaced if found not to be up to the task. For such a decision to be possible, it is necessary that New York be able to measure with some degree of confidence the performance of the person in the field. That is not easy, since the information that headquarters has will often come from the SRSG or from the parties. The latter will measure the SRSG's performance strictly in terms of whether or not it serves their interests.

Changing bureaucratic procedures is not the entire solution, however. UN officials, with some justification, often blame the lack of success in peacekeeping not on their organization but on a lack of political will and economic resources in the member states. When Secretary General Annan presented his proposals for overall UN reform in July 1997, one article quoted UN officials as saying:

> The bureaucracy has been made a scapegoat for recent UN failures in Somalia, Bosnia, Congo and Cambodia that were the fault not of UN workers, but of the unwillingness of the international community to confront the problems head-on. These are failures that cannot be corrected by turning loose management consultants to draw revised organizational tables and flow charts.[39]

Confronting problems head-on should include acknowledging all of the possibilities that may lead to a solution and devising realistic mandates. The member states, particularly those on the Security Council, should not hand the organization jobs to do just because they defy solution elsewhere. The member states should not instruct the UN to launch an operation simply to give the appearance that something is being done, but because they expect the UN can succeed.

Getting agreement between member states about common goals and common means is not easily accomplished. As Chayes noted with regard to Bosnia: "Even like-minded allies have often failed to reach consensus. Although they may agree that 'something must be done,' they are not always able to concur about what that 'something' is. This can lead to paralysis or palliative measures."[40] Getting countries to act with some unity of purpose is necessary, however, so that the peacekeepers have a chance, once deployed, to accomplish their mission. This is again easier said than done, since it requires countries to put the common good ahead of their individual interests. Maximizing the chances for success need not supersede a country's interests but should become one of them.

Avoiding Failure While Deployed

Having a strong mandate, adequate resources, and the right people will give a PKO a good chance of achieving the objectives of the mission. The SRSG must have the foresight and the authority to pursue the mission's priorities diligently. Secondary objectives like creating local capacity and taking a long-term developmental approach to problems must take a back seat to more immediate goals like demining key roads, disarmament, rapid demobilization and reintegration of former combatants, and moving ahead to elections.

If the elections are to be the culmination of the process, the UN has to be in a position to ensure that they are free and fair. The local actors will have to do much of the organization, but the international community will be paying the bills, so it must be able to ensure that the process is neither gold-plated nor obstructed by the parties. Election monitors should be primarily local rather than international. They are far cheaper, and it is important that they, rather than outside observers, be satisfied that the process has been free and fair.

The SRSG, together with the commander of the military component, should have the flexibility to adjust assignments and units to reflect the dynamic situation on the ground. Being bound by a plan drawn up in New York months before is a prescription for having the wrong troops in the wrong place doing the wrong things. This would have to be coordinated closely with the unit's government, however. That government may well prefer its men assigned to a riskless and useless task rather than to one that accomplishes something, if it endangers the soldiers involved. It is unclear that New York would be willing to delegate such authority to the field, however, or that troop contributors would go along with the reassignments.

If police observers are to be used to monitor the conduct of the local police, prevent human rights violations, and investigate those that occur, they will have to do a better job than the police that took part in ONU-MOZ and UNAVEM. The UN has succeeded at one such mission. The UN Observer Mission in El Salvador (ONUSAL) was without precedent in UN history in that it was "the first mission to accomplish its tasks of verification and observation of respect for human rights and international humanitarian law during an internal conflict.[41] The UN took on this responsibility almost as an afterthought. When the Salvadoran peace talks ground to a halt in July 1990, the negotiators proposed having the UN conduct human rights monitoring. Not only was the idea accepted, but "it succeeded in breaking the logjam in the negotiations."[42]

ONUSAL accomplished this by interpreting its mandate "as giving the highest priority to the protection of the civilian population and to the study of select cases involving humanitarian law."[43] ONUSAL's mandate gave it the powers to do so. It was given the capacity to verify respect for human rights; receive communications from any individual, group of individuals, or body complaining of human rights violations; visit any place or establishment freely and without prior notice; interview freely and privately any individual, group of individuals, or members of bodies or institutions; and make recommendations to the parties on the basis of the conclusions it reached with respect to cases or situations it may have been called upon to consider.[44]

The result of this mandate, effectively carried out despite the problem of diverse nationalities and inadequate training, was that the people of El Salvador were given a greater sense of security and confidence in the peace process and in the UN. The mandate, the performance, and the results of the ONUSAL experience all contrast sharply with what occurred in Angola and Mozambique.

ONUSAL had one other very significant advantage, at least over UN-AVEM and many other PKOs. As Flores points out:

> The willingness of the parties to reach an end to the armed conflict, a permanent characteristic of the Salvadoran negotiation process, has to be stressed. Absent in other peace negotiations, the desire of the Salvadoran parties for a peaceful solution is definitely one of the keys to the success of the ONUSAL mission.[45]

The conduct of the local actors and the external actors, along with the country's internal resources, constitutes the three factors discussed earlier that the UN cannot completely control. It can attempt to influence all three but generally does not do it well. In Mozambique, Ajello had a strong mandate and was willing to confront the parties when they failed to live up to their obligations. The dependency of Mozambique on donor aid gave the UN considerable leverage. Leverage means little, however, if the UN and the international community are unable or unwilling to use it.

Another source of leverage that is normally used with great reluctance is humanitarian aid. The selective provision of such aid helped end the war in Mozambique. However, the use of humanitarian aid in that case arose out of the consensus belief among the NGOs that RENAMO, because of its gross violations of human rights abuses, did not deserve to have food aid delivered to areas under its control. Such a consensus was not orchestrated by the UN and might be difficult to achieve in other instances.

In eastern Zaire, where the different use of humanitarian aid might have helped bring about a different result, not even the genocide committed by some of those receiving the aid was enough to create such a consensus. Finally, the government of Rwanda stepped in to prevent those responsible for genocide in Rwanda from using relief aid to provide themselves a base of support in Zaire. One could argue that innocent people would have suffered if aid were withheld, but many innocent people suffered after Rwandan troops and Zairian rebels forced people out of the refugee camps. The UN subsequently put great pressure on President Kabila to allow UN investigators the freedom to determine how many may have died, but it is likely the extent of the killing will never be known.

The UN also needs to address the question of outside actors in a peacekeeping situation. If the neighboring countries or regional powers play a positive role, they should be recognized and encouraged. If they play a negative role, they should be identified, chastised, and, if necessary, subjected to sanctions. This negative role can be an active one, in which the outside actor is assisting one of the parties to continue the conflict. It can also be a passive one, in which the outside actor simply ignores the fact that its territory is being used for the transshipment of arms.

Avoiding Failure After the Fact

Donors could use their aid both as a carrot and a stick to ensure that the parties live up to their peace agreement and implement it during the deployment phase. The international community usually finds this difficult to do, as national interests or humanitarian objectives take precedence. It finds using this leverage in the postdeployment phase even more difficult, though it may be necessary to ensure that what has been built while the peacekeepers were present is not destroyed after they have left. Most donors are reluctant to dictate to a sovereign government, even after the huge investment involved in a major PKO.

In the case of Cambodia, Shawcross noted in 1996:

> The donors of aid to Cambodia have not just the means but also, under the Paris Agreement, the responsibility to link assistance to the government's respect for its own expressed commitments to the rule of law. If they do not do so, violence, corruption and abuse of power will continue.[46]

It is now clear that they did not. Although the Cambodian government received almost half of its annual budget from the donors, few strings were attached.[47] Even after Hun Sen demonstrated how little respect he had for human rights and the rule of law, some major donors showed no inclination to use the leverage aid provided to improve the situation and salvage some of the accomplishments of UNTAC.

If there were sufficient commonality of purpose and political will, there would still be the question of how the coordination among donors would take form in the field. The traditional instruments of development assistance are not easily geared toward conditionality. Once programs are established, the bureaucracies responsible for them resist having them turned off for political reasons and will be even more resistant to doing so in coordination with other donors.

One of the Secretary General's July 1997 reform proposals was to have all the UN agencies in a country work from one office in order to better coordinate their programs. UN workers in the field will be even less willing than those in New York to tell governments things they don't want to hear, however, since they have to deal with those governments every day. Given the principle of sovereignty, the UN finds it difficult to be assertive, even when the government in question is putting peace at risk.

Aside from political will and common purpose on the part of the international community, a new definition of sovereignty may be required to allow the UN to play a stronger postdeployment role in a country that has benefited from peacekeeping. The traditional concept of sovereignty has eroded in recent years. Makinda (1996) notes:

> The message that Haiti, Northern Iraq and Somalia have conveyed is that the UN is probably ready to implement a broader concept of security that, among other things, includes economic development, social institutions, and good governance. They also indicate that the UN has recognized that respect for state sovereignty ought to be balanced against other issues, such as the provision of basic needs, respect for fundamental freedoms and, where necessary, a guarantee of minority rights.[48]

Makinda's three examples were all cases in which the United States had led the coalition of forces that intervened because there was no government or one that was seriously abusing its own citizens, and because the U.S. saw its own interests at stake. In today's world, a country like Haiti, from which refugees directly step onto the shores of the United States, would still be likely to merit such action. Because the Kurds in northern Iraq were imperiled, in part, because of the Gulf War, the U.S. might feel obligated to act under similar circumstances. However, under the Presidential Decision Directive issued after the deaths of the peacekeepers in Mogadishu, it is extremely improbable that the U.S. would be willing to lead another operation like UNOSOM. Rwanda demonstrated that even in the face of widespread suffering, there is now greater caution about launching such an initiative.

The question of a country's sovereignty after a PKO departs has probably not changed enough to permit the UN to play a sufficiently strong role to ensure that what has been built is not destroyed. Makinda describes the limitations of this changing definition of sovereignty:

> While a growing number of policy makers and analysts have been calling for a reinterpretation of state sovereignty and international security, uncertainty in the post–Cold War international system, past practice, and political imperatives in both the industrialized and developing worlds suggest that there will be no formal redefinition of these concepts. However subliminal and normative factors will continue to erode Westphalian sovereignty.[49]

This erosion will probably not be sufficient to permit the UN to take on a role with which it would still be uncomfortable. The irony of inviting several thousand blue-helmeted troops into a country to end its civil war will not prevent governments from resisting suggestions about how to sustain the peace after they have left.

Solutions that Won't Work

Many suggest that one of the problems of the UN is that it is undemocratic, in particular because of the power given to the Security Council and especially to its five permanent members. In "Agenda for Democracy," Boutros-Ghali wrote: "Democracy will not succeed if it is limited to within member states. We need democracy among member states. If global problems are solved by authoritarian means and national problems are solved by democracy, it will not work." Among the proposals to democratize the UN are expanding the Security Council, making more of its deliberations public, and shifting some of its authority to the General Assembly. If the council is to be expanded, a formula will have to be devised that can satisfy those left off it as well as those selected for the honor. That may be difficult because, while there is only one superpower, there are many countries that consider themselves important in their region and few of them are willing to be represented by someone else.

Whatever the formula, an expanded Security Council will make consensus on future peacekeeping operations and their mandates harder to achieve. A bigger council, with greater third world representation, may have more advocates for action. It also may have more countries that are reluctant to get involved in the teacup wars of the future. An expanded membership may make it difficult to maintain the collegial spirit that Hume observed among the 15 current members and make agreement on future peacekeeping harder to achieve.

What the advocates of democratizing the UN don't point out is that most UN members are at best limited democracies themselves. President Clinton in his 1997 address to the General Assembly noted that for the first time in the UN's history, there were more member states whose people live under democracy than did not. His speechwriters must have used a liberal definition of democracy. Freedom House, a human rights organization, in its annual ranking of countries puts each nation in one of three categories depending on its degree of democracy—free, partly free, or not free. At the end of 1996, Freedom House noted that more countries were free societies than ever before—79 of a total of 191 countries. The population of those 79 amounted to only 1.25 billion people, however, with 2.26 billion living in the partly free countries and another 2.26 billion in those states considered not free.[50]

To make the UN more democratic by giving more power to more of its members is therefore to attempt to make a democracy out of a group comprising representatives of mainly authoritarian governments. If democratization in the strictest sense were the goal, it might be more appropriate to suggest that partly free states have partial voting rights, and states that are not free have none.

The civil wars of today, which peacekeeping might help end, are a feature of the second and third worlds—the former Communist countries and the underdeveloped nations of the world. There have been no PKOs in the first world. However, 97 percent of the cost of peacekeeping is borne by the industrialized countries of the first world.[51] Since the majority of the members of the General Assembly are from the third world or the second, peacekeeping is a solution that can be advocated by this majority secure in the knowledge that they will not have to pay for it. One of the major reasons for the erosion of support for peacekeeping in the U.S. Congress has been the mushrooming costs of such operations, over which it has no control. A redistribution of the financial burden of peacekeeping might bring about more realism in considering how PKOs can be done better.

The financial burden is being redistributed in the UN, but not in a way that leads to more responsibility and realism. Third world countries have successfully lowered the dues paid by the poorest nations from $110,000 a year to $13,000.[52] This move may further exacerbate the strains between the American Congress, which has been demanding no growth in the UN's budget, and the vast majority of UN members. American efforts to lower its current obligation of 25 percent of the UN's regular budget collapsed after the Congress failed to approve a measure to pay up some of the U.S. arrears to the organization.

Even if the financial aspects can be worked out and the burden distributed in a way that people can agree upon, the confidence in the UN's ability to perform peacekeeping must be strengthened. Partly in recognition of the limitations on the UN, one proposal has been put forward for dealing with situations in Africa that require peacekeeping, which has been named the African Crisis Response Initiative (ACRI). Originally called the African Crisis Response Force, it was renamed because some found the use of the term "force" to be objectionable as a name for a group to be used for peacekeeping.[53]

The ACRI is designed to use the African troops under OAU or UN auspices with logistical support from the major powers. The attraction of the idea is that it provides the international community with an intermediate option between doing nothing and sending in its own troops. In the post-Somalia world of peacekeeping there is no enthusiasm for complicated, open-ended mandates or for casualties. African countries recognize this and say they are ready to act on their own behalf. As one OAU official said at a meeting of OAU defense chiefs to work out the details of the initiative, "From Burundi to Liberia, from the Democratic Republic of Congo to Congo Brazzaville, we have seen evidence of increasing reluctance of the rest of the world to become involved in African peace support operations."[54]

But even if some African countries are less sensitive to taking casualties in African peacekeeping operations than other nations, will they have better chances of success? The challenges will be no less daunting. If the task were quick and easy, there would be no shortage of nations willing to try. Can an underfunded army depending on someone else's logistics and training respond adequately? How can the three golden rules of updated peacekeeping operations apply if the legitimacy of the government is the central question, if the troops will often not be looked upon by their fellow Africans as impartial, and if the soldiers can protect only themselves when innocent civilians are most often the targets of attack?

The ACRI is clearly not the solution for all situations. In fact, there may be very few problems for which it will be an adequate answer. It may be one of the few responses available, however. Former UN Under Secretary General Brian Urquhart spoke at a UN conference on peace with the theme "Looking to the Future" in September 1997. Urquhart observed that the failure of only 3 of 17 recent UN peacekeeping operations has produced a "disastrous mood swing" toward cautiousness among member states enabling such unfortunate concepts as "coalitions of the willing" and "the reluctant sheriff—the US" to take hold at the UN.[55]

The future may be limited to coalitions of the willing, such as in Albania, or the reluctant sheriff taking on only those situations in which the American public can see a direct interest, such as in Haiti. The ACRI may play a part, but even if all the details are worked out, it will remain a solution looking for a problem it can solve. The future is likely to contain more attempts to use humanitarian aid as a substitute for political or military action such as protective engagement. The result will be more situations like eastern Zaire and Congo Brazzaville, where the regional actors such as Rwanda and Angola step in to assert their own interests and impose a military solution. In both cases, Angola intervened actively with men and arms as a means of stopping Savimbi from using these countries as transit points for his weapons shipments. As one article about the Angolan involvement pointed out "The United States and European governments—and the international institutions they dominate, such as the UN Security Council—have to a large degree become marginalized as African leaders decide on moves, including military actions, designed to further their own national interests."[56]

In November 1966, then Under Secretary General Annan told a UN committee:

> When the parties to a conflict were genuinely interested in achieving a settlement, mountains could be moved in the interest of peace. But even when they were not, that was not a reason for the rest of the world to neglect its responsibility towards international conflict areas.[57]

That is exactly what has happened. The failed attempts of the UN to deal with these situations through peacekeeping has brought about the Contraction Period, in which ignoring the problem may become the option of choice. In this era when the use of peacekeeping is so limited, ad hoc local solutions by local powers will be more frequently used, as has happened in both the Congos. Human rights, the welfare of refugees, and democracy will be among the victims of such conflicts and such solutions.

Barring an outbreak of collective amnesia among the international community or a strengthening of its political will, a new era of peacekeeping won't begin. A new era would begin sooner if peacekeeping could be done better. The ways to improve peacekeeping are far easier to list than to implement effectively.

The international community and the UN need to address both the external and the internal factors in a peacekeeping situation. The factors external to the operation of the PKO—the external actors, the internal resources, and the parties to the conflict—are elements that the UN cannot ignore. The neighboring countries, regional powers and other external actors have to be encouraged to play a constructive rather than a destructive role. Internal resources should not be allowed to be exported to sustain the fighting. Pressure must be brought to bear on the parties themselves to live up to the peace agreement that they have signed. Implicit in all these actions is the idea that the international community and the UN not simply be cheerleaders for the peace process but actively engaged in its implementation and willing to punish those who interfere with its implementation.

With regard to the internal factors that can affect the chances for a PKO to succeed, the UN could perform better during all three phases—before, during, and after the deployment of the peacekeepers. Before deployment the UN should accept only a strong role for itself in implementation of the peace agreement reached and then only after it has convinced itself that the parties in fact want peace and not just a respite from pursuit of their goals by military means. The agreement should include provisions for creating enough political space for an opposition to exist and to have enough of a stake in the system to want to see it preserved rather than feel the only alternative for the loser of an election is to return to war. The UN should be given wide responsibility to see that such conditions are created and maintained and that human rights in general are protected in the post-electoral period. The UN needs to craft a clear and realistic mandate and insist on a SOFA that protects its forces and minimizes its costs. The UN should pick the best people, especially for the Special Representative, as well as for the civilian, military, and police units and not simply fill its quota with the requisite numbers with more attention paid to their geographic diversity than to their quality.

During the deployment phase, the UN needs to be neutral but not impartial if that implies ignoring the transgressions of one side or never calling attention to them publicly. It should vigorously carry out its mandate and not simply cross its fingers. The UN must also insist on the ability to communicate directly and effectively (which means via AM radio broadcasts) with the people of the country in question. It also should take into account the effect of humanitarian assistance and coordinate its delivery so that it does not result in sustaining the conflict.

After deployment, the UN must remain active and aggressively push PCPB. It should not accept sovereignty as the reason for why the winners of the elections have the right to go back to the ways of doing things that brought about the civil war in the first place.

All of these actions may require overcoming the resistance to change in the way peacekeeping is currently conducted. While such reforms are necessary, it is unclear to what extent they are possible given the inherent limitations of the organization and the attitudes of the member states. Adlai Stevenson, the U.S. Representative to the UN in the mid-1960s, once said: "If the UN did not exist, we would have to invent it." To paraphrase him, if UN peacekeeping is to exist, we may have to reinvent it.

Some problems may be beyond resolution regardless of how well the organization improves its peacekeeping ability. Thus while the causes of peacekeeping's failures can be identified and remedies prescribed, the challenge of implementing the changes required rarely gets sufficient attention. Implementation is a problem that frequently is not fully overcome, and until it is better understood, peacekeeping will continue to be less of an instrument of the international community than it otherwise could be. The dilemma of protective engagement is one example. How the international community copes with having to be ready to kill some people in order to save others will defy easy answers regardless of what reform takes place.

Notes

Chapter 1

1. Report of the Secretary General on the UN Observer Mission in Angola (MONUA), S/1999/02, 24 February 1999, paragraph 3.
2. Ibid.
3. Never missing a chance for propaganda even in the midst of tragedy, the government produced a supposed UNITA deserter who claimed UNITA was holding some of the crew members captive. When the UN finally did reach the crash sites, it was clear that no one could have survived.
4. http://www.un.org/Depts/DPKO.
5. Report of the Secretary General on the UN Observer Mission in Angola, S/1999/49, 17 January 1999, paragraph 39.
6. Security Council Resolution 1229 (1999) of 26 February 1999.
7. "Current Peace-keeping Operations" and "Completed Peace-keeping Operations," prepared by the UN Department of Public Information, April 1997.
8. Rikhye, I. *The United Nations and Peacekeeping,* New York: St. Martin's Press, 1991, pp. 184–197.
9. Gelb, L. "Quelling the Teacup Wars." *Foreign Affairs,* November/December 1994, p. 5.
10. Durch, W. *The Evolution of UN Peacekeeping,* New York: St. Martin's Press, 1993, p. 9.
11. The greater level of cooperation within the Security Council was not limited to peacekeeping but was reflected in other council activities as well. Comparing the years after 1990 to the preceding ones, the number of formal meetings more than tripled, while informal sessions increased by a factor of five. The Council also adopted a far greater number of resolutions each year (an average of 64 between 1990 to 1994 as opposed to 13 annually in the years 1946 to 1989), and its members used their veto power far less (an average of 6 times a year before 1990 but on a total of only 3 occasions between mid-1990 and 1995.) The council also expanded the number of its subsidiary organs from 3 in 1988 to 14 in 1993, of which half were sanctions

committees (UNIDIR: "Managing Arms in Peace Processes: The Issues," New York: United Nations, p. 6).

12. Van Creveld, M. *The Transformation of War,* New York: The Free Press, 1991, p. 60.

13. Fetherston, A. *Towards a Theory of United Nations Peacekeeping,* New York: St. Martin's Press, 1994, p. 21.

14. Goshko, J. "Regional Conflicts Threaten 42 Million Around World, U.S. Study Finds," *Washington Post,* April 5, 1996.

15. Speech by USAID Administrator Brian Atwood, University of Maryland, November 2, 1995.

16. Albright, M. Testimony before the Subcommittee on Foreign Operations, Senate Appropriations Committee, Washington, March 8, 1995.

17. Pearce, D. *Wary Partners—Diplomats and the Media,* Washington: Institute for the Study of Diplomacy, 1995.

18. Modderno, F. "The Growing Clout of NGOs," *Foreign Service Journal,* July 1995, p. 34.

19. Modderno, F., op. cit., p. 35.

20. Boutros-Ghali, B. *Supplement to an Agenda for Peace,* New York: United Nations A/50/60, 1995.

21. Lippman, T. "U.S. May Send up to 5,000 Troops to Africa," *Washington Post,* November 14, 1996.

22. Mills, S. "The Financing of UN Peacekeeping Operations: The Need for Sound Financial Basis," Rikhye 1991:89.

23. Modderno, F., op. cit., p. 37.

24. http://www.un.org/Depts/dpko/faq.htm

25. 1997 World Fact Book, CIA.

26. Robbins, C. "Annan Unveils UN Proposal; It Is Unlikely to Satisfy U.S.," *Wall Street Journal,* July 17, 1997; Pisik, Betsy, "UN Overhaul Disappoints Many," *Washington Times,* July 17, 1997; and Goshko, J., "UN Reform Falls Short, Critics Say: Secretary General Leaves Staff," *Washington Post,* July 17, 1997.

27. Aita, J. "Secretary General Presents Major UN Reform Package" USIA Wireless File, July 16, 1997.

28. Rikhye, I. *The Thin Blue Line,* New Haven: Yale University Press, 1974.

29. Boutros-Ghali, B. *An Agenda for Peace,* A/47/277–S/24111. New York: United Nations, 1992.

30. Quinn, D. *Peace Support Operations and the U.S. Military,* Washington, D.C.: National Defense University Press, 1994.

31. Lewis, W. "Peacekeeping: Whither U.S. Policy?," Quinn 1994:185.

32. Diehl, P. "International Peacekeeping and Conflict Resolution—A Taxonomic Analysis with Implications," *Journal of Conflict Resolution,* Vol. 42, No. 1, February 1998, pp. 33–55.

33. McCain, J. "The Proper United States Role in Peacemaking," Quinn 1994:97.

34. Durch, W. *UN Peacekeeping, American Politics and the Uncivil Wars of the 1990s,* New York: St Martin's Press, 1996, p. 4.
35. Wren, C. "UN, Low on Funds and Successes, To Trim Peace Role," *International Herald Tribune,* November 25, 1995, quoting from a speech on November 2, 1995, by the Secretary General to the Business Council for the United Nations.
36. Author's interview with UN official, February 15, 1996.
37. Kaplan, R. "The Coming Anarchy," *Atlantic Monthly,* February 1994.
38. Druckman, D. and Stern, P. "Evaluating Peacekeeping Missions," *Mershon International Studies Review,* 1997, No. 41, p. 163.
39. Bratt, D. "Assessing the Success of UN Peacekeeping Operations," *International Peacekeeping,* 3(4), 1996, p. 64.

Chapter 2

1. Wiseman, H. "The United Nations and International Peacekeeping: A Comparative Analysis" in *The United Nations and the Maintenance of International Peace and Security,* UNITAR, 1987, pp. 264–99.
2. Fetherston 1994:16.
3. "Current Peace-keeping Operations" and "Completed Peace-keeping Operations," prepared by the UN Department of Public Information, April 1997.
4. Some writers use phrases such as "rankest cowardice" and "criminal irresponsibility" to describe the UN's policies and their failure to prevent the Rwandan genocide. See, for instance Gourevitch, P., "Stonewall Kabila," October 6, 1997, and "Continental Shift," August 4, 1997, *The New Yorker.*
5. Durch 1993:104.
6. Urquhart, B. *A Life in Peace and War,* New York: Harper Row, 1987, p. 133.
7. Ball, G. *The Past Has Another Pattern,* New York: Norton, 1983, p. 227.
8. Ball 1983:93.
9. Durch 1993:12.
10. Ibid., p. 349.
11. Wiseman 1987:289.
12. Rikhye 1974:5.
13. Many date this new level of cooperation to 1987 when indications that attitudes within the Soviet Union were changing were reflected in Gorbachev's speeches.
14. Hume 1994:214.
15. Van Creveld 1991:193.
16. Nordstrom, C. *The Paths to Domination, Resistance and Terror,* Berkeley: University of California Press, 1992, p. 261.
17. Evans, G. "Cooperative Security and Intrastate Conflict," *Foreign Policy,* Fall 1994, p. 4.

18. "Nation building," a term first applied in Latin America during the Cold War, began to be used more broadly to refer to the strengthening of institutions throughout the third world. It elevated peacekeeping from a technique to buy time for warring parties to permanently settle their differences, to the means through which those differences were resolved. It began to lose its meaning as the number of situations to which it was applied grew, and the resulting confusion within the UN caused the organization to lose sight of the limits of what peacekeeping could accomplish. This became especially true in those situations of near anarchy in which there was very little nation on which to build.

19. Speech by Anthony Lake to the TransAfrica Forum, Washington, D.C., June 29, 1995 in U.S. Department of State Dispatch, July 3, 1995, Vol. 6, No. 27, p. 539.

20. Pearce 1995:18.

21. Ibid., p. 24.

22. Mandelbaum, M. "The Reluctance to Intervene" *Foreign Policy,* Summer 1994, p. 14.

23. "The Year in Review 1966: UN Peace Missions," UN Department of Public Affairs, http://www.un.org/Depts/ dpko/yir96/peace96.htm

24. Lewis, P. "UN Authorizes Multinational Force for Albania," *New York Times,* March 29, 1997.

25. S/RES/1101 (1997) of March 28, 1997.

26. Op. cit.

27. Perlez, J. "Strongman in Albania Fights On," *New York Times,* May 3, 1997.

28. Perlez, J. "European Force for Albania Faces New Delays and Uncertainty," *New York Times,* April 4, 1997 and Perlez, J. "Rare Glimpse of Order Stirs Hope in Albanians," *New York Times,* August 17, 1997.

29. Randal, J. "With Mission Left Vague, First European Peacekeepers Arrive in Albania," *Washington Post,* April 16, 1997.

30. Perlez, J. "In Violent and Fearful Mood, Albania Goes to the Polls," *New York Times,* June 29, 1997 and Perlez, J. "Albanian Strongman Orders His Forces to Encircle the Capital," *New York Times,* July 3, 1997.

31. Cody, E. "Albania's New Socialist Prime Minister Vows Stability Without Foreign Troops," *Washington Post,* July 29, 1997.

32. Ibid.

33. Perlez, J., August 17, 1997, op. cit.

34. Walker, P. "Chaos and Caring: Humanitarian Aid Amidst Disintegrating States," *Journal of Humanitarian Assistance,* October 13, 1996, p. 3.

Chapter 3

1. Durch 1993:16.

2. Boutros-Ghali, B. *Supplement to an Agenda for Peace* (A/50/60), paragraph 77.

3. Author interview.

4. "Final Report on the In-Depth Evaluation of Peacekeeping Operation: Start Up Phase," UN Office of Oversight Services, March 17, 1995, paragraph 12.

5. Ibid., paragraph 14.

6. Author interview, October 13, 1995.

7. Hume 1994:11.

8. Skjelsbaek, K. "UN Peacekeeping: Expectations, Limitations and Results: Forty Years of Mixed Experience" in Rikhye 1991:66.

9. Licklider, R. "The Consequences of Negotiated Settlements in Civil Wars, 1945–93," *American Political Science Review,* Vol. 89, No. 3, September 1995, p. 685.

10. Ibid.

11. "Final Report on the In-Depth Evaluation of Peacekeeping Operation: Start Up Phase," UN Office of Oversight Services, March 17, 1995, paragraph 11.

12. Durch 1993:26.

13. Ignatieff, M. "The Hopeless War," *New York Times Book Review,* February 26, 1995.

14. Finnegan, W. "No Peace to Keep," *The New Yorker,* p. 9.

15. Callahan, D. "United It Stands" a review of "United Nations—The First Fifty Years" Meisler, S., New York: Atlantic Monthly Press, 1997, in the *New York Times Book Review,* October 15, 1995.

16. Eliasson, J. "Not UN Failure but Failure to Provide Means for the UN Task," *International Herald Tribune,* August 17, 1995.

17. Weiss in Daniel 1995:10.

18. "Comprehensive Report on Lessons Learned from United Nations Operation in Somalia," Lessons Learned Unit, Department of Peacekeeping Operations, December 1995, paragraph 10.

19. Durch 1993:427.

20. Durch 1993:430.

21. Zunes 1996:233.

22. Zunes 1996:228.

23. Stedman in Daniel 1995:42.

24. Lippman, T., "Support Dries Up for West Sahara's Struggle," Washington Post, December 4, 1995.

25. Zunes 1996:230.

26. Minter 1994:70.

27. Berdal in Daniel 1995:233.

28. Aita, J., "Major Confrontation Brewing over Boutros-Ghali Reelection," USIA Wireless File, June 21, 1996.

29. Sullivan, A. "U.S. Will Oppose a Second Term for U.N. Secretary-General," USIS Wireless File, June 21, 1996.

30. Goshko, J. "Boutros-Ghali Believed Near Bid for Second Term in UN Post," *Washington Post,* February 18, 1996.

31. Crossette, B. "U.S. Campaign Issue: Boutros-Ghali," *International Herald Tribune*, June 18, 1996.

32. Strobel, W. "U.S. Cautiously Explores Opposing Boutros-Ghali," *Washington Times*, June 14, 1996.

33. Crossette, B., op. cit.

34. Goshko, J., op. cit.

35. Boutros-Ghali, B. "Global Leadership After the Cold War," *Foreign Affairs*, March/April 1996, p. 86.

36. Ibid., p. 86.

37. Ibid., p. 91.

38. Ignatieff, M. "Alone with the Secretary-General," *The New Yorker*, August 14, 1995, p. 33.

39. Boutros-Ghali, B. "For the U.N. All Who Suffer Are Equals," *Washington Times*, August 1, 1995.

40. Ocaya-Lakidi, D. "UN and the U.S. Military Roles in Regional Organizations in Africa and the Middle East" in Quinn 1994:167.

41. Author interview, October 13, 1995.

42. Durch 1993:12.

43. Crossette, B., op. cit.

44. Aita, J. "Kofi Annan of Ghana Named New Secretary General of the UN," USIS Wireless File, December 13, 1996.

45. "Kofi Annan's Cautious Style," *New York Times* editorial, February 12, 1997.

46. Sciolino, E. "Despite Critics, New UN Chief Keeps His Style," *New York Times*, February 9, 1997.

47. "The Year in Review 1996: UN Peace Missions," p. 1.

48. Ibid.

49. Harrell and Howe in Daniel 1995:190.

50. Hume, C. "The Secretary-General's Representatives," *SAIS Review*, Summer-Fall 1995, p. 81.

51. Peace and Security Section of the UN's Department of Public Information, http://www.un.org/News/ossg/srsg.htm.

52. Hume, C., op. cit. p. 87.

53. Heininger 1994:35 While Cambodia was at least initially looked at as a success for the UN and Akashi, he went on to considerably less acclaim in peacekeeping in Bosnia though it may not have been entirely of his own making. As Richard Holbrooke describes it: "Akashi had been harshly treated by the press and castigated by critics of the UN for his weakness. But it was not entirely his fault: he was operating under tight constraints imposed by Boutros Ghali. Furthermore, Akashi was virtually ignored by General Janvier and the UN military" ("To End a War," page 200).

54. Author interview, November 1, 1995.

55. Author interview, January 23, 1997.

56. Sahnoun 1994:54–55.

57. Ibid.
58. Durch in Daniel 1995:154.
59. Ibid., p. 156.
60. Ibid., p. 156.
61. Author interview, November 30, 1994.
62. Neack 1995:178.
63. James 1995:246.
64. Neack 1995:186.
65. Author interview, June 16, 1996.
66. Pomfret, J. "Alleged Russian Corruption in Bosnia Worries NATO," *International Herald Tribune,* November 7, 1995.
67. Heininger 1994:76.
68. Author interview, October 10, 1995.
69. Licklider 1995:684.
70. Hoffman, M. "Third-Party Mediation and Conflict Resolution in the Post–Cold War World."
71. Hoffman, op. cit. p. 272.
72. Hume, op. cit. p. 21.
73. Touval, S. "Why the UN Fails," *Foreign Affairs,* September/October 1994, p. 45.
74. Whitman and Bartholomew in Daniel 1995:173.
75. "Final Report on the In-Depth Evaluation of Peacekeeping Operation: Start Up Phase," op. cit., paragraph 49.
76. "Comprehensive Report on Lessons Learned from United Nations Operation in Somalia," op. cit., paragraph 18.
77. Christopher, W. "The United Nations: The Momentum for Reform Must Accelerate," address at the 50th UN General Assembly, September 25, 1995, *U.S. Department of State Dispatch,* October 2, 1995, p. 711.
78. Boutros-Ghali, B. "Supplement to an Agenda for Peace" paragraph 44.
79. Wren, C. "Envision New Force for the UN," *International Herald Tribune,* October 1, 1995.
80. "Vital Force: A Proposal for the Overhaul of the UN Peace Operations System and for the Creation of a UN Legion," Project on Defense Alternatives, Commonwealth Institute, Cambridge, Mass., October 1995.
81. Urquhart, B. "For a UN Volunteer Military Force," *New York Review of Books,* June 10, 1993, p. 3.
82. Lie, T. *In the Cause of Peace,* New York: Macmillan, 1954, p. 98.
83. Urquhart, B. *A Life in Peace and War,* New York: Harper and Row, 1987.
84. Heininger 1994:32.
85. Author interview, November 30, 1995.
86. Shalev, Z. review of *Live from the Battlefield* by Peter Arnett, London: Corgi Books, 1995 in *The South African Journal of International Affairs,* Summer 1996, p. 196.

87. Berdal in Daniel 1995:234.
88. James, A. "Peacekeeping in the post–Cold War Era," *International Journal,* Spring 1995, p. 263.
89. "Managing Arms in Peace Processes: The Issues," UNIDIR, UN: New York, 1996, p. 25.
90. Davies, K. "Mobutu Accepts U.N. Cease-fire Call," *Washington Times,* March 6, 1997.
91. Ibid., p. 25.
92. Boutros-Ghali, B. *Supplement to an Agenda for Peace,* paragraph 33.
93. Durch 1993:12.
94. French, H. "After 6 Years of Civil War, A Lawless Liberia," *New York Times,* February 1, 1996, p. A3.
95. Heininger 1994:9.
96. UN Security Council Resolution 1059 of May 31, 1996.

Chapter 4

1. Minter, W. *Apartheid's Contras,* London: Zed Books, 1994, p. 89.
2. Birmingham, D. *Frontline Nationalism in Angola and Mozambique,* James Curry: London, 1992, p. 41.
3. Anstee M. manuscript, chapter two, p. 12.
4. Lodico, Y. draft of "A Peace That Fell Apart: The United Nations and the War in Angola," in Durch, W. *Peacekeeping, American Policy, and the Uncivil Wars of the 1990s,* New York: St. Martin's Press, 1996, p. 5.
5. Birmingham 1992:66.
6. Minter, W., op. Cit., p. 82.
7. Minter, W., op. cit., p. 93.
8. Ibid.
9. Newitt, M. *A History of Mozambique,* Indiana University Press, Bloomington, 1995, p. 523.
10. Newitt, M., op. cit., p. 524.
11. Hoile, D. *Mozambique—A Nation in Crisis,* Claridge Press, London, 1989, p. 11.
12. The problem of the ideological bias of the writer is frequently encountered. Questions such as who was responsible for Mondlane's and Machel's deaths, the extent of FRELIMO's military operations and success before independence, the strength of rival independence groups, the degree of Rhodesian and South African responsibility for the creation and continued existence of RENAMO, the amount of Malawian, American, and other outside support for RENAMO, and the motivation and depth of its political support among the Mozambican people are all treated remarkably differently. Reports of events seem to depend mainly on the prejudices of the writer, which are so

pervasive that the even-handed and objective observer appears to be the exception.

13. Newitt, M., op. cit., p. 541.
14. Isaacman, A. *Mozambique—From Colonialism to Revolution,* Westview Press, 1983, p. 106.
15. Bender, G. *Angola under the Portuguese—The Myth and the Reality,* London: Heinemann Educational Books, Ltd. 1978, p. 236.
16. Lodico, Y., op. cit., p. 6.
17. Human Rights Watch, "Angola: Arms Trade and Violations of the Laws of War Since the 1992 Elections," Washington, 1994.
18. Edis, R. "Mozambique's Successful Peace Process: An Insider's View," unpublished paper, February 1995, p. 1
19. Barnes, S. "Humanitarian Assistance as a Factor in the Mozambican Peace Negotiations: 1990–1992," unpublished paper, January 1996, p. 2.
20. Birmingham, D., op. cit., p. 68.
21. Flower, K. *Serving Secretly,* London: John Murray, 1987, p. 262.
22. There is considerable debate within the literature as to whether REN-AMO was simply a creation of Rhodesia and South Africa or whether it represented a significant percentage of Mozambicans who were willing to fight against FRELIMO rule. Anderson (1992:161), while oversimplifying, describes this phenomenon: "Some analysts have simply said that Mozambique's entire ruin is due to aggressive action of South Africa. Others say socialism failed and the rebels are an inevitable consequence of Africans trying to rule themselves." The ideological orientation of the writer seems to determine whether he or she is sympathetic to FRELIMO or RENAMO and therefore whether the latter is viewed simply as an instrument of apartheid or a reflection of popular discontent with one-party rule.
23. Minter, W., op. cit., p. 188. The level of external support and the number of RENAMO combatants will probably never be accurately established. Berman (1996:47) cites several sources that put the number of RENAMO soldiers at the time of the handover from Rhodesia to South Africa at between 250 and 500. Yet RENAMO registered 24,648 men in 1993 during the demobilization process. South Africa could have organized a fifty- to one-hundred-fold expansion of RENAMO, or the estimates of 500 or less could be significantly understated. A third alternative is that RENAMO inflated its troop levels with men willing to reap the benefits of immediate demobilization in order to demonstrate it was a large, indigenous, and popularly supported movement. Those writers sympathetic to the government or out to highlight the role of the apartheid regime in South Africa in the destabilization of its neighbors argue for greater that there was greater foreign involvement and less local support than RENAMO will admit to. This question will remain unresolved as there no inclination to examine the

past in Mozambique through some type of truth commission either on the part of the Government or RENAMO.

24. Minter, W., op. cit., p. 283.

25. Simpson (1993:323) described this problem well when he wrote: "Many of the explanations of this period have been put forward by the movement's sympathizers who emphasized the role of external factors, in particular the devastating part played by South African destabilization through the medium of RENAMO. However, more recent works, exemplified by the research of Christian Geffray and Alex Vines, have successfully shifted the focus of enquiry from foreign intervention to the domestic impact of unsuccessful policies, seen now as responsible for creating a groundswell of anti-FRELIMO sentiment which foreign interest were able to capitalise on."

26. Geffray, C. "La Cause des Armes au Mozambique: Anthropolgie d'une Guerre Civile," 1990, Karthala: Paris.

27. Author interview, July 14, 1996. On a reporting trip to Mozambique, a journalist asked Joe Hanlon, a prolific writer and long-time Mozambican expert, where he could find a typical village in which to interview people. Hanlon suggested a town in Inhambane Province that had changed hands several times during the war. The journalist visited it and found no great love for either FRELIMO or RENAMO among the villagers. After RENAMO got 38 percent of the vote in the parliamentary elections of 1994, the journalist wrote that this demonstrated some degree of popular support. According to the journalist, Hanlon wrote to his editor impugning his ability and integrity and tried to get the journalist fired. While Hanlon's effort to discredit an opposing point of view lacks subtlety, it is by no means unique among pro-FRELIMO scholars. Minter writes, "I regard journalists or scholars without knowledge of Portuguese or long-term residence in Angola or Mozambique as less likely sources of reliable information than those who have an intimate acquaintance with the countries" (Minter 1994:79). The vast majority of journalists will, of course, have neither. Almost no major media, other than that owned by the respective governments or an occasional stringer, are going to have a long term presence in countries like Angola and Mozambique that are only rarely the focus of the international press. To the contrary, those foreign journalists, whether employed by the government or not, with long term residence in Mozambique stayed because of ideological sympathy for FRELIMO and not because of the professional challenge. Since they wanted to remain and depended on the government for a visa, even if they were interest in objectivity they could easily be pressured. As a result, pro-government sympathies are constantly reflected in what they write and how they write it.

28. Honwana, J. "Discussion Paper: The International Community, Peacekeeping and Peacebuilding in Mozambique," unpublished paper, p. 16.

29. United Nations, *The UN and Mozambique, 1992–1995,* Blue Books Series, Vol. V, New York: UN, 1995, p. 10.

30. UN and Mozambique, 1995:17.
31. Berman 1996:25.
32. UN and Mozambique, 1995:21.
33. Berman 1996:42.
34. Ibid., p. 39.
35. UN and Mozambique, 1995:22.
36. Williams, A. "In Search of Peace: Negotiations and the Angolan Civil War," Pew Case Studies in International Affairs, Washington: Georgetown University, 1993, p. 9.
37. Ibid., p. 12.
38. Ibid., p. 13.
39. Cleary, S. "Angola—Prospects for Peace," *South African Yearbook of International Affairs 1997,* Johannesburg: South African Institute of International Affairs, 1997, p. 314.
40. Williams, A., op. cit., p. 17.
41. Bicesse Accords, section entitled "Concepts for Resolving the Existing Questions between the Government and UNITA," paragraph 4.
42. UN Reference Paper DPI/1552/AFR/PKO, July 1994, p. 1.
43. Lodico, Y., op. cit. p. 9.
44. Ibid., p. 15.
45. Author interviews.
46. Author interview, February 15, 1996.
47. Anstee, M. manuscript, p. 8.
48. Ibid., p. 5.
49. Author interview.
50. Anstee, M. manuscript, p. 56.
51. Ibid., p. 56.
52. Ibid., p. 58.

Chapter 5

1. Lodico, Y., op., cit. p. 23.
2. "The United Nations and Mozambique, 1992 – 1995," The UN Blue Book Series, Vol. V, New York: United Nations, p. 4.
3. A footnote in one UN research publication put it succinctly: "The sensitivities of the Government likely would have made for a difficult relationship with any SRSG. The selection of Aldo Ajello, who possessed a temperament and operating style not characteristic of a career diplomat, exacerbated the pre-existing tense situation. (His approach and demeanor, however, are also widely credited as a primary reason for the operation's success.)" "Managing Arms in Peace Processes: Mozambique," UN Institute for Disarmament Research, New York 1996, p. 28.

4. Jett 1995:3.
5. Author interview, February 15, 1996.
6. Ibid.
7. Mozambique Information Agency, July 29, 1994, Report on FAM Chief of Staff Press Conference from TELINFORMA No. 378/30.07.94.
8. Report of the Security Council Mission to Mozambique of 7 to 12 August 1994, S/1994/1009, August 29, 1994, paragraph 58.
9. Jett 1995:1.
10. Anstee, M. "Orphan of the Cold War," New York: St. Martin's Press, 1996.
11. Anstee 1996:535.
12. Ibid., p. 541.
13. Ibid., p. 527.
14. Ibid., p. 53.
15. Author interview in Luanda, July 10, 1996.
16. Anstee 1996:51.
17. Anstee, M. "Angola: The Forgotten Tragedy," *International Relations,* December 1993, p. 499.
18. Anstee 1996:39.
19. Ibid., p. 40.
20. Ibid., p. 112 In the manuscript for her book, when crediting the young academic for opening doors, she noted that this was something the UN had never done for her. This comment did not survive to make it into the book.
21. Anstee 1996:503.
22. Ibid., p. 529.
23. Ibid., p. 142.
24. Matloff, J. *Fragments of a Forgotten War,* London: Penguin, 1997, p. 174.
25. "United Nations Angola Verification Mission II," UN document, November 30, 1994, p. 15.
26. Nicoll, R. "UN Feels Heat in Angola," *The Mail & Guardian,* January 31, 1997.
27. Author interviews in Luanda, July 9, 1996.
28. Anstee 1993:527.
29. Lewis 1996:92.
30. Anstee 1993:500.
31. "The United Nations and Mozambique, 1992–1995," p. 3.
32. Ibid., pp. 30–31.
33. General Peace Agreement for Mozambique, Protocol IV, Paragraph II.4.
34. Author interview.
35. Author interview.
36. Jett 1995:3.
37. Lusaka Protocol, Definition of General Principles, paragraph 4.
38. UN Security Council Resolution 976 of February 8, 1995.
39. Author interview in Luanda, July 10, 1996.

40. "Final Report of the Secretary General on the United Nations Operation in Mozambique," S/1994/1449, December 23, 1994, paragraph 19.

41. Security Council Resolution 898, S/RES/898, February 23, 1994.

42. Ajello, A. "The Coordination of Humanitarian Assistance in Mozambique in the Context of the United Nations Peace-keeping Operation," April 26, 1995, p. 2.

43. Final Report of the Secretary General on the UN Operation In Mozambique, S/1994/1449, December 23, 1994, paragraph 20.

44. Jett, D. "Lessons Unlearned—Or Why Mozambique's Successful Peacekeeping Operation Might Not Be Replicated Elsewhere," *Journal of Humanitarian Assistance,* December 5, 1995, paragraph 12.

45. "The United Nations and Mozambique, 1992–1995," paragraph 158.

46. Human Rights Watch Report on Mozambique, December 1995, p. 31.

47. Anstee 1996:71.

48. Lodico, op. cit., p. 28.

49. Anstee 1996:70.

50. Anstee 1996:77.

51. Author interviews and "Report of the Security Council Mission to Mozambique of 7 to 12 August 1994," S/1994/1009, August 29, 1994.

52. Hanlon, J. "Mozambique Peace Process Bulletin," Issue 12—September 1994, p. 1.

53. Anstee, M. "The Experience in Angola, February 1992–June 1993," p. 161 in Whitman 1996.

54. Ajello (April 1995) op cit., p. 8.

55. "Final Report: Consolidated Humanitarian Assistance Programme 1992–94," United Nations Department for Humanitarian Affairs, December 1994, p. 5.

56. Jett, D. "Lessons Unlearned or Why Mozambique's Successful Peacekeeping Operation Won't Be Replicated," *Journal of Humanitarian Assistance,* December 1995 and author interviews in Maputo.

57. UNHCR enjoys a solid reputation and is one of the most respected UN agencies, not just because it brings humanitarian aid to people in desperate situations but because it does so effectively. UNHCR, unlike other UN organizations, enjoys the advantage of having a very well-defined task for a well-defined target population and a measurable result. The population it is to help (refugees) is easily defined, as is the assistance required (basic human needs). The time required is usually also well defined and limited (until they cease being refugees.) If the water, food, shelter, health care and sanitation facilities being provided are insufficient, the results are quickly felt and the refugees, particularly the youngest, begin to die. If more than one refugee under five years of age per 10,000 in that category dies a day, then UNHCR knows it has a problem and has to evaluate its efforts in each area to find the solution. All of these factors make it easy to measure and demonstrate both needs and results, which is usually more difficult with other UN programs.

58. "Minefields, Literal and Metaphoric," *U.S. News and World Report,* February 3, 1997, p. 42. It is interesting to note that this article cited the ICRC and the UN as the source of its statistics. The most common figure used in Mozambique for the number of mines was two million, and many experts thought that figure exaggerated.

59. Boutros-Ghali, B. "The Land Mine Crisis," *Foreign Affairs,* September/October 1994, p. 11.

60. "The United Nations and Mozambique, 1992–1995," p. 52.

61. Author interviews in Maputo and New York.

62. Author interviews in Maputo, New York, and Johannesburg.

63. Author interviews in Johannesburg, October 1997.

64. Author interviews in Maputo and Johannesburg.

65. Author interview. The problem of government inefficiency in dealing with mines is not confined to Mozambique. One demining expert noted that Zimbabwe was believed to have 1.5 million mines spread over 8500 square kilometers. After a government appeal, donors contributed ten million dollars. Two years later the Government had done little and the money remained unspent (Boulden, L. "Landmines: Lack of Will, Money," *Johannesburg Star,* p. 16).

66. Report of the Security Council Mission to Mozambique of 7 to 12 August 1994, S/1994/1009, August 29, 1994, paragraph 67.

67. "Minefields, Literal and Metaphoric," *U.S. News and World Report,* February 3, 1997, p. 42.

68. Sergio Viera, a FRELIMO deputy and former Minister of the Interior, in June 1966 asserted that there were fewer than 500,000 while a report by Africa Watch called the UN figure of 2 million inflated (Durch 1996:298).

69. Author interview.

70. Angola Peace Monitor, Issue No. 3, Vol. IV, November 27, 1997.

71. Author interview, July 8, 1995.

72. Ibid. This estimate problem is global as well as local. The campaign to ban land mines commonly used a figure of 100 million mines worldwide with an additional two million being added each year. Many demining experts disputed such figures, especially the latter one, given the lack of military activity that would be capable of causing such large growth (Heilbrunn, J. "Minefield of Dreams," *New Republic,* October 13, 1997, p. 4).

73. Author interview.

74. Ibid.

75. Author interview in Luanda.

76. "The United Nations and Mozambique, 1992–1995," p. 51 and the General Peace Accord, Protocol IV, Part vi II 2 b.

77. Jett 1995:3.

78. Ajello, A. "The Coordination of Humanitarian Assistance in Mozambique in the Context of ONUMOZ," in Whitman 1996:199.

79. "More Funds for Demobilized Mozambican Soldiers," Panafrican News Agency, January 18, 1997.
80. Anstee 1996:55.
81. Author interviews in Luanda, July 1996.
82. General Peace Accord, Protocol IV, Part vi I 2 d.
83. Berman, op cit., p. 4.
84. Daley, S. "In Mozambique, Guns for Plowshares and Bicycles," *New York Times,* March 2, 1997.
85. "Report on the Secretary General on the United Nations Operation in Mozambique," Document S/24892, December 3, 1992, paragraph 22.
86. Final Report of the President of the Cease-fire Commission, p. 10.
87. Ibid., p. 15.
88. Ibid., p. 12.
89. Daley, op cit. and Berman, op cit., p. 85.
90. Daley, op cit.
91. Berman, op cit., p. 85.
92. Anstee 1996:56.
93. General Peace Accord, Protocol IV, Part VI (I) 3.
94. Ajello, A. "Discussion Paper: The International Community, Peacekeeping and Peacebuilding in Mozambique," p. 34.
95. "The United Nations and Mozambique, 1992–1995," p. 204.
96. Ajello, A. "Discussion Paper: The International Community, Peacekeeping and Peacebuilding in Mozambique," p. 36.
97. "The United Nations and Mozambique, 1992–1995," p. 40.
98. Ibid., p. 40.
99. ONUMOZ Background Information Paper given to the Mission on the Security Council, August 8, 1994, p. 1.
100. Ibid., p. 41.
101. The "international members" of the Supervision and Control Commission (CSC) were the ambassadors from France, Germany, Italy, Portugal, the United Kingdom, the United States, and the OAU.
102. *AWEPA Mozambique Peace Process Bulletin,* Issue 11, August 1994, p. 4 echoed the FRELIMO line. Written by Joe Hanlon, the *Bulletin* is a useful resource, but like Hanlon's other writings is never free from the frequent insertion of his own peculiar political philosophy which lavishly favors the government.
103. Synge, for instance, in his *Mozambique—UN Peacekeeping in Action, 1992–94* seems to accept the point of view that the speech was more about power sharing than moving ahead with the peace process. It is worth noting that in his acknowledgments, he pays special recognition to Joe Hanlon, who attributes Mozambique's lack of development to a conspiracy by donors and international financial institutions (his most recent book on the subject is entitled *Peace Without Profit—How the IMF Blocks Rebuilding in Mozambique*)

and to Paul Fauvet, a long-time employee of the Mozambican Government's propaganda agency, AIM.

104. Author interview.

105. "The United Nations and Mozambique, 1992–1995," p. 41.

106. *Mozambique Peace Process Bulletin,* Issue 10, July 1994.

107. This predictably brought howls of protest from the government media, as well as from what the AWEPA *Mozambique Peace Process Bulletin* referred to as the "opposition press." With the exception of the fax newsletter *Impartial,* however, this "opposition press" consisted of one weekly newspaper and one daily fax newsletter (*Savana* and *Mediafax*). Both of these were staffed largely by former government journalists. While they were occasionally critical of the government, they were rabidly anti-RENAMO. *Impartial,* the only other publication not owned by the government, was equally fervent in its support of RENAMO. In other words reporting that was independent and objective simply did not exist within Mozambique. The attention of the foreign media was too ephemeral to fill the void and often relied on the same local journalists.

108. "The United Nations and Mozambique, 1992–1995," p. 41.

109. Lodico, p. 32.

110. Ibid., p. 32.

111. "The United Nations and the Situation in Angola, May 1991–June 1994," DPI/1552/AFR/PKO, UN: New York, June 1994, p. 3.

112. Anstee 1996:157.

113. Hume, C. *Ending Mozambique's War: The Role of Mediation and Good Offices,* Washington: U.S. Institute of Peace, 1994 (draft manuscript).

114. "The UN and Mozambique, 1992–1995," p. 42.

115. Edis, R. "Mozambique's Successful Peace Process: An Insider's View," p. 5.

116. Ibid., p. 5.

117. "The UN and Mozambique, 1992–1995," p. 33.

118. Letter to the author from Ambassador Edis, February 14, 1995.

119. Anstee 1996:64.

120. Ibid., p. 65.

121. Ibid., p. 65.

122. Ibid., p. 67.

123. Ibid., p. 68.

124. Author interview, July 8, 1996.

125. Anstee 1996:18.

126. Lodico, op. cit., p. 12.

127. Ibid., p. 14.

128. Ibid., p. 20.

129. Ibid., p. 21.

130. Anstee 1996:118.

131. Lodico, op. cit., p. 21.

132. Anstee 1996:90.
133. Ibid., p. 187.
134. Anstee 1996:25.
135. Anstee 1996:38.
136. Ibid., p. 199.
137. UNDP document of November 3, 1994.
138. Jett 1995:4.
139. "The United Nations and Mozambique," p. 61.
140. Ibid., p. 60.
141. See for instance Synge's version of those events that, as with the question of the government of national unity, unquestioningly accepts the version of the government apologists. In so doing he either misinterprets or deliberately distorts the American role by falsely characterizing the message I gave to Dhlakama and his advisors and by minimizing its impact.

Chapter 6

1. Zunes 1996:229.
2. Lodico, op. cit., p. 18.
3. U.S. Department of State, Bureau of Intelligence and Research, unclassified paper, "Conflict Resolution in Africa: Lessons from Angola," April 6, 1993.
4. Lodico, op. cit., p. 18.
5. Author interview, July 16, 1996.
6. Anstee 1996:147.
7. Friedman, T. "African Madness," *New York Times,* January 31, 1996.
8. "Angola: Trying," *The Economist,* July 15, 1995.
9. *Angola Peace Monitor,* Vol. III, Issue 7, March 27, 1997, p. 1.
10. *Angola Peace Monitor,* Vol. III, Issue 5, January 29, 1997.
11. FBIS,"Angola: Savimbi on Quartering of UNITA Troops, Future Role," Luanda Radio Nacional Network, 1900 GMT, March 14, 1996.
12. *Angola Peace Monitor,* Vol. III, Issue 8, April 25, 1997, p. 3.
13. Berman, E. "Managing Arms in Peace Processes: Mozambique," UNIDIR, New York: United Nations, 1996, p. 81.
14. Jett 1995:4.
15. Lodico, op. cit., p. 19.
16. Author interview.
17. Final Report of the President of the Cease-fire Commission, December 5, 1994, p. 16.
18. Ajello, April 1995, op cit., p. 1.
19. Anstee 1996:133.
20. Anstee 1996:124.
21. Anstee 1996:532.

22. Jett 1995:81. Even after it had won the elections, the Mozambican government remained committed to controlling the media. When donors complained about the size of the budget given the Information Ministry when the majority of Mozambicans had no access to either health care or education, the government sought to eliminate the issue without changing anything. It abolished the ministry but created an office under the prime minister with the same bloated budget and functions. The entire independent media consisted of two weekly newspapers (printed on government-owned presses) and two daily fax newsletters that had to compete with the heavily subsidized, government-owned media.
23. Jett 1995:24.
24. U.S. Department of State, "Angola Country Report on Human Rights Practices for 1996," January 30, 1997, p. 1.
25. U.S. State Department, "Angola Human Rights Practices, 1995," March 1996.
26. U.S. Arms Control and Disarmament Agency, "World Military Expenditures and Arms Transfers 1995," p. 111.
27. "Angola: Wealth Amid Poverty," Africa Information Afrique, January 8, 1996.
28. Author interview.
29. Author interview.
30. Human Rights Watch, "Arms Trade and Violations of the Laws of War Since the 1992 Elections," November 1994.
31. Graham, W. "Diamonds Could be Forever in Angola," *Johannesburg Star,* March 19, 1996.
32. "Angola: What's Mine Is Mine," *U.S. News and World Report,* February 17, 1997.
33. Author interview.
34. Washington Post Online World Fact Book.
35. U.S. Arms Control and Disarmament Agency, "World Military Expenditures and Arms Transfers 1995," p. 136.
36. Reno, W. "The Business of War in Liberia," *Current History,* May 1996, p. 215.
37. Shultz, G. *Turmoil and Triumph,* New York: Charles Scribner's Sons, 1993, p. 1124.
38. Ibid., p. 1116.
39. Ibid., p. 1117.
40. "The UN and Mozambique, 1992–1995," p. 68.
41. Anstee 1996:224.
42. Shultz 1993:1118.
43. Rupert, J. "Zaire Reportedly Selling Arms to Angolan Ex-Rebels," *Washington Post,* March 21, 1997, p. A1.
44. Whitelaw, K. "The Wars Behind the War," *U.S. News and World Report,* March 24, 1997, p. 43 and French, H., "Zaire's Power Vacuum Sucks in Neighbors," *The New York Times,* March 9, 1997.
45. French, H. "Support for Mobutu Erodes Further," *New York Times,* May 13, 1997.

46. Abrahamsson, H. and Nilsson, A. *Mozambique: The Troubled Transition—From Socialist Construction to Free Market Capitalism,* London: Zed Books, 1995, p. 46.
47. Wedgwood, R. "Lessons Learned in Peacekeeping: What Worked, What Didn't and Why? Session 6: The Case of Mozambique," informal transcript, June 9, 1995, p. 12.
48. Op. cit., p. 13.

Chapter 7

1. Walker, P. "Chaos and Caring: Humanitarian Aid Amidst Disintegrating States," *Journal of Humanitarian Assistance,* October 13, 1996, p. 1.
2. Scott, N. "Humanitarian Action and Security in Liberia 1989–1994," Occasional Paper #20, Thomas J. Watson Jr. Institute for International Studies, 1995, p. 39.
3. The international press has repeatedly reported on the corruption within ECOMOG, and particularly on the part of Nigerian troops which have always made up the bulk of the force. See for example Randal, J., "Liberian Fighting Raises Doubts on Peace Force," *Washington Post,* April 23, 1996; Friedman, T., *New York Times,* January 21, 1996.
4. Ludden, J. "West African Peacekeepers Falter in Strife-Torn Liberia," *Christian Science Monitor,* May 22, 1996 and French, H. "Liberia War: Nation Adrift," *New York Times,* May 12, 1996.
5. Author interview.
6. Tauxe, J. "Atomized Liberia Worse Than an Emergency," *International Herald Tribune,* May 17, 1966 and "U.S. Deplores Looting In Liberia," U.S. State Department announcement, May 23, 1996.
7. Rupert, J. "A Slim Chance for Liberia," *Washington Post,* January 27, 1997, p. A13.
8. Reuters, "Refugees Are Pawns, Prize in Great Lakes Conflict," 8:06 A.M. EST, December 16, 1996.
9. Rieff, D. "Camped Out," *The New Republic,* November 25, 1996, pp. 26–28.
10. Sullivan, A. "Conditional Approval for U.S. Troops in Zaire Relief Effort," USIS Wireless File, November 13, 1996 and Lippman, T. "U.S. May Send Up to 5,000 Troops to Africa," *Washington Post,* November 14, 1996.
11. Reuters, "Rwandan Refugees Confound U.N. Refugee Agency," 9:47 A.M. EST, December 13, 1996.
12. Duke, L. "Global Team Plans Aid for Refugees Hanging on at Zaire's Front Lines," *Washington Post,* December 2, 1996, p. A15 and Reuters, "France Says Over 500,000 Still Stranded in Zaire," 3:51 P.M. EST, December 20, 1996.
13. Reuters, "Rwandan Refugees Back From Tanzania," 4:17 A.M. EST, December 28, 1996.
14. Drogin, B. "Aid Groups in Rwanda Rethink Mission," *Los Angeles Times,* February 7, 1997.

15. Rieff, D., op. cit., p. 27.
16. Aita, J. "NGO's Appeal to Security Council for Help in Great Lakes," USIA Wireless File, February 13, 1997.
17. Ibid.
18. Solarz, S. and O'Hanlon, M. "Humanitarian Intervention: When Is Force Justified?," *The Washington Quarterly,* Autumn 1997, p. 11.
19. Ibid.
20. Scott, op. cit., p. x.
21. "A Report on the Liberian Peace Process," Africa Policy Information Center, December 28, 1996.
22. Author interview.
23. One USAID official in congressional testimony referred to RENAMO as the Khmer Rouge of Africa. Another former USAID officer, who headed its Office of Foreign Disaster Assistance, described RENAMO's abuse of child soldiers: "As many as 10,000 young boys, most under ten years old, had been forcibly recruited into rebel units and in a demented rite of initiation were forced to kill their own parents. By the time the boys entered early adolescence, a large number of them had killed as many as eight to ten people during systematic atrocities ordered by the rebel commanders" (Natsios 1997:164).
24. Barnes, S. "Humanitarian Assistance as a Factor in the Mozambican Peace Negotiations: 1990–1992," draft paper.
25. Ibid., p. 5.
26. Ibid., p. 2.
27. Ibid., p. 3.
28. Scott, op. cit., p. 32.
29. Prendergast, J. *Frontline Diplomacy—Humanitarian Aid and Conflict in Africa,* Boulder: Lynne Rienner Publishers, 1996.
30. Natsios, A. *U.S. Foreign Policy and the Four Horsemen of the Apocalypse: Humanitarian Relief in Complex Emergencies,* Westport: Praeger, 1997, p. 142.
31. Ibid., p. 143.
32. Ibid., p. 144.
33. Ibid., p. 161.
34. Ibid., p. 161.
35. Harriss 1995:4.
36. Durch 1996:6.

Chapter 8

1. Diehl, P. *International Peacekeeping,* Baltimore: Johns Hopkins University Press, 1993 and Durch 1996:17.
2. Ghali in Durch 1993:124.
3. Op. cit.

4. Maren, M., "Somalia: Whose Failure?" *Current History,* May 1996, p. 202.
5. Augelli, E. and Murphy, C. "Lessons of Somalia for Future Multilateral Assistance Operations," *Global Governance,* Volume 1:3 1995, p. 342.
6. "United Nations Assistance Mission for Rwanda," UN Department of Public Affairs background paper.
7. Op. cit.
8. "The Year in Review 1996: UN Peace Missions," UN Department of Public Affairs.
9. Op. cit.
10. Op. cit.
11. UN Department of Public Information, "Current Peace-keeping Operations." The six are UNMOGIP (India/Pakistan), UNFICYP (Cyprus), UNDOF (Golan Heights), UNIKOM (Iraq/Kuwait), UNIFIL (Lebanon), and UNTSO (Middle East).
12. Ghali in Durch 1993:128.
13. Boutros-Ghali, B. "Supplement to the Agenda for Peace," paragraph 52.
14. Schear, J. in Durch 1996:175.
15. Op. cit.
16. Op. cit.
17. Schear, J. in Durch 1996:172.
18. Shawcross, W. "Tragedy in Cambodia," *New York Review of Books,* November 14, 1996, p. 41.
19. Smith, J. "$3 Billion Effort Fails to Pacify Cambodia," *Washington Post,* June 14, 1997, p. A13.
20. Smith, J., op. cit.
21. Ibid.
22. Mydans, S. "Cambodia Faction Claims Victory as Fighting Halts," *New York Times,* July 7, 1997.
23. Richberg, K. "Cambodia: U.N. Success Story Fouled," *Washington Post,* July 13, 1997, p. A1.
24. Thayer, N. "Drug Suspects Bankroll Cambodian Coup Leader," *Washington Post,* July 23, 1997.
25. Branigin, W. "Hun Sen Gambles Cambodia Can Withstand Sanctions," *Washington Post,* July 12, 1997, p. A14.
26. Branigin, W., op. cit.
27. See for instance the work of the UN Research Institute for Social Development (UNRISD) in its Rebuilding War-torn Societies Project; Del Castillo, G. "Post-Conflict Peace-Building: The Challenge to the UN," *Cepal Review,* August 1995; Barakat, S. and Hoffman, B. "Post-Conflict Reconstruction: Key Concepts, Principal Components and Capabilities," paper presented at the International Colloquium on Post-Conflict Reconstruction Strategies, Vienna, June 1995; "An Inventory of Post-conflict Peace-building Activities" prepared by the Task Force on Post-Conflict Peace-Building.

28. Del Castillo, G. "Post-Conflict Peace-Building: The Challenge to the UN," *Cepal Review,* August 1995.
29. Op. cit.
30. Op. cit., paragraph 121.
31. UNRISD, "Rebuilding War-Torn Societies," An Action Research Project on Problems of International Assistance in Post-Conflict Situations, Geneva, March 1995.
32. "The United Nations and Mozambique, 1992–1995," p. 302.
33. Jett 1996:1.
34. U.S. Department of State, "Mozambique Human Rights Practices, 1995," March 1996.
35. U.S. Department of State, "Mozambique Country Report on Human Rights Practices for 1998."
36. "Mozambique's Rocky Road to Democracy," *Afrika News Network,* June 24, 1997.
37. Ibid.
38. UN Research Institute for Social Development, Programme for Strategic and International Security Studies, Mozambique Case Study, "Mocambique: Imagem do Pais," Maputo, January 5, 1996.
39. Ibid.
40. Berman, E. *Managing Arms in Peace Processes: Mozambique,* UNIDIR/96/22, New York: United Nations Institute for Disarmament Research, 1996, p. xvii.
41. UN Security Council Resolution 976 (1995) of February 8, 1995, paragraph 6.
42. Angola Country Report on Human Rights Practices for 1996, U.S. Department of State, January 30, 1997, pp. 5–6.
43. "Country Reports on Human Rights Practices for 1996," U.S. Department of State, Washington: U.S. Government Printing Office, 1997, p. 187.
44. Op. cit., p. 7.
45. Author interview.
46. Security Council Resolution 1106 (1997) of April 17, 1997.
47. Corey, C. "Extraordinary Progress Towards Unity Seen in Angola," USIS Wireless File, April 24, 1997.
48. Angola Peace Monitor, Volume III, Issue 9, May 30, 1997.
49. Lippman, T. "Angolan Armor Joins Drive in Zaire, U.S. Officials Say," *Washington Post,* May 2, 1997, p. A1; French, H. "Support for Mobutu Erodes Further," *New York Times,* May 13, 1997; Rupert, J. "Angolan Role Raises Ante in Zairian Strife," *Washington Post,* March 16, 1997, p. A27; Rupert, J. "Casualties Illustrate Foreign Role in Zaire," *Washington Post,* March 18, 1997, p. A13.
50. Daley, S. "Zaire's Fall Jolts a Neighbor Nation's Fragile Peace," *New York Times,* June 8, 1997; Phillips, B. "War Cries from Angola," *The Mail &*

Guardian, June 6, 1997; Angola Peace Monitor, Volume III, Issue 9, May 30, 1997.

51. All Africa Press Service, "Efforts Underway to Save Angola's Peace," June 16, 1997; Gordon, C. "Angola in a State of Near-War," *The Mail & Guardian,* June 20, 1997; Munaku, T. "Angola Seen Sliding Back Into War," Panafrican News Agency, June 27, 1997.
52. *Angola Peace Monitor,* Volume III, Issue 10, June 30, 1997.
53. Op. cit.
54. Daley, S. "Angola Peace Effort Headed for Crisis," *New York Times,* August 1, 1997 and Gordon, C. "Savimbi and Dos Santos Warn of New Angolan War," *The Mail & Guardian,* August 1, 1997.
55. UN Security Council Resolution 1118 (1997).
56. Report of the Secretary General on UNAVEM III, S/1997/438, June 5, 1997, paragraph 14.
57. Op. cit., Addendum paragraphs 1 and 2.
58. Op. cit., paragraph 32.
59. *Angola Peace Monitor,* Vol. III, Issue 8, April 25, 1997.
60. Op. cit.
61. Author interview in Luanda.
62. *Angola Peace Monitor,* Volume III, Issues 9, 10 and 11.
63. *Angola Peace Monitor,* Volume III, Issue 11, July 17, 1997.
64. Progress Report of the Secretary General on the United Nations Observer Mission in Angola (MONUA), S/1997/640 of August 13, 1997, paragraph 38.
65. Reuters, "Angolan Ex-Rebels Quit Town, Win Delay," *Washington Post,* September 30, 1997, p. A16.
66. Aita, J. "Security Council Stops New Sanctions on UNITA," USIS Wireless File, September 30, 1997.
67. *Angola Peace Monitor,* Issue No.2, Vol. IV, November 3, 1997.
68. Angola Peace Monitor, Issue No.3, Vol. IV, November 27, 1997.
69. Duke, L. "Angola Said to Sway War Next Door," *Washington Post,* October 15, 1997, p. A23.
70. UNAVEM II, UN document of November 30, 1994.
71. Schmidt, S. "DNC Donor With an Eye on Diamonds," *Washington Post,* August 2, 1997, p. A1.
72. S/1997/640 of August 13, 1997.
73. "Toward War, Again, in Angola," *Washington Post,* August 13, 1997, p. A20.

Chapter 9

1. Solarz and O'Hanlon suggest the death rate should exceed the murder rate in the United States although it is unclear how this would work in practice

since there is never statistical certainty about casualties in the midst of a civil war. See Solarz, S. and O'Hanlon, M. "Humanitarian Intervention: When Is Force Justified?" *The Washington Quarterly,* Autumn 1997.

2. "The Year in Review 1996: UN Peace Missions," http://www.un.org/Depts/dpko/yir96/peace96.htm.

3. Applebaum, A. "Is the UN Really Necessary?" *The Spectator,* July 31, 1995.

4. USIS Wireless File, "Richardson Remarks on New UN Reform Package" and "U.S. Gives UN Reform Plan Tentative Stamp of Approval," July 16, 1997 and "U.S. Official Praises Annan's UN Reform Efforts," August 1, 1997.

5. Pisik, B. "UN Overhaul Disappoints Many," *Washington Times,* July 17, 1997, and Robbins, C. "Annan Unveils UN Proposal; It Is Unlikely to Satisfy U.S.," *Wall Street Journal,* July 17, 1997.

6. Crossette, B. "Despite Assurances, UN Workers Fear Downsizing," *New York Times,* July 18, 1997.

7. Goshko, J. "UN Reform Hinges on Competing Interests," *Washington Post,* July 21, 1997.

8. Comments by Ghanian Ambassador Jacob Wilmot as quoted in USIS Wireless File, "Secretary General Presents Major UN Reform Package," July 16, 1997.

9. Muller, J. W. "The Reform of the United Nations," New York: Oceana Publications, 1992.

10. "Comprehensive Review of the Whole Question of Peacekeeping Operations in all their Aspects," Report of the Special Committee on Peacekeeping Operations, A/51/130 of May 7, 1996, paragraph 7.

11. "The Lessons Learned Unit," http://www.un.org/Depts/dpko-/llu2.htm.

12. UN Press Release SC/6261 of August 30, 1996.

13. Ibid.

14. "Supplement to an Agenda for Peace," paragraph 77.

15. Gamba 1995:50.

16. "Report of the Special Committee on Peace-keeping Operations," A/51/130 of May 7, 1996.

17. Rohter, L. "Haiti's Woes Persist as UN Troops Depart," *New York Times,* December 4, 1997.

18. UN Security Council Press Release SC/6410 of August 14, 1997.

19. Ibid.

20. Ibid., p. 4.

21. Organization for Security and Cooperation in Europe, Western European Union, European Union, and the North Atlantic Treaty Organization.

22. Ibid., p. 1.

23. UN Press Releases GA/SPD/96 of November 18, 1996, and GA/PK/145 of April 10, 1997.

24. The current Secretary of State, when she was Ambassador to the UN, paraphrasing the American expression "mean as a junk yard dog," referred to the

Office of Internal Oversight after its first year of existence as a "junk yard puppy," leaving the impression it lacked teeth and aggressiveness.

25. Crossette, B. "In War on Corruption and Waste, UN Confronts Well-Entrenched Foe," *International Herald Tribune,* November 3, 1997.

26. Lindstrom, G. "Building and Developing a National Capacity," http://www.un.org/Depts/Landmine/ NewsLetter/2.

27. Author interviews.

28. Synge 1997:174. Synge's employment as a UN consultant may explain his enthusiasm for a strategy that clearly is not key to successful peacekeeping.

29. Crossette, B. "In War on Corruption and Waste, UN Confronts Well-Entrenched Foe," *International Herald Tribune,* November 3, 1997, p. 5.

30. Ibid.

31. Hume 1994:53.

32. Author interview, February 13, 1997.

33. Statement to the Special Meeting of the General Assembly on Reform, July 16, 1997, paragraph 115.

34. Sanderson 1995:33.

35. "Supplement to an Agenda for Peace," UN A/50/60-S/1995/1, January 3, 1995, paragraph 46.

36. Sanderson, J. "UNTAC: Debriefing and Lessons—The Military Component View," *International Peacekeeping,* February–May 1995, p. 32.

37. Righter, R. *Utopia Lost: The United Nations and World Order,* New York: Twentieth Century Fund Press, 1995, p. 339.

38. Sanderson 1995:33.

39. Goshko, J., op. cit.

40. Chayes, A. "Beyond Reform: Restructuring for More Effective Conflict Intervention," *Global Governance,* May–August 1997, p. 117.

41. Flores, T. "ONUSAL—A Precedent for Future UN Missions?" *International Peacekeeping,* December 1994–January 1995, p. 5.

42. Aspen Institute, "Honoring Human Rights and Keeping the Peace—Lessons from El Salvador, Cambodia and Haiti," p. 5.

43. Flores 1994:5.

44. Ibid.

45. Ibid.

46. Shawcross, op. cit., p. 46.

47. Shawcross, op. cit., p. 45.

48. Makinda, S. "Sovereignty and International Security: Challenges for the UN," *Global Governance,* May–August 1996, p. 164.

49. Ibid., p. 165.

50. Reuters, 2330 GMT, December 17, 1996.

51. Durch, W. *Handbook on UN Peace Operations,* Washington: Henry L. Stimson Center, 1995, p. 12.

52. Crossette, B. "US Effort to Reduce Its UN Dues Dies," *New York Times,* December 19, 1997.

53. Rupert, J. "U.S. Troops Teach Peacekeeping to Africans," *Washington Post,* September 26, 1997, page A16.

54. Hartnack, M. "OAU Peacekeeping Plan," *Business Day,* October 22, 1997, p. 12.

55. UN Press Release NGO/300 PI/1033 of September 15, 1997

56. Rupert, J. "Acting More Independently, African Nations Quicker to Intervene," *Washington Post,* October 21, 1997, page A14.

57. UN Press Release GA/SPD/96 of November 18, 1996.

Selected Bibliography

Abrahamsson, H. and Nilsson, A. *Mozambique: The Troubled Transition,* London: Zed Books, 1995.

Action for Southern Africa. *Angola Peace Monitor.*

Ajello, A. "Contribution and Comments on the Paper on New or Restored Democracies," unpublished paper.

———. "Lessons Learned in Peacekeeping: What Worked, What Didn't and Why?—The Case of Mozambique," unpublished transcript, June 9, 1995.

———. "The Coordination of Humanitarian Assistance in Mozambique in the Context of the United Nations Peacekeeping Operation," unpublished paper.

———. "The Peace Process in Mozambique," unpublished paper, August 8, 1995.

Alden, C. "Mozambique: An Abiding Dependency," in *Southern Africa at the Cross-roads,* Larry Benjamin and Chris Gregory, eds., Johannesburg: Justified, 1992.

———. and Simpson, M. "Mozambique: A Delicate Peace," *JMAS* 31:1 March 1993.

Anstee, M. *Orphan of the Cold War—The Inside Story of the Collapse of the Angolan Peace Process, 1992–93,* New York: St. Martin's Press, 1996.

Applebaum, A. "Is the UN Really Necessary?," *The Spectator,* July 31, 1995.

Aspen Institute, "Honoring Human Rights and Keeping the Peace—Lessons from El Salvador, Cambodia and Haiti," Aspen Institute, 1996.

AWEPA, Mozambique Peace Process Bulletin 1993–1995.

Augelli, E. and Murphy, C. "Lessons of Somalia for Future Multilateral Assistance Operations," *Global Governance,* Vol 1:3 1995.

Ball, G. *The Past Has Another Pattern,* New York: Norton, 1983.

Bender, G. *Angola Under the Portuguese—The Myth and the Reality,* London: Heinemann Educational Books, 1978.

Birmingham, D. *Frontline Nationalism in Angola and Mozambique,* London: James Curry, 1992

Black, D. "Widening the Spectrum: Regional Organizations in Peacekeeping Operations," *Peacekeeping & International Relations,* May/June 1996, p. 7.

Black, R. *Angola,* World Bibliographical Series, Vol. 151, Oxford: Clio Press, 1992.

Bowen, M. "Beyond Reform: Adjustment and Political Power in Contemporary Mozambique," *Journal of Modern African Studies,* 1992, pp. 255–79.

Boutros-Ghali, B. "Global Leadership after the Cold War," *Foreign Affairs*, March/April 1996.

———. "Supplement to An Agenda for Peace," New York: UN, 1995.

———. "An Agenda for Peace," New York: UN, 1992.

———. "For the UN All Who Suffer Are Equals," *Washington Times*, August 17, 1995.

———. "Ways to Improve the United Nations," *International Herald Tribune*, August 17, 1995.

Boutwell, J., Klare, M. T., and Reed, L. *Lethal Commerce: The Global Trade in Small Arms and Light Weapons*, Cambridge, MA: American Academy of Arts and Sciences, 1995.

Bratt, D. "Defining Peacekeeping Success: The Experience of UNTAC," *Peacekeeping & International Relations*, July/August 1996.

———. "Assessing the Success of UN Peacekeeping Operations," *International Peacekeeping*, 3(4), 1996.

———. "Explaining Peacekeeping Performance: The UN in Internal Conflicts," *International Peacekeeping*, 4(3), 1997.

Carlsson, I. "The UN at 50: A Time to Reform," *Foreign Policy*, Fall 1995.

Chayes, A. "Beyond Reform: Restructuring for More Effective Conflict Intervention," *Global Governance*, May-August 1997.

Childers, E. and Urquhart, B. *Development Dialogue*, "A World in Need of Leadership—Tomorrow's United Nations," 1990:1–2; "Towards a More Effective United Nations," 1991:1–2; "Renewing the United Nations System," 1994:1, Ford Foundation.

Christopher, W. "The United Nations: The Momentum for Reform Must Accelerate," address at the 50th UN General Assembly, September 25, 1995.

Cilliers, J. and Mills, G. *Peacekeeping in Africa—Volume 2*, Braamfontein: South African Institute of International Affairs, 1995.

Clarke, W. and Herbst, J. "Somalia and the Future of Humanitarian Intervention," *Foreign Affairs*, March/April 1996.

Cleary, S. "Angola—Prospects for Peace?," *South African Yearbook of International Affairs 1997*, South African Institute of International Affairs, 1997.

Cole, B. *The Elite: The Story of the Rhodesian Special Services*, Transkei: Three Knights Publishing, 1984.

Committee on Global Governance, *Our Global Neighborhood*, Oxford: Oxford University Press 1995.

Crocker, C. *High Noon in Southern Africa*, New York: Norton, 1992.

Daniel, D. *Beyond Traditional Peacekeeping*, New York: St. Martin's Press, 1995.

della Rocca, R. *Mozambico—Dalla Guerra Alla Pace*, Torino: Edizioni San Paolo, 1994.

Department of State, *United States Participation in the United Nations*, Washington: U.S. Government Printing Office, 1995.

Diehl, P. *International Peacekeeping,* Baltimore: Johns Hopkins University Press, 1993.

Diehl, Paul, et al., "International Peacekeeping and Conflict Resolution—A Taxonomic Analysis with Implications," *Journal of Conflict Resolution,* Vol. 42, No. 1, February 1998, pp. 33–55.

Dobbins, J. "Haiti: A Case Study in Post–Cold War Peacekeeping," speech at Institute for Study of Diplomacy, Georgetown University, September 21, 1995

Druckman, D. and Stern, P. "Evaluating Peacekeeping Missions," *Mershon International Studies Review,* 1997.

Durch, W. *The Evolution of UN Peacekeeping,* New York: St. Martin's Press, 1993.

———. *UN Peacekeeping, American Politics, and the Uncivil Wars of the 1990s,* New York: St. Martin's Press, 1996.

Eban, A. "The UN Idea Revisited," *Foreign Affairs,* September/October 1995.

Edis, R. "Mozambique's Successful Peace Process; An Insider's View," unpublished paper.

Eliasson, J. "Not UN Failure but Failure to Provide Means for the UN Task," *IHT,* August 17, 1995.

Erskine, E. *Mission with UNIFIL,* London: Hurst & Company, 1989.

Evans, G. "Cooperative Security and Intrastate Conflict," *Foreign Policy,* Fall 1994.

Falk, P. and Campbell, K. "The United States, Soviet Union, Cuba and South Africa in Angola: The Quagmire of Four Party Negotiations, 1981–88," Pew Case Studies in International Affairs, Georgetown University, 1988.

———. "The United States, Soviet Union, Cuba and South Africa in Angola: Negotiator's Nightmare; Diplomat's Dilemma, 1974–80," Pew Case Studies in International Affairs, Georgetown University, 1988.

Fetherston, A. *Towards a Theory of United Nations Peacekeeping,* New York: St. Martin's Press, 1994.

Finnegan, W. *A Complicated War,* Berkeley: University of California Press, 1992.

Freedom House. "Freedom in the World—The Annual Survey of Political Rights and Civil Liberties, 1994–95."

Freeman, C. "The Angola/Namibia Accords," *Foreign Affairs,* Summer 1989.

Fromuth, P. *A Successor Vision: The United Nations of Tomorrow,* Lanham: University Press of America, 1988.

Geffray, C. *La Cause des Armes au Mozambique,* Paris: Credu-Karthala, 1990.

Gersony, R. "Summary of Mozambican Refugee Accounts of Principally Conflict-Related Experience in Mozambique: Report Submitted to Ambassador Moore and Dr. Chester A. Crocker," Department of State Bureau for Refugee Programs, April 1988.

Hampson, F. O. *Nurturing Peace,* Washington: United States Institute of Peace Press, 1996.

Hanlon, J. *Apartheid's Second Front,* London: Penguin, 1986.

———. *Mozambique: Who Calls the Shots?* London: James Curry, 1991.

Hare, P. *Angola's Last Best Chance for Peace,* Washington: U.S. Institute of Peace Press, 1998.

Harriss, J. *The Politics of Humanitarian Intervention,* London: Pinter, 1995.

Heininger, J. *Peacekeeping in Transition—The United Nations in Cambodia,* New York: Twentieth Century Fund Press, 1994.

Henkin, A. *Honoring Human Rights and Keeping the Peace—Lessons from El Salvador, Cambodia, and Haiti,* Washington: The Aspen Institute, 1995.

Higdon, S. "Angola: Conflict Resolution and Peace-building," London: Saferworld, September 1996.

Hirsch, J. and Oakley, R. *Somalia and Operation Restore Hope—Reflections on Peacemaking and Peacekeeping,* Washington: United States Institute of Peace Press, 1995.

Hiscocks, R. *The Security Council—A Study in Adolescence,* London: Longman, 1983.

HMSO *Wider Peacekeeping,* 1995.

Hoffman, M. *Dilemmas of World Politics: International Issues in a Changing World,* Oxford: Clarendon Press, 1992.

Holbrooke, R. *To End a War,* New York: Random House, 1998.

Honwana, J. "Peacekeeping and Peacebuilding: Two Faces of the Same Coin," *Track Two,* March/June 1995.

Howe, H. "ECOMOG and Its Lessons for Regional Peacekeeping," unpublished paper.

Howe, J. "The United States and United Nations in Somalia: The Limits of Involvement," *The Washington Quarterly,* Summer 1995.

Human Rights Watch, *Conspicuous Destruction—War, Famine and the Reform Process in Mozambique,* New York: Human Rights Watch, 1992.

———. Angola: Arms Trade and Violations of the Laws of War Since the 1992 Elections, New York: Human Rights Watch, 1994.

Hume, C. "The Secretary General's Representatives," *SAIS Review,* Summer-Fall 1995.

———. *The United Nations, Iran and Iraq—How Peacekeeping Changed,* Bloomington: Indiana University Press, 1994.

———. *Ending Mozambique's War: The Role of Mediation and Good Offices,* Washington: U.S. Institute of Peace, 1994.

Ignatieff, M. "Alone with the Secretary General," *New Yorker,* August 14, 1995.

———. "The Hopeless War," *New York Times Book Review,* February 26, 1995.

Isaacman, A. and B. *Mozambique: From Colonialism to Revolution, 1900–1982,* Boulder: Westview, 1982.

James, A. "Peacekeeping in the Post–Cold War Era," *International Journal,* Spring 1995.

Jett, D. "Lessons Unlearned or Why Mozambique's Successful Peacekeeping Operation Won't Be Replicated," *Journal of Humanitarian Assistance,* December 1995.

———. "Cementing Democracy: Institution-Building After the Mozambican Elections," *Harvard International Review,* Fall 1995.

Kaplan, I. *Area Handbook for Mozambique,* Washington: U.S. Government Printing Office, 1977.

Kaplan, R. "The Coming Anarchy," *Atlantic Monthly,* February 1994.

Kapuscinski, R. *Another Day of Life,* London: Pinter, 1988.

Kennedy, P. and Russett, B. "Reforming the United Nations," *Foreign Affairs,* September/October 1995.

Kitchen, H. *Angola, Mozambique and the West,* New York: Praeger, 1987.

Kyle, S. "Economic Reform and Armed Conflict in Mozambique," *World Development,* Vol. 19, No. 6, pp. 637–49, 1991.

Lewis, W. *Military Implications of United Nations Peacekeeping Operations,* Washington: National Defense University, 1993.

Licklider, R. "The Consequences of Negotiated Settlements in Civil Wars, 1945–1993," *American Political Science Review,* September 1995.

Lind, M. "Twilight of the UN," *New Republic,* October 30, 1995.

Lippman, T. "U.S. May Send up to 5,000 Troops to Africa," *Washington Post,* November 14, 1996.

Lodico, Y. "The United Nations Angolan Verification Mission (UNAVEM II) Prospects for the Next Mission," draft of "A Peace That Fell Apart," Durch:1996.

Lyons, T. "Somalia—State Collapse, Multilateral Intervention, and Strategies for Political Reconstruction," Brookings Occasional Papers, The Brookings Institution, 1995.

Mackinlay, J. and Chopra, J. "Second Generation Multinational Operations," *The Washington Quarterly,* Summer 1992.

Maier, K. *Angola: Promises and Lies,* London: Serif, 1996.

Makinda, S. "Sovereignty and International Security: Challenges to the UN," *Global Governance,* May-August 1996.

Mandelbaum, M. "The Reluctance to Intervene," *Foreign Policy,* Summer 1994.

Marcum, J. The Angolan Revolution, Cambridge MA: MIT Press, 1969, 1978.

Maren, M. "Somalia: Whose Failure?," *Current History,* May 1996.

Matloff, J. *Fragments of a Forgotten War,* London: Penguin, 1997.

Mazula, B. *Mocambique—Eleicoes, Democracia e Desenvolvimento,* Maputo: Inter-Africa Group, 1995.

Meisler, S. "Dateline UN: A New Hammarskjold?," *Foreign Policy,* Spring 1995.

Metz, S. *The Future of the United Nations: Implications for Peace Operations,* Carlisle: Strategic Studies Institute, 1993.

Minter, W. Operation Timber: Pages from the Savimbi Dossier, Trenton: Africa World Press, 1988.

———. Apartheid's Contras—An Inquiry into the Roots of War in Angola and Mozambique, London: Zed Press, 1994.

Modderno, F. "The Growing Clout of NGOs," *Foreign Service Journal,* July 1995.

Muller, J. *The Reform of the United Nations,* New York: Oceana Publications, 1992.

National Democratic Institute for International Affairs. *The United Nations and Namibia,* Washington, D.C., 1990.

Natsios, A. *U.S. Foreign Policy and the Four Horsemen of the Apocalypse,* Westport: Praeger, 1997.

Neack, L. "UN Peacekeeping: In the Interest of Community or Self?," *Journal of Peace Research,* May 1995.

Newitt, M. *A History of Mozambique,* Bloomington: Indiana University Press, 1995.

Okuma, T. *Angola in Ferment,* Boston: Beacon Press, 1962.

Pakenham, T. *The Scramble for Africa,* New York: Random House, 1991.

Pearce, D. *Wary Partners—Diplomats and the Media,* Washington, D.C.: Congressional Quarterly Inc., 1995.

Picco, G. "The UN and the Use of Force," *Foreign Affairs,* September/October 1994.

Quinn, D. *Peace Support Operations and the U.S. Military,* Washington, D.C.: National Defense University Press, 1994.

Ratner, S. *The New UN Peacekeeping: Building Peace in Lands of Conflict after the Cold War,* New York: St. Martin's Press, 1995.

Reno, W. "The Business of War in Liberia," *Current History,* May 1996.

Rieff, D. "An Age of Genocide," *The New Republic,* January 29, 1996.

Righter, R. *Utopia Lost: The United Nations and World Order,* New York: Twentieth Century Fund Press, 1995.

Rikhye, I. and Harbottle, M. *The Thin Blue Line—International Peacekeeping and Its Future,* New Haven: Yale University Press, 1974.

Rikhye, I. *The Theory and Practice of Peacekeeping,* New York: St. Martin's Press, 1984.

Rikhye, I. and Skjelsbaek, K. *The United Nations and Peacekeeping—The Lessons of 40 Years of Experience,* New York: St. Martin's Press, 1991.

Roo Lon, C. *Foreign Intervention in African Conflicts: A Case Study of the Angolan Conflict,* University of Georgia, 1989.

Roper, J. *Keeping the Peace in the Post–Cold War Era: Strengthening Multilateral Peacekeeping,* New York: Trilateral Commission, 1993.

Russell, F. "The Dilemma of Humanitarian Assistance in Modern Peacekeeping," *Peacekeeping and International Relations,* March/April 1996.

Russett, B. "Ten Balances for Weighing UN Reform Proposals," *Political Science Quarterly,* Summer 1996.

———. and Sutterlin, J. "The UN in a New World Order," *Foreign Affairs,* Spring 1991.

Sahnoun, M. *Somalia: The Missed Opportunities,* Washington, D.C.: United States Institute of Peace Press, 1994.

Sanderson, J. "UNTAC: Debriefing and Lessons—The Military Component View," *International Peacekeeping,* February-March 1995.

Savimibi, J. *Por um Futuro Melhor,* Lisbon: Nova Nordica, 1986.

Shaw, M. and Cilliers, J. *South Africa and Peacekeeping in Africa—Volume 1,* Johannesburg: Institute for Defence Policy, 1995.

Shawcross, W. "Tragedy in Cambodia," *New York Review of Books,* November 14, 1996.

Shultz, G. *Turmoil and Triumph,* New York: Macmillan, 1993.

Simpson, M. "Foreign and Domestic Factors in the Transformation of Frelimo," *The Journal of Modern African Studies* 31, 2(1993), Cambridge University Press.

Smock, D. and Crocker, C. *African Conflict Resolution—The U.S. Role in Peacemaking,* Washington, D.C.: U.S. Institute of Peace, 1995.

Snider, D. *The United Nations at Fifty: Sovereignty, Peacekeeping, and Human Rights,* Washington, D.C.: Center for Strategic and International Studies, 1995.

Solarz, S. and O'Hanlon, M. "Humanitarian Intervention: When Is Force Justified?," *The Washington Quarterly,* Autumn 1997.

Sullivan, J. *Embassies Under Siege,* Washington, D.C.: Brassey's, 1995.

Synge, R. *Mozambique—UN Peacekeeping In Action, 1992–94,* Washington, D.C.: United States Institute of Peace Press, 1997.

Talbott, S. "The Case for the U.S. in the UN," speech at Henry L. Stimson Center, Washington, D.C., October 3, 1995.

Touval, S. "Why the UN Fails," *Foreign Affairs,* September/October 1994.

UN Economic and Social Council. "Final Report on the In-depth Evaluation of Peacekeeping Operations," March 1995.

———. "In-depth Evaluation of Peacekeeping Operations: Termination Phase," February 1996.

UNHCR. *The State of the World's Refugees 1995,* New York: Oxford University Press, 1995.

UN Department of Peacekeeping Operations. "Comprehensive Report on Lessons Learned from United Nations Operation in Somalia," December 1995.

UNIDIR. "Managing Arms in Peace Processes: Somalia," New York: 1995.

———. "Small Arms and Intra-State Conflicts," March 1995.

UN Department of Public Information. "The United Nations and the Situation in Angola, May 1991-June 1994," reference paper.

———. UN Information Notes, "United Nations Peacekeeping Update: May 1994."

UN Research Institute for Social Development. "Mocambique: Imagem Do Pais," Mozambique Case Study, January 5, 1996.

Urquhart, B. "The United Nations and Future Peace," *SAJIA,* Spring 1993.

———. *A Life in Peace and War,* New York: Harper & Row, 1987.

U.S. Congress. "Reform of United Nation Peacekeeping Operations: A Mandate for Change," August 1993.

———. "Management and Mismanagement at the United Nations," Hearing before House Committee on Foreign Affairs, March 5, 1993.

———. "U.S. Participation in Somalia Peacekeeping," Hearing before Senate Foreign Relations Committee, October 19–20, 1993.

U.S. Department of State. Annual Human Rights Reports for Angola and Mozambique, 1995, 1996, 1997, and 1998.

———. "Conflict Resolution in Africa: Lessons from Angola," INR paper, April 6, 1993.

U.S. Institute of Peace. "Dialogues on Conflict Resolution: Bridging Theory and Practice," Washington: USIP March 1993.

———. "Conflict and Conflict Resolution in Mozambique," Washington: USIP April 1993.

Utting, P. *Between Hope and Insecurity: The Social Consequences of the Cambodian Peace Process*, Geneva: UNRISD, 1994.

Vail, L. *Capitalism and Colonialism in Mozambique*, London: Heinemann, 1980.

Van Creveld, M. *The Transformation of War*, New York: The Free Press, 1991.

Vines, A. *Renamo Terrorism in Mozambique*, London: James Curry, 1991.

Wainhouse, D. *International Peacekeeping at the Crossroads*, Baltimore: Johns Hopkins University Press, 1973.

Walker, J. "International Mediation of Ethnic Conflicts," *Survival*, Spring 1993.

Weiss, T. *The United Nations in Conflict Management*, New York: International Peace Academy, 1990.

———. *From Massacres to Genocide*, Washington, D.C.: The Brookings Institution, 1996.

Whitman, J. *After Rwanda—The Coordination of United Nations Humanitarian Assistance*, New York: St. Martin's Press, 1996.

Williams, A. "In Search of Peace: Negotiations and the Angolan Civil War," Pew Case Studies, Georgetown University, 1993.

Wiseman, H. *Peacekeeping, Appraisals and Proposals*, New York: Pergamon Press, 1983.

Wolfers, M. and Bergerol, J. *Angola in the Frontline*, London: Zed Press, 1983.

Zartman, W. "Conflict Reduction: Prevention, Management, and Resolution," *Conflict Resolution in Africa*, Washington, D.C.: Brookings 1991.

———. *Resolving Regional Conflicts: International Perspectives*, Newbury Park: Sage Publications, 1991.

———. and Touval, S. *International Mediation in Theory and Practice*, Boulder: Westview Press, 1985.

Zunes, S. "Western Sahara: Peace Derailed," *Current History*, May 1996.

Index